Magic in the Kitchen

Magic
IN THE KITCHEN

PHOTOGRAPHS BY *Jan Bartelsman*

with Stephanie Lyness, Sherrill A. Rose, and Kimberly Yorio

ARTISAN   NEW YORK

DESIGN BY *Ph*.D

PUBLISHED BY ARTISAN
A Division of Workman Publishing, Inc.
708 Broadway
New York, New York 10003
www.artisanbooks.com

Library of Congress Cataloging-in-Publication Data

Bartelsman, Jan.
        Magic in the kitchen / Jan Bartelsman.
                    p. cm.
        ISBN 1-57965-173-9
1. Cooks—United States—Pictorial works. 2. Cookery. I. Title.

        TX649.A1 B37 2001
        641.5'092'273—dc21
        2001034344

Printed and bound in China

DESIGNED BY Ph.D

First edition
10 9 8 7 6 5 4 3 2 1

Contents

Preface

From a young age onward, I have been driven to eat good food. Not because my grandmother was a great cook and took me out looking for berries, nuts, and mushrooms in the woods, as is the case with some of the great chefs in this book, but because my mother was a lousy cook. I used to hang around outside the few restaurants near my house, just to catch the smell of good food being prepared and make plans for the day that I would actually go inside and taste it. Then, when I was nine, my attentions shifted from food to photography—my great-aunt Jopie had given me a camera and a developing set to process film. I was hooked, but I didn't abandon my first love altogether. When I got older, my two passions merged. Not only did I achieve my goal of eating in great restaurants, I got to meet and photograph the best food artists in the world.

This project had a great start. On our first trip from Amsterdam to New York to begin the photo shoots, my colleague, Cees, and I took a taxi from Kennedy airport directly to Times Square where the James Beard Awards (the prestigious awards ceremony for chefs) were being held. Our publisher had invited us so we would get an immediate feel for the culinary world we were entering. As we approached the venue, we noticed that all the men were wearing suits or tuxedos, which we hadn't thought of bringing. Luckily, a few paces farther up the sidewalk we heard a man yelling, "Men's designer suits for sale!" We reappeared a bit later, dressed to the nines.

The next morning at our first shoot, we found that our stars were still lucky. As I unpacked my view camera at New York City's Union Pacific, I saw that it had been smashed during the trip. This was potentially an extremely embarrassing situation. Just at that moment, chef Rocco DiSpirito walked in looking very puzzled and asking us why we were a day early. Someone had apparently put the wrong date on his calendar. Because he was too busy to shoot right then, he asked us to reschedule and invited us to return later for lunch (salmon with rhubarb—delightful). We agreed, and used the unexpected hiatus to buy a new camera and an unbreakable case.

The chefs in this book all make sensational food and are artists of the highest caliber. Never in my life have I experienced such wonderful meals and great wines. I floated rather than walked out of their restaurants, a sort of delirious grin on my face. All I could actually say was, "Wow." I have had occasion to eat very well in Europe, but this was different. I was especially surprised by the chefs' daring mix of ingredients—I thoroughly enjoyed the experience of looking at a menu and wondering how some weird combination (as it would surely be regarded from a traditional European perspective) could be good, only to find out later that it could be great. Bob Kinkead's Walnut-and-Horseradish-Crusted Rockfish with Sherry-Beet Sauce is a perfect example of this. Discussing this issue with some of the European chefs in the book who have been working in the United States for many years, I came to appreciate the fact that the brilliant new combinations I had enjoyed can be attributed in part to the artistic freedom that chefs get from their American audience, which is less rooted in strict culinary tradition.

Cees and I had so much fun working with these chefs that sometimes we could hardly stop laughing during a shoot. And it was interesting to explore the many connections between the worlds of cuisine and photography. The art of food preparation is actually comparable to the creation of our photomontage portraits. Being inspired by ingredients, combining and preparing them in such a way as to end up with something more than the sum of these ingredients, with something sublime on the plate, is what these chefs are so great at doing. The main ingredients of our portraits are the chefs themselves, our inspiration coming from their restaurants, food, and ideas. Although we wouldn't dare compare our results with those of these chefs, we also try to combine our photographic elements into a whole that is more than the sum of its parts.

I would like to thank the chefs for their generous participation and for making this culinary and photographic tour of the United States one of the most enjoyable projects we've ever worked on.

Jan Bartelsman

Introduction

The forty remarkable chefs featured on these pages were chosen because their work, taken as a whole, describes American cuisine today in the richness of its diversity. The food varies greatly from chef to chef. It is characterized by different flavors and new, personal combinations of tastes. Some food is strongly defined by a particular cultural inheritance, while other food is not. The chefs are borrowing ingredients and techniques from all over the world and integrating them into a new cuisine, a uniquely American cuisine.

This American cuisine revealed its character in the work of Julia Child, who inspired a new kind of creativity in American cooking. Child showed us how to use French technique to create new and unfamiliar foods in our kitchens. She cooked French food with an attitude that was entirely American: Practical and unflappable in the face of culinary disaster, she was serious about the food, but also matter-of-fact, democratic, unceremonious, and never precious. She showed us how to borrow from the cuisine of another culture and make it our own. She made it fun to cook new foods. The gift of our American perspective is that our approach to food is mostly unfettered by tradition. Child gave us the confidence to experiment and cook in ways that we were not born to. Once we had the confidence to cook French food, we had the confidence to experiment, borrowing ingredients, techniques, and tastes from wherever we liked and integrating them into a new cuisine that has become our own.

One hundred, or even fifty years ago, diversity in American cooking wore a different face than it does now. Each region

had its indigenous foods: there was chicken and dumplings in the South, gumbo in Louisiana, and bagels in New York City. (There was also, of course, that generation of white Americans living in the fifties, for whom American food was a rather bland, homogenized cuisine that was mostly devoid of any particular cultural style or flavor.) But until recently, America was spacious enough for those regional cuisines to coexist in relative separateness from each other. You could tell what the ethnic population of a neighborhood was by the foods in the local grocery store. And restaurants served the food of whatever culture they were representing, whether it be Asian, Latino, European, or some regional style of American cooking.

At the turn of this century, however, with urban centers pushing out into the outlying areas and once relatively quiet parts of the country booming, diverse cultural populations in America are living ever more closely with one another. Ingredients from a variety of cultures aren't being sold in just specialty food stores; they are on the shelves of major American supermarkets, too. So lemongrass, several varieties of Asian noodles, tomatillos, Indian spices, and chile pastes from around the world have become standard items in any grocery store. And restaurant chefs are being excited and influenced by the multiplicity of ingredients available to them.

Eric Ripert, the French-born chef at Le Bernardin in New York City, says he no longer cooks French but rather New York cuisine, acknowledging the influence on his cooking of a variety of cultures other than French, notably Southeast Asian and Moroccan. Ming Tsai, the chef at Blue Ginger in Boston, tells the story of how he, having worked as a kid in his family's Chinese restaurant in America, went to Paris to study cooking at the Cordon Bleu and eventually wound up working at a restaurant called Natasha in Paris. He began to experiment with the tastes he grew up on and used those ingredients in the creation of new dishes for the restaurant. The food was a success; Tsai had developed his own cooking style, French technique colored by Asian ingredients.

Even chefs whose food is more traditionally western European are using nontraditional combinations of ingredients. Gary Danko, for example, of Gary Danko's in San Francisco, makes dishes that are based on fairly classic European tastes that reflect his desire for simplicity in cooking. Even so, he uses ingredients and techniques from three different cultures in his recipe for Fillet of Beef with Stilton Butter: the technique is French, the Stilton is English, and the pancetta used to wrap the beef is Italian.

When Tom Colicchio at Gramercy Tavern in New York City uses Indian spices in a lobster dish, he borrows a selection of spices often used in Indian cooking, such as bay leaf, cayenne, fennel, coriander, and mustard seed. He uses that particular combination of spices because he likes the way they taste, not because he is referencing an authentic Indian food. He doesn't use the spices as an Indian cook would, rather he integrates them into his own cooking style that is also grounded in French technique. The dish doesn't look or feel Indian, despite the Indian flavoring, nor does it feel particularly French. It is original Colicchio—that is, it's American.

In divorcing ingredients from the context of their parent culture, the ingredient is then free to be used by Americans in a variety of new ways. So when Marcus Samuelsson at Aquavit in New York City borrows a variety of Asian and Southeast Asian ingredients to make a curry paste for his Pickled Herring and Potato Salad, whatever meaning, associations, and tradition those ingredients have had in their cuisines of origin is lost. Samuelsson has made them into something new and surprising.

In addition to borrowing from other cultures, these chefs bring their own culinary inheritance to the mix—sometimes actually changing what is native to their native land. Ben Barker, chef at Magnolia Grill in North Carolina, was born in the South. His cooking is strongly influenced by the traditions of that region, in particular, by a farm-to-table approach to cuisine rooted in a strong relationship to local farmers. At Magnolia Grill, the local produce still inspires the creation of the dishes. But as Barker and other chefs in the area have become inspired to cook with ingredients from other cultures, the growers have been called upon to grow these new ingredients. So "local" and "regional" ingredients for Durham, North Carolina, now also include lemongrass, fresh turmeric, galangal, and kaffir lime leaves, as well as the more traditional American produce. By literally grafting these ingredients onto American soil, farmers working with chefs such as the Barkers have made these ingredients American.

Cook these recipes and you will be able to taste the different cultures as they play off one another in the food. The contrast and juxtaposition of cultures and ingredients make the flavors stand out and set each other off. Try an experiment: Rick Tramonto, executive chef at Tru in the Chicago area, has contributed two soup recipes to this book—a Porcini Cappuccino and a Sweet Corn Soup with Sweet and Hot Peppers. He serves them as part of a foursome of soup-appetizer tastes put together in order to give restaurant clients the experience of a progression of flavors. Eaten on their own, they are certainly delicious; but if you eat them side by side, the corn soup tastes sweeter in comparison to the rich, earthy flavor of the mushrooms, and the flavor of the porcini becomes more pronounced. We know better how porcini taste by the ways in which they do not taste like corn. The same is true for tasting other cultures: The flavors are highlighted in juxtaposition to one another. So, for instance, Ming Tsai's Lilikoi Brown Butter Vinaigrette is made with a base of browned butter, or beurre noisette, that is cooked until it turns a light brown color and takes on a nutty taste, and flavored with passion fruit juice. The rich, buttery flavor of beurre noisette is a classic French taste. In savory dishes, we are used to accenting the butter with an acid, lemon juice or vinegar, to cut its richness. In Tsai's vinaigrette,

the nutty, French flavor of the butter and the sweet, exotic taste of the Hawaiian passion fruit are highlighted in contrast to each other—doubly so, because the combination is an unexpected one.

The recipes on these pages celebrate American cuisine at the beginning of the new century. When you cook the food, you'll be delighted to discover how delicious, varied, quirky, and full of character it is. And what is really interesting and unique is that, as you cook the recipes and eat the food, you'll experience and taste the remarkable culinary movement that is happening in American cooking today. This movement, which began with Julia Child, is now reaching full fruition. *Magic in the Kitchen* documents and immerses you in the magic that these chefs are creating in their restaurants. Not only can you cook their food in your own home, but you'll have an opportunity to meet the chefs as well, through photo portraits and interviews. Read about these talented men and women and the influences that have shaped their cooking. Taste their creativity. And, as Julia says, *"Bon Appétit!"*

Stephanie Lyness

Julia Child
TEACHER, AUTHOR, AND MENTOR TO GENERATIONS OF COOKS

When I went to college, that was back in the 'thirties, women didn't have careers. But during World War II we were needed, so I joined the OSS, the newsprint service. I was in Ceylon and Indian China during the war, and that's where I met my husband. Then, because he was brought up in France and spoke French, we were sent to Paris after the war, with the U.S. Information Service. Paris was lovely. And I just couldn't get over the food. It was wonderful. I went right away to the Cordon Bleu. I didn't want to take a housewife's course, and luckily there were some American GIs who had been given two years of free education, and wanted to go into food, and I was able to work with them. We had a wonderful old chef. And that really started me out. Then I met my colleague Simone [Simca] Beck, and we teamed up.

Then friends from America came over and said, "We want to learn to cook, but we don't speak French, so we don't want to go to the Cordon Bleu. You teach us." So Simca, who was always ready to do anything, said, "Fine!" and we started our own school. That turned into our book, *Mastering #1*. It took about eight or nine years to get it written. We were learning by doing. Other cookbooks didn't go into as much detail as we did, but I was about thirty-one or thirty-two and I wanted detail, like exactly how far the chicken is from the flame, things like that.

The timing of the publication was very important, because the Kennedys were in the White House and anything they did was news. They had a wonderful French chef, René Verdon. And people were finally going abroad because it took so much less time by plane. So it all came together and there I was, doing the kind of cooking people were suddenly interested in.

I've never had my own restaurant, I know too much about it, and I'm too old now! Anyway, I'm not a chef. I'm a cook and a teacher. We use the term "chef" very loosely in this country. A chef is the head of a restaurant, with people under him or her.

Ben and Karen Barker **MAGNOLIA GRILL** | Durham

Karen and I pursued our culinary education and our romance simultaneously. We met at culinary school twenty years ago in New York. On the first day of class, we sat next to each other, and we've been cooking together ever since. Wherever we've worked, Karen has always been the pastry chef and I've been a cook or the chef. We never presented ourselves as a team per se, but we are in fact a team now.

What we do a lot of here is the juxtaposition of land and sea.

We're a southern restaurant, and we cook in a contemporary fashion. We always try to use the foundation of our "southern-ness," the agrarian and fishing resources of the area. We have a wealth of extraordinary shellfish here, primarily shrimp, crabs, clams, and oysters from our coast, and I love to cook with all of those—not only because they are abundant, but because of the opportunity to showcase them in a contemporary expression of regional cooking. I love those great, big, fat sea scallops, their sweetness, that great silky texture, and that really clean taste of the ocean. It makes a terrific foil for a butternut hash that is accented by country ham. This is a good dish—and the shells are cool, too. I come from a family of farming people, and most often, vegetables were the principal element of our dinner table. There was always a protein component, but it usually was *not* the centerpiece as it is in most restaurant cooking. A full complement of side dishes and a myriad of fresh vegetables is my memory of what those tables were about. My cooking, as a consequence, tends to present vegetables as the star of the plate. How we put them together to blend their textures and their sweetness or earthiness or crunch is often, I think,

what differentiates our food. Karen's desserts are also reflective of traditional American-style baking. She does a lot of homey desserts with big flavors, always seasonally based.

When we graduated from culinary school, we contemplated going to California or elsewhere, but North Carolina seemed like an as yet unexplored opportunity for restaurateurs. We started out here by converting an old health-food store into the restaurant. It had generous amounts of wall space, but we had no money to buy artwork, so we started soliciting local artists to use the space as a gallery of sorts, and it's turned into a wonderful design adjunct. The "exhibitions" revolve every six to eight weeks, and that reflects the idea of seasonality and brings us back to the food. We've got a great friend who every year hangs his whimsical fish sculptures, made of old, broken surfboards, in the restaurant. They're extraordinary. And of course, we sell a lot of seafood when his work is on display.

15

PAN-SEARED SEA SCALLOPS WITH BUTTERNUT "HASH" | Serves 4

A palette of anise flavors—the fennel in the hash, the tarragon in the leeks and sauce, and the sprinkle of toasted anise seeds on the scallops—reveals all the facets of that flavor and bring out the natural sweetness of the vegetables and the scallops.

FOR THE LEEKS VINAIGRETTE

1 tablespoon tarragon vinegar

1 tablespoon olive oil

4 baby leeks (about 6 ounces), trimmed and washed, or 1 medium leek,
    trimmed, white and light green part only, and cut lengthwise in half

½ teaspoon kosher salt

Pinch of freshly ground black pepper

FOR THE SAUCE

½ cup thinly sliced shallots

2 tablespoons olive oil

1 bay leaf, preferably fresh

Reserved muscles from the scallops (see below)

1 teaspoon fennel seeds, pulsed in a spice or coffee grinder to crack

¾ cup dry vermouth

¼ cup tarragon vinegar

1 cup chicken stock

1 tablespoon lobster coral (optional)

2 tablespoons unsalted butter, softened

½ teaspoon kosher salt

Pinch of freshly ground black pepper

FOR THE HASH

¼ cup olive oil

1 cup diced (¼-inch) butternut squash

2 tablespoons diced (¼-inch) country ham

Kernels from 1 ear corn (about ½ cup)

¼ cup diced (¼-inch) fennel, blanched

2 tablespoons diced (¼-inch) roasted, peeled poblano
    or red bell pepper

¼ cup finely chopped frisée

2 tablespoons tarragon vinegar

1 tablespoon minced fresh tarragon

1 tablespoon chopped fresh flat-leaf parsley

¼ teaspoon kosher salt

⅛ teaspoon freshly ground black pepper

FOR THE SCALLOPS

8 large dry-packed scallops (about 1½ ounces each), muscles removed and
    reserved for sauce

Coarse sea salt and freshly ground black pepper

1 tablespoon olive oil

Tarragon oil for drizzling

½ teaspoon anise seeds, lightly toasted and ground

Fresh chervil sprigs for garnish (optional)

PREPARE THE LEEKS: Combine the vinegar and oil in a medium bowl and reserve. Bring about 1 inch of water to a boil in a medium saucepan fitted with a steamer basket. Place the leek(s) in the basket, cover, and steam until tender, 4 to 5 minutes for baby leeks, about 8 minutes for a larger leek. Drain well in a colander.

While still warm, cut the leek(s) on the bias into 1-inch sections and toss in the vinaigrette. Season with the salt and pepper and set aside.

PREPARE THE SAUCE: Put the shallots, olive oil, bay leaf, and reserved scallop muscles in a small nonreactive saucepan, place over medium heat, and cook until the shallots are softened, 3 to 4 minutes. Add the fennel seeds, vermouth, and vinegar, bring to a simmer, and cook until the liquid has reduced to a syrup. Add the chicken stock and reduce by about one-half. Strain the sauce into a clean small saucepan, pressing down on the solids to extract all of the liquid, and set aside.

If using the lobster coral, put it in a mini-processor or bowl with the butter and process or cream together. Set aside at room temperature.

PREPARE THE HASH: Heat 2 tablespoons of the oil in a medium frying pan over medium-high heat. Add the squash and ham and sauté until the squash is softened and lightly colored, 4 to 5 minutes. Add the corn, fennel, and roasted pepper and sauté until the corn is just tender, 2 to 3 minutes. Add the frisée, vinegar, the remaining 2 tablespoons oil, and the herbs and toss to combine. Season with the salt and pepper. Set aside.

PREPARE THE SCALLOPS: Pat the scallops dry on paper towels and sprinkle with salt and pepper. Heat a heavy frying pan over medium-high heat. Add the olive oil and tilt the pan to coat it with the oil. Add the scallops and cook, turning once, until well browned but still translucent in the center, about 2 minutes on each side. Remove scallops; keep warm.

16

FINISH THE DISH: Place a 3-inch ring mold on a warm serving plate. Add one-quarter of the leeks and press them gently into an even layer. Fill the mold with some of the hash and level it. Gently remove the mold. Cut each of 2 scallops in half crosswise, and place them evenly around the hash. Repeat and make three more plates.

Bring the sauce to a boil over high heat. Use an immersion hand blender or whisk to emulsify the butter and the lobster coral, if using, into sauce. Season with the salt and pepper.

Spoon the sauce around the hash and scallops. Drizzle the tarragon oil around the plates. Sprinkle the scallops with the anise seeds, garnish with chervil, if using, and serve hot.

Sweet scallops frame a tower of butternut squash hash.

FRIED OYSTERS ON CREAMY WINTER SUCCOTASH WITH BARBECUE VINAIGRETTE | Serves 4

This succotash is a bit of work, but it's a superb rendition of that classic lima bean dish. It has a delicately sweet, fresh taste. The usual fresh corn kernels are replaced by hominy, which gives the dish a satisfying soft, starchy texture that contrasts with the crisp coating on the oysters.

This is a practical dish for entertaining because the succotash and barbecue vinaigrette can be made ahead. The only last-minute work is frying the oysters.

FOR THE VINAIGRETTE
1 head garlic, tips of cloves sliced off
¼ cup cider vinegar
2 tablespoons honey
1 tablespoon tamarind concentrate
½ teaspoon dried red pepper flakes
¼ cup reserved oyster liquor (see below), strained
2 tablespoons tomato paste
¼ cup peanut oil
½ teaspoon kosher salt
¼ teaspoon freshly ground black pepper
2 to 4 dashes Tabasco sauce, or to taste

FOR THE SUCCOTASH
2 tablespoons peanut oil
½ cup diced (¼-inch) country ham (about 3 ounces)
¼ cup diced (¼-inch) fennel
¼ cup diced (¼-inch) carrot
¼ cup diced (¼-inch) onion
¼ cup diced (¼-inch) red bell pepper
1 tablespoon minced garlic
½ teaspoon dried red pepper flakes
1 bay leaf
2 cups fresh or thawed frozen baby lima beans
1 to 1¼ cups chicken stock
1 cup canned white hominy, drained and rinsed
¾ cup heavy cream
Kosher salt and freshly ground black pepper

FOR THE OYSTERS

About 4 cups peanut oil for deep-frying

1 cup stone-ground coarse cornmeal

½ cup all-purpose flour

½ teaspoon kosher salt

¼ teaspoon cayenne pepper

¼ teaspoon freshly ground black pepper

1½ pints shucked oysters, drained, liquor reserved

1 tablespoon chopped fresh flat-leaf parsley

1 teaspoon fresh thyme leaves

1 cup coarsely chopped arugula leaves (about 1 small bunch)

½ to 1 teaspoon cider vinegar

¼ cup chopped scallions

4 small watercress sprigs for garnish

PREPARE THE VINAIGRETTE: Preheat the oven to 400°F.

Wrap the head of garlic in aluminum foil and roast until softened, 40 to 45 minutes. Let cool slightly.

Squeeze the roasted garlic out of the skins. Measure 2 tablespoons and set aside; reserve the remainder for another use.

Combine the vinegar, honey, tamarind, pepper flakes, and oyster liquor in a small saucepan. Bring to a boil and simmer for 5 minutes. Transfer to a blender. Add the 2 tablespoons roasted garlic and the tomato paste and blend until combined. With the blender running, gradually drizzle in the oil to emulsify. Blend in the salt, pepper, and Tabasco sauce. Set aside at room temperature until ready to serve.

PREPARE THE SUCCOTASH: Heat the oil in a large saucepan over medium heat. Add the ham and cook until lightly browned, 1 to 2 minutes. With a slotted spoon, remove the ham from the pan; set aside. Add the fennel, carrot, onion, and red pepper to the pan and cook until softened and beginning to caramelize, 2 to 3 minutes. Add the garlic, red pepper flakes, and bay leaf and cook for 1 minute.

Add the lima beans and just enough chicken stock to barely cover. Bring to a simmer and cook until the lima beans are just tender, 4 to 5 minutes for frozen limas, slightly longer for fresh.

Meanwhile, combine the hominy and cream in a small saucepan. Bring to a boil, reduce the heat, and simmer, stirring occasionally, until the cream is reduced and thickened, 4 to 5 minutes.

Add the hominy to the pan with the lima bean mixture. Season to taste with salt and pepper. Cover to keep warm and set aside.

PREPARE THE OYSTERS: Preheat the oven to 200°F.

Pour 3 to 4 inches of oil into a large deep saucepan. Heat to 350°F on a deep-frying thermometer.

Combine the cornmeal, flour, salt, cayenne, and black pepper in a bowl. Working with 10 to 12 oysters at a time, dredge them in the cornmeal mixture, shake off the excess, and fry until crisp, 1 to 1½ minutes. Remove from the oil with a slotted spoon or spider and drain on brown paper bags. Transfer to an ovenproof plate and keep warm in the oven while you finish frying the oysters.

FINISH THE DISH: Reheat the succotash over medium-low heat. Add the parsley, thyme, ham, arugula, and vinegar to taste. Season again with salt and pepper. Divide the succotash among four hot serving bowls. Pile the fried oysters on top. Sprinkle with the scallions, drizzle some of the barbecue vinaigrette around the plate and serve the rest in a bowl. Garnish each plate with the watercress sprigs.

The oysters are sauced with a barbecue vinaigrette and a light green parsley-infused roasted garlic oil.

Ben Barker

18

My passion for food . . . I always had it. My grandmother had it. We grew up making most of our own products at home, from prosciutto to flour to cornmeal. When I first started in the business, I was not a professional. Then I got into the knife skills and all of that . . . but the fascination that I entered with—the romance of the food—was always a big part of me.

Lidia Bastianich

Lidia Bastianich

I like all aspects of food. . . . I like the science of cooking and I like the anthropology of food. . . . I took courses, I even gave courses in the anthropology of food. I think that food is so much more than what you have on a plate. It reflects the culture of a people, a nation. It reflects the ground, the topography—you know, what drives people. It is nourishing, but it is also pleasurable. It can become art, and it reflects the people who produce it. So I was interested in all of those aspects. Of course, I'm interested in the preservation of some of those things now because one thing leads to another. I'm sort of traditional about products and recipes specific to Italy, because that's where my focus is. I feel that my job, after more than thirty years of running restaurants and businesses, is, in a sense, to safeguard the Italian culinary culture and bring it to Americans. Whether it is through my restaurants, or my television show, or my books, that's what I communicate.

In Italy, I like to go foraging for mushrooms. I love mushrooms. I also go foraging for mushrooms here. Truffles? In Italy, truffles are harvested in Piemonte, basically, but also in the Marches, and there are also some truffles in the area that I come from. It is so great to find one. It is beautiful, very exciting, with the dogs, when you go. The excitement of the dogs is amazing. The dog will run back and forth, back and forth, until you come closer to where the truffle is, and then he'll start digging, and then, of course, you dig, and you pull it out, and the dog just jumps and licks and licks, as if to say, you know, "We got one! We got one!" And then all he gets is a little piece of bread, the dog, and he's quite happy.

When they train them, as small dogs, they put a small piece of a truffle in their bread so that they really develop their sense of what it is. They used to hunt for truffles with pigs, but the pigs would eat them. That was a problem.

One of my aunts was a wonderful chef who cooked for the then-royal families, if you will, who came down to Trieste from Austria-Hungary, so I was always involved in cooking on a level that was more than just home cooking. My family came to the United States in 1958, and I actually went on to school and studied biology and chemistry and the sciences. But I gravitated to restaurants, working part-time and summers in bakeries and restaurants. Then I met my former husband, who was in the industry, and that was how it began. In 1971, when I was twenty-three, I opened my first restaurant with him. Though I was working full-time in the restaurant, I was not a chef. We had hired a chef, and I worked along with him for two or three years, and I picked up a lot. But I also realized how much I needed to learn. So I went back and took courses. I went to Queens College and to Hunter, then I went to Italy to school, to learn the art of making pasta—even though I had been making pasta all the time at home! . . . I think the skills I needed were the knife skills, the butchering, pastry, those are the things I went back for.

21

BECCO, FELIDIA, and ESCA | New York
LIDIA'S | Kansas City, Pittsburgh

PAN-SEARED VEAL TENDERLOIN WITH CASTELMAGNO CHEESE FONDUTA, TRUFFLE-SCENTED SALSIFY, AND SHAVED WHITE TRUFFLES | Serves 4

This dish combines the élan of a restaurant meal with the ease of a home-cooked meal. And perhaps because of that, it feels like the best of home cooking. Veal tenderloin is an exquisitely tender, tasty (and expensive) cut of veal that you'll probably need to special-order from your butcher. In the restaurant, it's served with salsify (in pieces or mashed, as in the recipe below), seasoned with white truffles, and sauced with a cream sauce with a bare hint of cheese.

Fresh white truffles are a wonderful extravagance, but with the truffle butter, you'll find that the dish has a lot of truffle flavor even if you have to do without them. Truffle butter is sold in small jars or plastic containers in gourmet food stores.

FOR THE SALSIFY
Juice of ½ lemon
1 pound salsify (see Note)

2 tablespoons truffle butter
1 teaspoon kosher salt
¼ teaspoon freshly ground black pepper
1 tablespoon freshly grated Parmigiano-Reggiano

FOR THE VEAL
1 tablespoon unsalted butter
1 tablespoon extra-virgin olive oil
2 pounds veal tenderloin, cut into 4 pieces
Kosher salt and freshly ground black pepper

FOR THE FONDUTA
1½ cups heavy cream
½ cup grated Castelmagno cheese or ½ cup freshly grated Parmigiano-Reggiano plus 1 tablespoon Gorgonzola or blue cheese
2 large egg yolks, lightly beaten

2 ounces white truffles (optional)

PREPARE THE SALSIFY: Fill a bowl with cold water and add the lemon juice. Peel the salsify and cut into 3-inch lengths, dropping it into the lemon water as you work to keep it from darkening.

Drain the salsify. Cook in a saucepan of boiling salted water until tender but not mushy, about 20 minutes. Drain and set aside.

PREPARE THE VEAL: Heat the butter and oil in a large frying pan over medium heat. Sprinkle the veal all over with salt and pepper. Add the veal to the pan and cook, turning once, until cooked to medium-rare, 8 to 10 minutes.

MEANWHILE, FINISH THE SALSIFY: Melt the truffle butter in a medium frying pan over medium heat. Add the salsify and roughly mash with a fork until it is no longer in pieces but is not a puree either. Season with 1 teaspoon salt, the pepper, and Parmigiano. Remove from the heat and cover to keep warm.

PREPARE THE FONDUTA: Bring the cream to a boil in a saucepan over medium-high heat. Add the cheese and stir to melt. Remove the pan from the heat. Whisking the sauce constantly so that the egg doesn't curdle, pour the eggs in the sauce and whisk to blend.

To serve, spoon the mashed salsify into the center of four serving plates. Place the veal on top and pour the fonduta over the veal. Shave the white truffles over all, if using.

NOTE: Salsify is available in farmers' markets and some supermarkets in the spring. If you can't find it, you might substitute celery root, which is often available from fall through spring and tastes lovely with the veal and truffles.

Veal tenderloin with fingers of salsify and wilted greens

STRANGOZZI WITH PORCHETTA, GRAPE TOMATOES, AND PECORINO CHEESE | Serves 4

Strangozzi is a type of pasta from Umbria that resembles tagliatelle, but is shorter, and thicker as well, so that it has a kind of "crunch" when you eat it. The semolina dough is very rich in eggs and rather wet in comparison to standard pasta doughs. The strangozzi are hand-rolled and cut, but because the dough is not rolled terribly thin, rolling and cutting them by hand is not much more work than making pasta using a machine.

The strangozzi is dressed with a simple, spicy tomato sauce that goes together very quickly. If you don't like your food hot, cut the red pepper flakes by half, or more.

FOR THE PASTA

1 cup semolina flour

1½ teaspoons porcini mushroom powder (from 2 to 3 dried porcinis, ground in a spice or coffee grinder)

8 large egg yolks

All-purpose flour for rolling the pasta

FOR THE SAUCE

2 tablespoons extra-virgin olive oil

1 garlic clove

4 ounces thickly sliced porchetta or prosciutto cotto, cut into ¼-inch strips

8 ounces New Jersey (or other) grape tomatoes or cherry tomatoes, cut in half

1 tablespoon dried red pepper flakes

½ cup chopped fresh flat-leaf parsley

One 3- to 4-ounce chunk pecorino Toscano (preferably aged 6 months) for grating

PREPARE THE PASTA: Combine the semolina flour and mushroom powder. Pile in a mound on a marble or wooden work surface and make a well in the center of the mound. In a small bowl, beat the egg yolks with a fork until blended. Add to the well. Using the fork, gradually draw the flour mixture from the sides of the well into the eggs. As you work, the egg mixture will become thicker. Continue beating until there is just a thin ring of flour around the egg mixture and the dough is too thick to mix with a fork. If the

dough gets too stiff before almost all of the flour is incorporated, drizzle a tiny amount of warm water over the egg mixture and continue working the flour into the dough. (You may not need any water.)

Work the remaining flour into the dough with your hands just until a rough, firm dough forms. The dough should be wet but not sticky. Rub your hands together to remove any dough scraps and add to the mound of dough. Shape the dough into a rough ball, cover loosely with plastic wrap, and set aside for 1 hour.

Flour your hands and the (cleaned) work surface lightly with all-purpose flour. Roll out the dough about ⅛ inch thick with a rolling pin. Cut it into 4-by-6-inch sheets; you should get 5 sheets. Lay the sheets out to dry until the dough stiffens a bit, 15 to 30 minutes.

Use a large sharp knife to cut the dough into strips 6 inches long and about ½ inch wide. Flour the pasta lightly as needed to keep it from sticking, and stack the strangozzi on top of one another until ready to cook.

PREPARE THE SAUCE: Heat 1 tablespoon of the oil in a medium frying pan over medium heat. Add the garlic and sauté until golden, 1 to 2 minutes. Add the porchetta and cook to render the fat, 3 to 5 minutes. Add the tomatoes and red pepper flakes and continue cooking, stirring often, until the tomatoes soften, 5 to 6 more minutes.

Meanwhile, bring a large pot of salted water to a boil.

FINISH THE DISH: Add the pasta to the boiling water and cook until al dente, about 5 minutes. When the pasta is just about cooked, place the pan with sauce over medium-high heat. Drain the pasta, add to the pan with the sauce and stir to coat with the sauce. Add the parsley and the remaining 1 tablespoon olive oil and remove from the heat.

Divide the pasta and sauce among four serving bowls. Grate pecorino over the top and serve hot.

Lidia Bastianich

Rick Bayless

FRONTERA GRILL and TOPOLOBAMPO | Chicago

I grew up in the restaurant business. I'm fourth generation in a family of restaurant people. It gets into your blood, I guess. And although I have always made my living by cooking, I have also always been interested in teaching.

Mexican cuisine is very misunderstood in the United States. What we call Mexican food here is really derivative of what was eaten in the area of Mexico that has since become the southwestern part of the United States, when that territory was a sort of Mexican outback or frontier. The cuisine of that region is a cousin, a distant cousin, to the food that has traditionally been eaten south of the border. In an area just north of Mexico City, there is a line that archaeologists and anthropologists say denotes where Mesoamerica starts. South of this line all the great pre-Columbian cultures survived, and it's also where all the really interesting food comes from, to my way of thinking. This cuisine has deep roots, and it deserves respect because it is extremely diverse and complex with a focus on herbs and wild greens and varieties of chiles no one has ever heard of. It is also a very regional cuisine. Its pinnacle is its sauces, called *moles,* which are simmered for many hours and are usually kept over from one day to the next because they get better the following day.

Avocados are essential in Mexican cooking. When the Spaniards arrived, they brought fat with them. Before then, Mexicans cooked with avocado, which the Spaniards hailed as the "butter of the poor." Nowadays we might call it the "butter of the rich"—we know it's actually much healthier for you than butter is, and it suffers no lowly status. It adds a beautiful, creamy element to all of the Mexican dishes it's used in. Everyone who has tasted guacamole knows how rich and unctuous the avocado really is.

Chiles are another essential component; they define Mexican cuisine more than anything else. Mexico is the native land of the chile. Certainly, more types of chiles were domesticated there than in any other place in the world. And the number of varieties ultimately points to the fact that they are used for flavor, not for heat. When Christopher Columbus came to the New World, he was looking for black pepper, something that was really *picante.* Finding chiles, he took only the small, really hot, least flavorful representatives as a substitute for the black pepper, and basically distributed them around the world in his travels. And that is why people everywhere think about chiles in terms of their heat, whereas in Mexico, they are thought of in terms of their flavors.

QUICK-FRIED SHRIMP WITH SWEET TOASTY GARLIC | Serves 6

These good, garlicky shrimp are quickly fried in *mojo de ajo,* an oil that is cooked slowly with lots of garlic and then seasoned with lime juice and smoky chipotle chiles. Slow cooking makes the garlic sweet and infuses the oil with its flavor. This recipe makes more mojo de ajo than you'll need to cook the shrimp. It will keep in the refrigerator for about 2 weeks (the oil will become solid but will liquefy at room temperature). Reheat the cold mojo de ajo over low to medium heat and use it for sautéing.

FOR THE MOJO DE AJO

¾ cup peeled garlic cloves (about 2 large heads)

1 cup extra-virgin olive oil

½ teaspoon kosher salt, or to taste

Juice of 1 lime

2 canned chipotle chiles en adobo, seeded and cut into thin strips

FOR THE SHRIMP

2 pounds shrimp, peeled and deveined, with tail portion left on

Kosher salt

3 tablespoons chopped fresh cilantro or parsley

Fresh cilantro leaves for garnish

2 limes, cut into wedges, for serving

PREPARE THE MOJO DE AJO: Chop the garlic into ⅛-inch bits, either with a sharp knife or by dropping the cloves into the feed tube of a food processor with the motor running. Transfer to a small saucepan, add the oil and salt, and cook over medium-low heat, stirring occasionally, until the oil gently bubbles (like mineral water) and there is just a hint of movement on the surface. Adjust the heat to keep the mixture at a gentle simmer and continue to cook, stirring occasionally, until the garlic is soft and the color of light brown sugar, about 30 minutes.

Add the lime juice and simmer until most of it evaporates, about 5 minutes. Stir in the chiles and season to taste with salt.

Keep the mojo de ajo warm over low heat while you prepare the shrimp.

PREPARE THE SHRIMP: In a large nonstick frying pan, heat 1½ tablespoons of the mojo de ajo oil over medium-high heat. Add half of the shrimp, sprinkle generously with salt, and cook, stirring gently and continuously, until the shrimp are just cooked through, 3 to 4 minutes. Stir in half of the cilantro or parsley. Transfer to a deep serving platter. Repeat the process with the remaining shrimp.

To serve, with a slotted spoon, scoop the warm bits of garlic and chiles from the mojo de ajo and drizzle them over the shrimp. Arrange the lime wedges around the platter and garnish with cilantro leaves.

FLAVORED GORDITAS WITH ROASTED POBLANO GUACAMOLE | Serves 8 as a snack or 4 as a main dish

Gorditas are fat masa tortillas that are shallow-fried, then slit open, like a pocket pita, and stuffed. These are stuffed with guacamole, cheese, onion, and arugula seasoned with lime and salt.

FOR THE GORDITAS
6 thick slices smoky bacon (about 8 ounces)
1 pound (2 cups) fresh smooth-ground corn masa, or 1¾ cups powdered masa harina mixed with 1 cup plus 2 tablespoons warm water

FOR THE GUACAMOLE
1 large poblano chile
3 garlic cloves, unpeeled
2 large ripe avocados
1 to 2 tablespoons fresh lime juice
½ teaspoon kosher salt

2 cups young arugula leaves (or fresh basil, mizuna, or tender spinach), stems removed
Fresh lime juice to taste
Kosher salt
⅓ cup chopped onion
⅓ cup finely crumbled or grated Mexican queso añejo or other dry grating cheese, such as pecorino Romano or Parmigiano-Reggiano
Vegetable oil for frying

PREPARE THE GORDITAS: Heat a medium frying pan over medium heat. Add the bacon and cook until crisp. Drain on paper towels, cool, and then finely chop.

Heat a well-seasoned or nonstick frying pan over medium heat.

Knead the masa until it has the consistency of soft cookie dough, adding a little water if necessary. Knead in half of the chopped bacon; reserve the remaining bacon. Divide the dough into 8 portions and roll into balls; cover with plastic to keep from drying.

PREPARE THE GUACAMOLE: Roast the poblano over an open flame or on a baking sheet 4 inches below a very hot broiler, turning, until the skin is evenly blistered and blackened, about 5 minutes for an open flame, 10 minutes under a broiler. Cover with a kitchen towel and let stand for about 5 minutes. Rub off the blackened skin, then pull or cut out the stem and the seed pod. Tear the poblano open and quickly rinse to remove any remaining seeds and bits of skin. Roughly chop it.

Heat an ungreased griddle or frying pan over medium heat. Add the garlic cloves and roast, turning frequently, until the cloves are softened and slightly darkened in spots, about 15 minutes. Cool, then peel. Combine with the poblano in the bowl of a food processor and pulse several times to coarsely puree. Scrape into a medium bowl.

Halve the avocados and scrape the flesh into the bowl. Using an old-fashioned potato masher or the back of a spoon, coarsely mash the avocados with the garlic and poblano. Taste and season with the lime juice and salt. Press plastic wrap directly against the surface of the guacamole and refrigerate until you are ready to fry the gorditas.

FINISH THE GORDITAS: Line a tortilla press with 2 sheets of plastic cut to fit the plates of the press. Place 1 ball of dough in the tortilla press and gently press into a gordita about 4 inches in diameter and about ¼ inch thick. Remove the gordita—still between the sheets of plastic—from the tortilla press, and peel off the top sheet of plastic. Flip the gordita onto the fingers of one hand, then gently peel off the second sheet of plastic. (Or, place a 7-inch square of plastic [a plastic freezer bag works well] on the work surface. Put a ball of dough in the center and flatten it. Then press the dough into a disk 3½ to 4 inches in diameter. Flip onto your hand.) In one flowing motion, roll the gordita off your fingers and into the hot frying pan. Fry for about 1½ minutes, then flip and fry for another 1½ minutes, or until lightly browned on both sides. Transfer to a plate. Press and fry the remaining gorditas in the same way. Cover with plastic wrap and set aside while you prepare the guacamole.

FINISH THE DISH: Toss the arugula with a sprinkling of lime juice and salt. Rinse the onion in a strainer under cold water, then shake to remove the excess moisture. Have the guacamole, cheese, and the remaining bacon within reach.

In a medium deep, heavy frying pan or large saucepan, heat ½ inch of oil over medium-high heat until the oil is hot enough to make the edge of a gordita sizzle (about 350°F on a deep-frying thermometer). Fry the gorditas one at a time, turning them once after about 15 seconds, until crisp but not hard, about 45 seconds total. They will puff up a bit, like pita bread. Drain on paper towels.

With a small sharp knife, cut a slit into the edge of each gordita, cutting halfway around the circumference of the disk to open a pocket. Fill each gordita with 2 heaping tablespoons of guacamole and a little of the dressed arugula, then sprinkle in cheese, onion, and bacon. Arrange the gorditas on a platter and serve.

Rick Bayless

Daniel Boulud

DANIEL, CAFÉ BOULUD, and DB BISTRO MODERNE | New York

I am not a butter freak. I am very careful with that. Nevertheless, I would love to meet a chef who says he never uses butter. . . . I don't think his food will be that tasty, especially the desserts. If it is tasty, then it is probably a lie about not using butter.

I was very interested in cooking from a very young age. I was around food all the time, and I was always a sort of helpful hand in the kitchen. Because I was living in the country, I had a sense of the cycle of the seasons. That is how it is when you pick your own vegetables and raise your own livestock. We also went foraging for all kinds of wild things as well. My grandparents had a café, a small hangout, a local stop. My grandmother did the cooking, and then later my mother took over. The kitchen there was always full of the wonderful smell of food, and, of course, when you eat and prepare the food you have also grown yourself, it is always more interesting. There is more of a connection to it.

During the summer, we canned fruits: cherries, peaches, plums, apricots, green beans, everything as it came into season so that you could last the winter with your food. You might do the green beans with herbs, the apricots in a light syrup with some vanilla, pears with cinnamon, peaches with perhaps a bit of lemon peel. In the winter we put up celery stalks and things like that, so the winter vegetables were also preserved. Today, fewer and fewer people do canning, because in the supermarket you have everything available all the time. But before, if you wanted green beans in the winter . . . Canning was a big thing.

I am inspired by the market, by the ingredients, the seasons, the food, and then, after that, a combination of flavors. Right now we are serving a Maine crab salad that is seasoned with a little bit of lemon juice and olive oil and a touch of tarragon and chervil. It comes with a light celery root rémoulade, which is surrounded by a *gelée* of Granny Smith apples and green celery. It has the very refreshing side of the apples and the celery, and it has the earthiness of the celery root and the crab. It is a little bit briny and refreshing and nice. When I was developing this dish, I wanted something very delicate that would allow the brininess and the taste of the crab to come through. Separately, the other ingredients also have their own light, personal flavor, but when they are all put together, they make sort of a progressive combination of taste and texture.

29

PANCETTA-WRAPPED TUNA WITH POTATO-RAMP PUREE | Serves 6

A piece of tuna loin is wrapped in pancetta and roasted whole as you would a roast of meat. The pancetta flavors the tuna as it keeps it from drying out. The tuna is served with mashed potatoes seasoned with pureed ramps—scallionlike members of the onion family that taste slightly of garlic. (If you can't find ramps, you can substitute scallions with a bit of garlic.) Fingerling potatoes are often sold in supermarkets these days, but Yukon Golds will work if you can't find them.

FOR THE TUNA

8 to 10 ounces slab pancetta or bacon, thinly sliced
One 1¼ pound "roast" of tuna loin (in an even cylindrical piece approximately 6 inches long, 1½ inches wide, and 1½ inches thick) (see Note)
Kosher salt and freshly ground white pepper
1 tablespoon unsalted butter

FOR THE POTATO-RAMP PUREE

1¾ pounds potatoes, preferably fingerlings
¾ cup whole milk
8 tablespoons (1 stick) unsalted butter, cut into 8 pieces
3 ounces ramps, trimmed, or 3 ounces scallion greens plus 1 garlic clove, finely chopped
1 bunch Italian parsley, stemmed
¼ cup extra-virgin olive oil
Kosher salt and freshly ground white pepper

FOR THE SAUCE

6 ounces chanterelles, trimmed and cleaned (halved or quartered if large)
1 tablespoon finely chopped shallots, rinsed and dried

Kosher salt and freshly ground white pepper
¼ cup sherry vinegar
¼ cup dry white wine
¼ cup chicken stock
2 tablespoons unsalted butter
2 tablespoons finely chopped fresh chives

PREPARE THE TUNA: On a piece of plastic wrap large enough to enclose the tuna, lay out the slices of pancetta vertically, with each slice slightly overlapping the one next to it. Season the tuna very lightly with salt and pepper and place it across the center of the meat. One by one, wrap each slice of pancetta around the tuna, keeping the rows even. Secure the pancetta by tying the wrapped tuna at 1-inch intervals with kitchen twine, just as you would a meat roast. Wrap the plastic wrap around the tuna and refrigerate while you prepare the potatoes and ramps.

PREPARE THE POTATOES: Peel the potatoes and cut into ½-inch pieces. Put the potatoes in a large pot of cold salted water, bring to a boil, and cook until the potatoes are tender enough to be pierced with the point of a knife, about 15 minutes.

When the potatoes are almost done (after about 10 minutes), combine the milk and butter in a small saucepan and bring to a boil over medium-high heat. As soon as the mixture reaches a boil and the butter melts, remove from the heat.

When the potatoes are cooked, drain them and return them to the pot. Set the pot over medium heat and, shaking the pot to keep the potatoes from sticking, heat just until the

potatoes are dry, 1 to 2 minutes. Spoon the potatoes into a food mill fitted with the fine disk or a potato ricer and pass the potatoes into a large bowl. Pour in the hot milk mixture in a slow, steady stream, stirring continuously. Press a piece of plastic wrap directly against the surface of the potatoes and set the bowl aside in a warm place, or keep the potatoes warm in a covered heatproof bowl set over a pan of simmering water.

PREPARE THE RAMPS: Bring a small saucepan of water to a boil. Add the ramps (or scallion greens) and boil until tender, 3 to 4 minutes. Scoop the ramps (or scallions) out of the pot with a slotted spoon (keep the water at a boil) and run them under cold water to cool and set the color. Dry thoroughly on paper towels.

Add the parsley to the boiling water and cook for 2 minutes. Drain the parsley, then run under cold water to cool and set the color. Dry thoroughly on paper towels and set aside.

Preheat the oven to 350°F.

FINISH THE PUREE: In a medium frying pan, heat 1 tablespoon of the olive oil over medium heat. If using ramps, add them and cook, stirring, 3 minutes. If using scallion greens, first sauté the garlic until it is tender but not colored, about 2 minutes, then toss in the scallion greens and cook, stirring, for 3 minutes. Scrape the ingredients into the bowl of a small food processor or blender. Add the parsley and the remaining 3 tablespoons olive oil and puree, scraping down the sides of the container as needed.

Stir the puree into the potatoes and season with salt and pepper. Cover and keep warm while you cook the tuna.

COOK THE TUNA: Melt 1 tablespoon of the butter in a large ovenproof frying pan over medium heat. When the pan is hot, add the tuna and sear for 2 minutes on each of its 4 sides.

Put the pan in the oven and roast for 5 minutes for rare, 7 minutes for medium-rare. Remove the pan from the oven and place the tuna on a warm serving platter.

PREPARE THE SAUCE: Pour off half of the fat from the pan, place the pan over medium-low heat, and add the chanterelles. Cover and cook until the mushrooms are almost tender but not colored, 3 to 5 minutes. Add the shallots, season to taste with salt and pepper, and continue cooking until the shallots are softened, 1 to 2 minutes. Add the vinegar and simmer until reduced by about three-quarters. Add the wine, bring to a boil, and boil until the pan is almost dry. Add the stock and cook until reduced by one-half. Remove the pan from the heat and swirl in the remaining 2 tablespoons butter, a piece at a time, to emulsify. Stir in the chives.

To serve, cut the tuna into 12 slices with an electric knife or very sharp, long, thin-bladed knife. Place a spoonful of the potato-ramp puree in the center of each of six serving plates. Lean 2 slices of tuna against each scoop of puree and spoon the chanterelles and sauce around.

NOTE: Ask your fish purveyor to cut you a piece of tuna from the tail end of the loin so that it is relatively narrow. A wider cut will overcook on the outside before the inside warms.

Pancetta-wrapped tuna with sautéed fiddlehead ferns, wild asparagus, and ramps, along with a spike of bacon

31

MAINE PEEKY TOE CRAB SALAD WITH GREEN APPLE–CELERY GELÉE | Serves 4

In this salad, apples appear in a variety of forms: a gelée (in which apple juice is lightly thickened with gelatin), baked and glazed thin-sliced chips, and raw. At the restaurant, the crab salad is shaped with a 2¾-inch ring mold, but at home, you can serve it more simply.

FOR THE GELÉE
4 Granny Smith apples, cored
Pinch of vitamin C powder (see Note)
1 lime
One 2-ounce sheet gelatin or ½ teaspoon
    powdered gelatin
1 small celery stalk, peeled and finely diced

FOR THE APPLE CHIPS
2 tablespoons confectioners' sugar
½ McIntosh apple, very thinly sliced
    (on a mandoline)

FOR THE CRAB
1 pound peeky toe or other excellent-
    quality fresh crab, picked over for
    shells or cartilage
Fresh lemon juice to taste
Extra-virgin olive oil to taste
Kosher salt and freshly ground white pepper

1 head frisée, white and light yellow parts only
½ McIntosh apple, cored and cut into
    matchsticks
2 tablespoons walnuts, toasted and roughly
    chopped

PREPARE THE GELÉE: Coarsely chop 3½ of the apples. Finely dice the remaining ½ apple and set aside.

Put the chopped apples in the bowl of a food processor and process to a puree,

scraping down the sides of the bowl as needed. Add the vitamin C powder and process to blend. Line a strainer with a double thickness of damp cheesecloth, set the strainer over a bowl, and pour in the puree. When most of the liquid has gone through the strainer, press against the solids to extract the remaining liquid. Pour out and set aside 1 cup of the juice; drink the remaining juice or use for another purpose.

Slice off the top and bottom of the lime and remove the peel and all the pith. Slice between the membranes to release the lime sections. Remove any seeds and finely dice the sections. Set aside.

Drop the sheet gelatin into a bowl of cold water to soften or soften the powdered gelatin in 1 tablespoon cold water.

Meanwhile, warm ¼ cup of the apple juice in a small saucepan over low heat. Stir in the softened gelatin. When the gelatin is dissolved, pour the mixture into a bowl. Add the remaining ¾ cup apple juice and stir in the reserved diced apple, the celery, and lime. Chill until the gelatin sets and the gelée is syrupy, then cover and refrigerate until needed.

PREPARE THE APPLE CHIPS: Preheat the oven to 175°F.

Dust a nonstick baking sheet with 1 tablespoon of the confectioners' sugar and lay out the apple slices in a single layer, without overlapping. Sprinkle the slices with the remaining 1 tablespoon confectioners' sugar. Bake until the slices are crisp and very lightly browned, 1½ to 2 hours. Remove from the baking sheet while still warm and let cool on a flat surface.

PREPARE THE CRAB: Gently toss the crab with the lemon juice and olive oil. Season to taste with salt and white pepper.

ASSEMBLE THE DISH: Place a mound of the crab in each of four shallow soup bowls. Spoon one quarter of the gelée around the crab. Garnish each plate with a bouquet of frisée, some apple matchsticks, and an apple chip. Sprinkle with the toasted walnuts and serve. Enjoy the remaining chips as a snack.

NOTE: Vitamin C powder, found in health food stores, keeps apples from turning brown.

Crab salad topped with mixed lettuces, a baked apple slice, and raw apple cut into matchsticks

Daniel Boulud

I still flash back to the first time I burned the bread. I didn't do it twice. That's the way it was at that time. You didn't make mistakes. You strove for perfection at any cost. I'm learning to temper myself now away from that, but those are lessons that were hard-learned.

Jeffrey Buben

Jeffrey Buben

VIDALIA and BISTRO BIS | Washington, D.C.

In my kitchen today, I know I am not an example of the perfect chef. I have a tendency to be demanding and crazy and lose my temper and get very emotional about things when they don't go right.

I went to school at the Culinary Institute of America in Hyde Park, and apprenticed with a Dutch chef from Rotterdam. He was old school, a very frugal chef. Talented, bohemian, a brilliant mind, but a self-destructive personality. The typical stereotype of the excessive, drunken chef—just out of control. He could drink two or three bottles of wine in a day and still function. His cooking was brilliant. We cooked beautiful game at a private hunt club in upstate New York. We cooked earthy, wonderful food, very rustic, deep flavors. He was tough, but I was eighteen, nineteen, years old, and was inspired.

I still flash back to the first time I burned the bread. I didn't do it twice. That's the way it was at that time. You didn't make mistakes. You strove for perfection at any cost. I'm learning to temper myself now away from that, but those are lessons that were hard-learned. I try to tell my staff that you have to be disciplined. Cooking is an art that requires craftsmanship. You have to be true to your craft in order to be good.

ROAST SPRING CHICKEN AND VIOLA'S DUMPLINGS | Serves 4

"My grandmother Viola made this dish when I was a kid, but she didn't make it like we make it. Her way would be more country-style. We turned chicken and dumplings into haute cuisine."

This elegant rendition of a simple farmhouse chicken stew calls for small whole chickens that are roasted rather than stewed.

Viola made European-style dumplings that are very different from the fluffy, eggless American dumplings that you may be used to. European-style dumplings are soft on the outside with a firmer, drier, almost bready interior. They are simmered in stock just until the raw taste of the flour disappears and the interior firms. If cooked longer than that the outside of the dumplings will get gummy and mushy, while the inside will change very little.

FOR THE VEGETABLE GARNISH
3 medium carrots, peeled
3 medium parsnips, peeled
2 celery stalks, peeled
4 ounces thin asparagus, trimmed and cut into
    1½-inch lengths
12 pearl onions, peeled

4 tablespoons (½ stick) unsalted butter
½ cup diced (¼-inch) slab bacon
4 ounces white mushrooms, trimmed and
    halved or quartered, depending on size
Kosher salt and freshly ground black pepper

FOR THE CHICKENS
Four 1½- to 2-pound baby chickens or
    Cornish game hens (see Note)
Kosher salt and freshly ground black pepper
4 fresh thyme sprigs
4 bay leaves, preferably fresh

FOR THE SAUCE
2 tablespoons unsalted butter
¼ cup minced shallots
½ cup dry white wine
1 cup strong chicken stock
1 cup heavy cream
Kosher salt and freshly ground black pepper

FOR THE DUMPLINGS
1 cup sifted all-purpose flour
1½ teaspoons baking powder
½ teaspoon kosher salt
⅓ cup milk
1 large egg
8 cups chicken stock

2 tablespoons minced fresh chives for garnish

PREPARE THE VEGETABLES: Cut the carrots and parsnips lengthwise in half and then crosswise into pieces about 1½ inches long. Cut these pieces lengthwise in halves or quarters, depending on size, to make slender equal-sized lengths. Cut the celery lengthwise in half and then into 1½-inch lengths.

In a saucepan of boiling salted water, blanch the carrots until tender, 5 to 6 minutes. Transfer to a bowl with a slotted spoon. One at a time, blanch the parsnips, celery, asparagus, and onions, transferring the vegetables to the bowl when tender, 5 to 6 minutes for the parsnips, about 4 minutes for the celery, 2 to 3 minutes for the asparagus, and 8 to 12 minutes for the onions, depending on size; refresh the cooked asparagus under cold running water to stop the cooking. Set the vegetables aside.

PREPARE THE CHICKENS: Preheat the oven to 400°F.

Put a roasting or cast-iron pan large enough to hold the chickens without touching in the

oven and heat until the pan is very hot, about 10 minutes. Meanwhile, wash the chickens and pat dry. Season the cavities with salt and pepper and place 1 herb sprig and bay leaf in each. Sprinkle all over with salt and pepper.

When the roasting pan is hot, put the chickens in the pan and roast until the juices run clear when the birds are pierced in the thigh with a fork, about 50 to 60 minutes. Remove from the oven, cover loosely with aluminum foil, and let rest until ready to serve.

MEANWHILE, PREPARE THE SAUCE: Melt the butter in a medium saucepan over medium-low heat. Add the shallots and cook until translucent, 2 to 3 minutes. Add the wine, bring to a boil, and reduce to a glaze. Add the stock and cream and reduce by one-half. Season to taste with salt and pepper. Set aside.

PREPARE THE DUMPLINGS: Sift the dry ingredients together into a medium bowl. Beat the milk and egg in a measuring cup with a fork. Add to the flour mixture and stir with the fork to make a fairly stiff dough.

Bring the stock to a simmer in a large saucepan. Using two spoons, drop 1-inch balls of the dough into the simmering broth. Cover and simmer until cooked through, 8 to 10 minutes. Turn off the fire under the saucepan and leave the dumplings in the broth until ready to serve.

FINISH THE DISH: Melt the butter for the vegetables in a large frying pan over medium-high heat. Add the bacon and cook for about 2 minutes to render the fat. Add the mushrooms and cook for 1 minute. Add the vegetables and sauté until hot and lightly browned. Season to taste with salt and pepper.

Meanwhile, rewarm the sauce over medium heat.

Arrange the chickens on a large serving platter. Scatter the vegetables around. Remove the dumplings from the stock with a slotted spoon and arrange around the birds. Spoon the sauce over the chicken, sprinkle with the minced chives, and serve.

NOTE: You can use baby chickens, sold as *poussins* at many specialty food stores, or Cornish game hens. If your Cornish game hens are closer to 2 pounds apiece than 1½ pounds, add 10 minutes to the roasting time.

VIDALIA'S BAKED ONION | Serves 4

This signature appetizer is made with the sweet onion that gave the restaurant its name. It is served when the onions are in season, from early April through November or December, with a sweet-and-sour sauce that accentuates the sweetness of the onion. If Vidalias are not available in your market, you can substitute another variety of sweet onion, such as Walla Walla, Maui, or Grano.

FOR THE ONIONS
4 large Vidalia onions
4 tablespoons unsalted butter
4 teaspoons chopped fresh thyme
4 teaspoons chopped fresh rosemary
2 tablespoons chopped garlic
3 tablespoons dark brown sugar
½ cup sherry vinegar
¼ cup beef stock

FOR THE SAUCE
2 tablespoons unsalted butter
12 large shiitake mushrooms, stemmed and
  thinly sliced
¼ pound country ham, cut into thin strips
  about 1½ inches long
¼ cup peeled, seeded, and diced ripe tomato
1 tablespoon drained tiny capers

¼ cup chopped fresh chives
Kosher salt and freshly ground black pepper

PREPARE THE ONIONS: Preheat the oven to 375°F.

Slice off the tops of the onions. Using a small knife to make the original cut for each strip, gently peel back the skins in strips about ½ to ¾ inch wide, all the way to the root ends, leaving the skins attached at the roots.

Cut four 12-inch squares of aluminum foil. Put 1 tablespoon of the butter, 1 teaspoon each of the chopped thyme and rosemary, one-quarter of the garlic, and one-quarter of the brown sugar in the center of each foil square. Set an onion root end up on top of each. Gently lift the strips of skin up above each onion as you bring the four corners of the foil squares over to meet at the root. Then crimp the foil around the root of the onion to make a "neck" with the strips of skin sticking out. Spoon 2 tablespoons of the vinegar and 1 tablespoon stock into each packet.

Place the foil packets on a baking sheet and bake until the onions are tender, about 1¼ hours. Remove the onions from the foil, carefully reserving the juices, and place on serving plates. Set aside in a warm spot.

PREPARE THE SAUCE: Melt the butter in a medium frying pan over medium-high heat. Add the mushrooms and ham and cook until the mushrooms are tender, 4 to 5 minutes. Add the reserved juices from the onions, bring to a boil, and reduce until thickened. Add the tomato, capers, and chives, stirring to mix. Season to taste with salt and pepper.

To serve, spoon the sauce around the onions.

Jeffrey Buben

37

Tom Colicchio

GRAMERCY TAVERN and CRAFT | New York

It all starts with the product: finding great ingredients and then working from the ingredients and trying to work with them in combinations, but always in a natural way. I don't want the food to appear too fussed with or too played with. A trained eye will know there's a lot going on, but to the untrained eye it should look very simple.

You can start with one ingredient, an artichoke, for example, and braise it in some white wine with some vegetables and olive oil. And once you have that artichoke ragout, you can think about what you're going to do with it. You can simply serve it the way it is—it is very good on its own. Or you can chill it down, take the cooking liquid, and turn it into a vinaigrette, which is another technique. You can add lobster to it and have a lobster-artichoke salad. Or you can use the cooking liquid to braise fish. There are many things you can do once you have the artichokes.

Or you might begin with three ingredients, and by using different techniques on each of the ingredients, create different dishes or different riffs on the one dish. For instance, take lobster/pasta/peas. If I'm cooking at home, I might do this: cook the lobster, chop it up, boil some peas, boil some pasta, and toss it all together with some olive oil. It's a good, simple dish. But if you take the lobster bodies and make a lobster stock, and then make a lobster sauce, add it to the lobster/pasta/peas, you have a better dish, a more complex dish, and it just takes a little more time and effort. We could also place the focus on the peas. We could make a chilled pea soup and take some lobster, cook it, combine it with some orzo and some herbs, and use it to garnish the soup. Same three ingredients, just put together in a different way.

I had a recipe tester working with me [on *Think Like a Chef*] who just watched me and went off and wrote the recipes—I hate writing recipes. As I was cooking, she would point things out to me. She would say, "What are you doing?" And I'd say, "Roasting some vegetables." And she'd say: "No, no, no. There's something that you're doing, you're adding something to the pan a little at a time, or you're controlling the heat a different way, no one teaches you how to do this, why are you doing it?" So I had to really think about why I do things.

PAN-ROASTED TURBOT WITH BLACK TRUFFLE VINAIGRETTE | Serves 6

Turbot is a delicate-flavored, fine-fleshed European flatfish that is likely to be difficult to find. If you do see it, it will be expensive, but grab it anyway—it's a delicious fish. Halibut is a good substitute if you can't find it.

The fish is cooked over medium rather than high heat because slower cooking enhances the flavor of the fish. Make sure to dry the fish well so that it doesn't stick to the pan.

You will find jarred preserved black truffles in specialty stores without much problem. They are sold in a little of the juice in which they are cooked; use that juice in the vinaigrette.

FOR THE TRUFFLE VINAIGRETTE
1 tablespoon chopped fresh or preserved black truffle (about ⅓ ounce)
3 tablespoons black truffle juice (optional)
2 tablespoons white wine vinegar
¼ teaspoon kosher salt
⅛ teaspoon freshly ground black pepper
½ cup extra-virgin olive oil

FOR THE SWISS CHARD
1½ pounds Swiss chard, trimmed and washed

1½ tablespoons unsalted butter
Scant ½ teaspoon kosher salt
⅛ teaspoon freshly ground black pepper

FOR THE TURBOT
¼ cup peanut oil
Six 8- to 10-ounce pieces turbot or halibut, on the bone
Kosher salt and freshly ground black pepper
4 tablespoons (½ stick) unsalted butter
2 large fresh thyme sprigs, plus 6 small sprigs for garnish

PREPARE THE VINAIGRETTE: Combine the chopped truffle, truffle juice, vinegar, salt, and pepper in a small bowl. Gradually whisk in the oil and set aside.

PREPARE THE CHARD: Cut off the stems of the chard and peel them with a vegetable peeler. Cut the stems into matchstick-sized pieces. Tear the leaves into large pieces.

Bring a large pot of water to a boil. Add the chard stems and boil until barely tender, about 3 minutes. Remove with a slotted spoon or spider to a colander and drain; transfer to a bowl. Add the leaves to the boiling water and cook until limp, 1 to 2 minutes. Drain and add to the bowl with the stems. Set the chard aside.

PAN-ROAST THE FISH: Heat 2 tablespoons of the oil in each of two large frying pans over medium heat. Pat the fish dry with paper towels and sprinkle on both sides with salt and pepper. Add the fish to the pans skin-side down and cook for 3 minutes, then turn the fillets and cook for 3 more minutes. Turn the heat to low. Add 2 tablespoons of the butter and 1 large sprig of thyme to each pan and continue cooking the fillets, turning them once again so that they brown evenly. Baste with the lightly browned butter, until they are opaque throughout, about 4 more minutes for 1-inch-thick fillets, somewhat longer for thicker fillets (cut into the fish with a small knife to check). Transfer the fish to a cutting board and remove the skin and bones. Set the pans aside.

MEANWHILE, FINISH THE CHARD: Just before serving, melt the butter in a large frying pan over medium heat. Add the chard stems and leaves, salt, and pepper and cook, tossing, until the chard is warmed through, about 1 minute.

To serve, place the boned fillets on 6 serving plates. Arrange the chard alongside. Drizzle the fish with some of the browned butter from the pans and then with the truffle vinaigrette. Garnish each plate with a sprig of thyme and serve.

SPICED LOBSTER WITH GREEN TOMATO CHUTNEY

For this dish of Indian-spiced lobster, lobster bodies are simmered with orange zest, fresh ginger, cardamom, and a mixture of crumbled bay leaf, cayenne, toasted mustard, coriander, and fennel seeds, and ground in a spice or coffee grinder to make a stock. The stock is reduced by about two-thirds, allowed to steep for 10 minutes, then strained and enriched with crème fraîche and lobster butter.

The lobster tails are wrapped in plastic wrap (the plastic seals the flesh, so as not to wash away flavor) and parboiled along with the claws in boiling salted water. The shelled tails and claws are then sautéed in butter and olive oil with bay leaves and more lobster spice.

Just before serving, the sauce is frothed in a blender or with a hand-held mixer, and finished with whole pink "peppercorns" (actually a mild tasting red berry). The lobster is arranged on the plate with the sauce and fava beans that have been blanched, tossed in butter, and seasoned with salt and pepper. The sauce is spooned around. The dish is garnished with a room-temperature green tomato chutney made from green tomatoes cooked with a red bell pepper, sugar, white wine vinegar, garlic, fresh and dried chile pepper, fresh ginger, fresh tarragon and thyme, and cardamom, mustard, coriander, and fennel seeds.

Tom Colicchio

Gary Danko

There is a lot of drama in running a restaurant. It's like a Broadway musical: no matter what sort of dysfunctional crises we may encounter at any given moment, it is my job to put on a performance. I cannot let it show that there is anything unusual going on in the kitchen—you know, that the plumbing is backing up. . .

In the library at CIA [Culinary Institute of America], I came across a book that changed my life. It was written by Madeleine Kamman. She was interested, as I am, in the art and science of cooking, and was one of the first people to put the *hows* and *whys* of cooking into practical application. Example: When I went to CIA they showed how to make a hollandaise sauce, but they didn't tell why it might break. They would show you how to fix it if it did break, but there was no technical information on why that hollandaise sauce breaks. I wanted to know that, the *how* and the *why*, because then you can become a better cook. And that comes a step before technique. When you learn those principles, you can be proactive in that hollandaise breaking by knowing what's going to make it happen. And what makes it break is that eventually, as it sits there, it loses its moisture, and it is the water that keeps the emulsion in suspension. That is a very simple illustration. Madeleine went even further into things, like that if a crème anglaise breaks, it could be that you tasted it, put your finger into your mouth, and then back into the bowl. The enzymes in your saliva jar this reaction that separates the crème. This is all part of the art and science of cooking.

I worked in a place in Vermont called Tucker Hill. Vermont is like an unsung California. In California, they get all the praise. . . . Vermonters make some beautiful products, but they don't get the praise. I felt like I was in a chef's paradise. Being close to Maine, we had very beautiful seafood. All the seafood that all the New York chefs are touting right now, I was getting them back then when nobody else was tapping that source. I had scallops, halibut, fresh crabmeat, live scallops in the shell, and then I had all the people who would churn butter for the restaurant, or make cheese, or bake bread in their wood-burning oven. So it was a paradise there.

FILLET OF BEEF WITH STILTON BUTTER AND CANDIED SHALLOTS | Serves 6

This is a straightforward, elegant dish of steak and potatoes topped with a stilton butter and garnished with shallots cooked in red wine, port, and crème de cassis.

Red wine–candied shallots are traditionally cooked with a gastrique—a combination of sugar and vinegar that gives the shallots a sweet-and-sour flavor. Here, the shallots are cooked without the sugar and vinegar; the shallots' own sweetness is accented by careful caramelization and balanced by the acidity of the red wine.

Glace de viande is a very reduced meat stock that you can find at many specialty food stores. For a lighter dish, the gratin can be made with stock in lieu of cream.

FOR THE POTATO GRATIN
1 garlic clove, smashed with the side of a large knife
2 tablespoons unsalted butter, softened
3 pounds Red Bliss or Yukon Gold potatoes
2 cups heavy cream
1 tablespoon kosher salt
½ teaspoon freshly ground black pepper
¼ teaspoon freshly grated nutmeg

FOR THE CANDIED SHALLOTS
2 cups veal or chicken stock
⅓ cup dry red wine
⅓ cup cassis liqueur or syrup
⅓ cup port wine
4 tablespoons (½ stick) unsalted butter
2 pounds shallots, peeled, root ends trimmed but left attached
1 bay leaf
½ teaspoon dried thyme
½ teaspoon grated lemon zest

FOR THE STILTON BUTTER
8 tablespoons (1 stick) unsalted butter, softened
3 ounces Stilton cheese, crumbled (about ⅔ cup)
1½ teaspoons Cognac
1½ teaspoons chopped fresh chervil or 1 teaspoon chopped fresh parsley
    plus ½ teaspoon chopped fresh tarragon

1½ teaspoons chopped fresh tarragon
1½ teaspoons minced fresh chives
½ teaspoon kosher salt

FOR THE STEAK
Six 5-ounce fillet steaks, about 1¼ inches thick
6 thin slices prosciutto (about 4 ounces), cut lengthwise in half
1 tablespoon olive oil
Kosher salt and freshly ground black pepper

FOR THE SAUCE
4 garlic cloves, minced
½ cup dry Madeira
¾ cup glace de viande
2 teaspoons chopped fresh rosemary
2 tablespoons unsalted butter
Kosher salt and freshly ground black pepper

PREPARE THE POTATO GRATIN: Preheat the oven to 350°F. Rub a large gratin dish with the garlic clove, then rub the dish with the butter.

Peel and thinly slice the potatoes on a mandoline or vegetable slicer and layer them evenly in the gratin dish. Season the cream with the salt, pepper, and nutmeg and pour it over the potatoes.

Place the dish in the oven and bake the gratin until the cream is absorbed and the crust is golden brown, about 2 hours. Remove and keep warm; increase the oven temperature to 400°F.

MEANWHILE, PREPARE THE SHALLOTS: Combine the stock, wine, cassis, and port in a large measuring cup and set aside.

Melt the butter in a medium frying pan over medium-high heat. Add the shallots and toss to coat with the butter. Cook, tossing often, until the shallots are golden brown, 5 to 6 minutes. Add about ¾ cup of the wine-stock mixture, along with the bay leaf, thyme, and lemon zest. Bring to a boil, reduce the heat, and simmer until the liquid has reduced to a glaze. Add another ¾ cup of the liquid and reduce again. Continue until all of the liquid has been used and the shallots are tender, about 1 hour and 15 minutes. Set aside.

44

PREPARE THE STILTON BUTTER: Combine all of the ingredients in the bowl of a food processor and process until blended. Set aside.

PREPARE THE STEAK: Wrap each steak with 2 strips of prosciutto. Secure the prosciutto with toothpicks.

Heat a large ovenproof frying pan over medium-high heat for 3 minutes. Rub the steaks on both sides with the oil and season with salt and pepper. Add the steaks to the hot pan and sear for 2 minutes on each side. Remove from the heat and put 1 tablespoon of the Stilton butter on top of each steak (reserve the remainder for another use).

Put the pan in the oven and cook until the steaks are medium-rare, about 4 minutes. Transfer the steaks to a serving platter; set the pan aside. Carefully remove the toothpicks from the steaks. Cover loosely with aluminum foil to keep them warm while you make the sauce.

PREPARE THE SAUCE: Place the frying pan over medium heat. Add the garlic and sauté for 1 minute. Add the Madeira and simmer until reduced by one-half. Stir in the glace de viande, rosemary, and butter and continue simmering until the sauce is thick enough to nap the steak. Season to taste with salt and pepper.

To serve, spoon the sauce over the steaks. Spoon the shallots around and serve hot, with the potato gratin.

Fillet of beef served with a mix of sautéed seasonal vegetables along with the shallots

45

ROAST QUAIL STUFFED WITH WILD MUSHROOMS | Serves 6

These days, quail are conveniently sold semi-boneless (completely boned except for the legs), making them easy to eat as well as to stuff. Here, the quail are stuffed with a wild mushroom ragout, roasted whole, and served with young vegetables. You could also serve the quail with potato gratin (see page 44).

You'll need to start the recipe a day before you plan to serve it to give the quail time to marinate.

FOR THE MARINADE

¼ cup red wine (preferably a cabernet or
    pinot noir)
2 garlic cloves, chopped
1¼ teaspoons kosher salt
5 teaspoons Dijon mustard
1¼ teaspoons dried thyme
1½ teaspoons ground coriander
¼ cup olive oil

12 semi-boneless quail, wing tips removed

FOR THE MUSHROOM RAGOUT

2 tablespoons olive oil
1 pound wild mushrooms, such as chanterelle,
    shiitake, oyster, or cremini trimmed and
    coarsely chopped
2 garlic cloves, minced
1 tablespoon chopped fresh parsley
1 teaspoon kosher salt
½ teaspoon freshly ground black pepper

2 tablespoons olive oil
Kosher salt and freshly ground black pepper

FOR THE SAUCE

2 cups chicken or veal stock
2 tablespoons unsalted butter
Kosher salt and freshly ground black pepper

ONE DAY AHEAD, PREPARE THE MARINADE AND MARINATE THE QUAIL: Combine all of the marinade ingredients in a small bowl. Brush the quail with the marinade and place in a bowl. Cover with plastic wrap and refrigerate overnight.

THE NEXT DAY, PREPARE THE MUSHROOM RAGOUT: Heat the oil in a large frying pan over medium-high heat. Add the mushrooms and cook until they are limp and the juices they released have evaporated, 8 to 10 minutes. Stir in the garlic, parsley, salt, and pepper. Let cool completely.

COOK THE QUAIL: Preheat the oven to 350°F.

When the ragout is cool, spoon it into the body cavities of the quail. Then roughly truss the quail: Cross the legs of each quail at the "ankles" and press the legs toward the breast to make a compact package and enclose the stuffing. Center a piece of kitchen twine under the "ankles" and bring the ends of the twine up and around to tie the ankles together. Run the ends of the twine along the breasts of the quail and over the wing joints, and tie the two ends together at the neck.

Heat 1 tablespoon of the oil in each of two small ovenproof frying pans, preferably nonstick, over medium-high heat. Add the quail and brown all over, about 2 minutes. Place the pans in the oven and roast the quail until the breast meat is medium-rare, about 12 minutes.

Sprinkle the quail with salt and pepper and transfer to a serving platter. Remove the kitchen twine. Cover loosely with aluminum foil to keep the quail warm while you make the sauce.

PREPARE THE SAUCE: Pour off the fat from the pans. Add 1 cup of the stock to each pan and simmer, scraping the bottom of the pans with a wooden spoon to pick up any browned bits, until reduced by about one-half. Combine all of the stock in one pan, whisk in the butter, and season to taste with salt and pepper.

To serve, spoon the sauce over the quail.

Two quail, stuffed, browned and roasted, and served with young vegetables

Gary Danko

In the end, your cooking reflects where home is and conveys who you are. Someone might ask, "Well, who are you?" And you might say, "Well, let me show you what I eat."

Robert Del Grande

Robert Del Grande

We try to show what cooking is like in Texas, and that means that we don't try to compete with France or Italy or other places; we just do our own thing. There is a food writer I know from way back, a really interesting fellow, and he said that if someone were to blindfold you and fly you on a plane to a restaurant somewhere that you should be able to tell where you are by tasting the food in that restaurant. To him, it was important that a restaurant in a certain region should speak of that region. I was very attracted by that idea. It really made sense to me. I don't serve an international, global cuisine that could be transported anywhere and not lose something. When I moved to Texas, I was basically a Californian. Texas seemed kind of foreign to me, how things worked. The longer I lived here, the more things became more natural and intuitive, and less foreign. Texas has a whole sense of country to it, it's kind of Mexico/Texas, and there's that Mexican feel to the food in terms of chilies and spice. . . . Compared to New England or San Francisco, the way we do things is much different.

Of course, we don't live in a vacuum. We are influenced by all sorts of things. And we always look for inspiration from other places. Our salmon, for example, comes mostly from the Pacific Northwest or from the Northeast. But we don't cook it in the style of the Pacific Northwest. We do it our own way. You have to look at that salmon and say, not, "How do I make it Texan?" but,

"If I lived in Texas, how would I want to eat it, naturally?" I feel that the salmon is a little bit oily and not very racy, that it needs some spice, and we make this black chile salsa which is kind of whacky, and for some reason it works. We buy the black chiles from Mexico and we actually toast some bananas, too, and some other things that we puree into this salsa—it's kind of smoky and spicy, and with the salmon, it's great. When I look at it, I think, "Yeah, this is probably not New York City."

When I used to go up to San Francisco, I'd have breakfast, fried eggs and bacon, and I'd put salt and pepper on them and eat the eggs with the bacon, and toast or whatever. Now, I had fried eggs at home this morning and I got a little bottle of hot chile sauce out of the refrigerator and put it on the eggs. . . . Very few people around here would eat eggs without putting hot chile sauce on them. Eggs and chiles, oh yeah, a spicy Texas breakfast! It's real cultural.

49

CAFÉ ANNIE, TACO MILAGRO, and RIO RANCH | Houston   **CAFÉ EXPRESS** | Various locations in the Southwest

SEARED SEA SCALLOPS WITH AVOCADO RELISH AND JICAMA SALAD | Serves 4

Here is a scallop appetizer with flavors from Texas and Mexico: guacamole, cilantro, jicama, and lime. A rich-flavored walnut oil sets off the sweetness of the jicama.

FOR THE AVOCADO RELISH

1 ripe Hass avocado
¼ cup minced white onion
1 serrano chile, stemmed and minced
    (with seeds to taste)
1 tablespoon finely chopped fresh cilantro
1 tablespoon olive or walnut oil
Juice of ½ lime (1 to 1½ tablespoons)
½ teaspoon kosher salt
⅛ teaspoon freshly ground black pepper
½ ripe tomato, chopped

FOR THE JICAMA SALAD

2 cups peeled and diced (¼-inch) jicama
1 tablespoon walnut oil
4 teaspoons fresh lime juice
½ teaspoon kosher salt
¼ teaspoon dried red pepper flakes

FOR THE SCALLOPS

8 large sea scallops (about 12 ounces total)
Kosher salt and freshly ground black pepper
2 tablespoons olive oil

FOR THE CILANTRO GARNISH

2 loosely packed cups fresh cilantro sprigs
    (about ½ bunch)
1 teaspoon walnut oil
½ teaspoon fresh lime juice
Pinch of kosher salt

PREPARE THE RELISH: Peel and pit the avocado and roughly dice it. Put the avocado into a bowl with all of the remaining ingredients except the tomato and use a large spoon to mix, mashing the avocado to make a coarse salsa. (Do not overwork the avocado; leave bits of it unmashed.) Stir in the chopped tomato. Place a sheet of plastic wrap directly against the surface of the relish to keep the avocado from darkening and refrigerate the relish until ready to serve.

PREPARE THE SALAD: Combine all of the ingredients in a bowl and toss gently to combine. Set aside at room temperature.

PREPARE THE SCALLOPS: Sprinkle the scallops with salt and pepper. Heat the oil in a large frying pan over high heat until very hot. Add the scallops and cook until well browned on both sides, 1 to 2 minutes on each side. Reduce the heat to low and continue cooking until the scallops are firm but still give under light pressure, 2 to 3 more minutes.

MEANWHILE, PREPARE THE GARNISH: Combine all of the ingredients in a bowl and toss.

ASSEMBLE THE DISH: Slice each scallop horizontally in half. Make a pile of jicama salad in the center of each of four serving plates. Tightly arrange 4 slices of scallops around each salad. Place a spoonful of the avocado relish onto each scallop slice. Set a small pile of the cilantro garnish on top of each salad and serve immediately.

The textural contrasts in the dish are lovely—the silky, smooth avocado and scallop are balanced by the crunch of the jicama salad.

PHEASANT ROASTED WITH CINNAMON AND BACON WITH RED CHILE–PECAN SAUCE

A whole pheasant is rubbed with a spice-rub mixture of cinnamon, ancho chile powder, salt, and pepper and roasted in a slow oven until partially cooked through. Then the legs and breasts are removed from the carcasses, the legs returned to the oven to finish cooking, and the breasts set aside. The carcasses are used to make a rich brown pheasant stock flavored with bacon.

For the sauce, toasted pecans, the pheasant stock, and cascabel or dried Santa Fe chiles are simmered together, then pureed and creamed.

Just before serving, the pheasant legs and breasts are brushed with a maple syrup–balsamic vinegar glaze spiced with cinnamon. The birds are broiled to crisp the skin and then put in the oven to finish cooking.

The breasts are sliced and fanned on the plates along with the legs. Each plate is garnished with a coil of bacon slices, sprigs of watercress, and a pool of the chile sauce.

Robert Del Grande

Traci Des Jardins JARDINIÈRE | San Francisco

I was raised in the Central Valley of California, and cooking was at the center of my family's social life. My father is a farmer. My grandfather from Louisiana loved to cook more than anything else. An aunt and uncle of mine loved going to good restaurants. They all definitely influenced my decision to be a chef. In my family, food was very important.

I didn't start cooking professionally until I was seventeen. I didn't go to [cooking] school. I started a series of traditional apprenticeships, working with French chefs in America. Then I went to Europe, and New York, and then I came back to California. In France, all the restaurants I worked in were three-star; they have such a high proportion of workers—service staff and kitchen personnel—compared to the number of covers they do, so it is very different in style from what we do in the United States. Of course, it was wonderful to experience the culture and food of France, and it definitely influences what I do.

New York is a little different, fast paced. I find that in California, you're much more connected to the food sources, the farmers and the producers, and there is a greater awareness of where the food is coming from and how it is being produced. Here you really have a lot of contact with the people who are growing the food, the processes they go through, whether they are cheese makers or farmers or somebody who is producing meat.

I still prefer mushrooms from Europe to those grown here. I think they have a lot more flavor. If you can get fresh porcini from Italy or cèpes from France, they have a very different flavor from the ones from here, as do chanterelles and wild field mushrooms.

We have an aging room for our cheeses, which we buy from around the world—France, Australia, Italy, Holland, England, Spain—and the American artisans as well. So we have a good array of cheeses. It's one of my passions, having lived in France, and when I opened my restaurant, I really wanted to have a nice facility to be able to care for them properly. So much of what you do for cheese is to care for it properly. So I created the aging room. Cheese is one of our specialties.

55

PAN-ROASTED CHICKEN WITH MORELS, SPRING PEAS, AND HEIRLOOM POTATOES | Serves 4

Ideally, this is a recipe to make in the spring, when fresh morels, peas, and pea sprouts are all in the market and you can find tiny fresh spring onions, too. But you can make this at other times of the year using pearl onions, year-round varieties of cultivated mushrooms such as portobello, cremini, and/or oyster, and, spinach in lieu of the pea sprouts.

FOR THE SAUCE

2 tablespoons vegetable oil
2 pounds chicken bones, necks, or backs, chopped into 2-inch pieces with a cleaver or a large heavy knife
1 carrot, roughly chopped
1 celery stalk, roughly chopped
2 shallots, roughly chopped
1 garlic clove, crushed
1 cup dry white wine
5 cups chicken stock
2 fresh thyme sprigs
6 parsley stems

1 tablespoon unsalted butter
Kosher salt and freshly ground black pepper

FOR THE VEGETABLES

1 pound baby Russian Banana potatoes or other fingerling or small new potatoes
2 cups shelled fresh peas
1 pound morel mushrooms, trimmed
3 tablespoons unsalted butter
½ cup chicken stock
12 tiny spring onions, trimmed of all but ½ inch of green, or 12 pearl onions, peeled
Kosher salt
Freshly ground black pepper
2 tablespoons clarified unsalted butter
4 ounces pea sprouts or stemmed spinach (4 firmly packed cups)

FOR THE CHICKEN

4 boneless chicken breasts, with skin, first wing joint still attached (see Note)
Kosher salt and freshly ground black pepper
1 tablespoon clarified unsalted butter

PREPARE THE SAUCE: Preheat the oven to 450°F.

Heat a heavy roasting pan over medium-high heat. Add the oil and bones and cook, stirring occasionally, until the bones are golden brown, about 10 minutes. Add the carrot, celery, shallots, and garlic. Put the pan in the oven and roast, stirring every now and then, until the bones and vegetables are well caramelized, 25 to 30 minutes.

Remove the pan from the oven, add the wine, and place over medium-high heat. Bring to a boil and deglaze, scraping up the browned bits stuck to the bottom of the pan. Transfer to a large saucepan, place over medium heat, and simmer until the wine is reduced to a glaze. Add the chicken stock, thyme, and parsley stems. Bring to a simmer and skim off the fat and froth with a small ladle. Then simmer until reduced by three-quarters. Strain through a fine-meshed strainer into a clean saucepan and set aside.

PREPARE THE VEGETABLES: Place the potatoes in a saucepan, add cold water to cover, and salt the water. Bring to a boil and simmer, partially covered, until the potatoes are tender, 15 to 25 minutes, depending on size. Remove the potatoes from the saucepan with a slotted spoon; reserve the water for cooking the peas. Set the potatoes aside until cool enough to handle, then peel them; if they are large, cut them into bite-sized pieces. Place in a bowl.

Return the potato water to a boil, add the peas, and cook until just tender, 1½ to 2 minutes. Drain and immediately plunge into a bowl of ice water to stop the cooking. When the peas are chilled, drain and set aside.

Meanwhile, dunk the morels into a bowl of cold water and lift them out leaving any sand at the bottom of the bowl. Repeat the process 3 more times, replacing the water with fresh cold water each time. Drain well.

Melt 1 tablespoon of the butter in a large frying pan over medium-high heat. Add the morels and cook until they begin to sizzle and brown slightly, 2 to 3 minutes. Reduce the heat to low, add ¼ cup of the chicken stock, and cook until the morels are tender, about 2 more minutes. Transfer to a bowl and set aside. Set the pan aside.

Put the onions in a medium saucepan with 1 tablespoon of the butter, place over medium heat, and cook, stirring, for 2 minutes. Sprinkle with ½ teaspoon salt and ¼ teaspoon pepper, or to taste. Add 2 tablespoons water for spring onions, ½ cup water for pearl onions, cover, and cook until the onions are tender, about 4 minutes for spring onions, 15 minutes for pearl onions. Drain and transfer the onions to the bowl with the mushrooms.

PREPARE THE CHICKEN: Preheat the oven to 450°F.

Sprinkle the chicken breasts on both sides with salt and pepper. Heat a large heavy ovenproof frying pan over medium-high heat. When the pan is very hot, add the clarified butter and swirl it to coat the bottom of the pan. Add the chicken breasts skin side down and cook until the skin is a rich golden brown, 4 to 5 minutes. Put the pan in the oven and roast until the chicken is cooked through, 12 to 15 minutes.

MEANWHILE, FINISH THE VEGETABLES: Heat a large frying pan over medium-high heat. When it is very hot, add the clarified butter. Add the potatoes and cook until golden brown, about 5 minutes. Season with ½ teaspoon salt and ¼ teaspoon pepper, or to taste.

While the potatoes are cooking, add the remaining 1 tablespoon butter to the frying pan used for the mushrooms and heat over medium heat. Add the morels and onions and cook, stirring, until heated through. Add the peas and pea sprouts or spinach and cook, stirring, until wilted. Stir in the remaining ¼ cup chicken stock, the peas, and potatoes and toss.

FINISH THE SAUCE: Bring the sauce to a boil and swirl in the butter to emulsify. Season with salt and pepper.

To serve, spoon the vegetable mixture onto warm serving plates. Slice the chicken and fan it on top of the vegetables. Drizzle the sauce around and serve hot.

NOTE: Ask your butcher to prepare the chicken breasts so that they are boned, with just the first, meaty joint of the wing still attached. (Or you can bone supermarket breasts, and cut off the last two joints of the wings yourself.)

PORCINI MUSHROOM AND SQUAB TARTS WITH AN HERB SALAD SEASONED WITH AGED BALSAMIC VINEGAR

For these savory open-faced tarts, 3½-inch puff pastry rounds are baked until crisp. A mushroom duxelles, seasoned with fresh thyme and parsley and bound with a little reduced cream, is spread in a thin layer over the pastry. Sautéed sliced fresh porcini mushrooms are fanned out on top, so that the tips of the slices touch the edge of the pastry rounds. Breast of squab, sautéed medium-rare and thinly sliced, is fanned on top, in the center of the tart, so that the porcini slices peek out from underneath. An herb salad of celery leaves, celery sprouts, chervil, parsley, chives, and chive blossoms is sprinkled over the tops of the tarts and around the plates. Aged balsamic vinegar is drizzled around the plates to finish.

Traci Des Jardins

57

Rocco DiSpirito **UNION PACIFIC** | New York

The idea of balance in food is starting to carry over into my life as well. I recognize that in order to achieve longevity, you have to work a balance into your life, the same way I work it into the food.

Ethnic cooking is extremely popular these days, and I think that's because it is exciting. It is often characterized by a marvelous tension that comes from the juxtaposition of sweet, sour, salty, and bitter flavors. If you look at all ethnic food, whether Asian, Indian, South American, there's this acidity and sugar and salt that are constantly repeating in the food, and that is very exciting and I take a lot of cues from that. These are the four flavors that the palate recognizes, and balancing them properly is what makes food taste exciting. I like to keep this in mind when I'm cooking. When I need one of these four flavors, I don't limit myself in terms of its origin. If I feel a dish could use something salty, I might use Thai fish sauce, or seaweed from Normandy, or dried fish from Sweden. . . .

I use seasonal products. With spring coming, I started to think about Copper River salmon. This salmon has an intense natural fattiness that needs something to temper it, and it occurred to me that rhubarb, which comes into season at the same time, would do that perfectly. It's got an acidity that tempers the salmon's fattiness, makes it taste cleaner. It also tempers the salmon's rich, gamy flavor. Salmon needs something very, very tart, so what could be better than rhubarb? I could have chosen lemon juice— it's also acid—but I thought the additional "fruitiness" of the rhubarb made for an interesting and exciting combination. You have to make things exciting.

In my free time, I mostly eat at other restaurants. There was a long period of time when I had no idea what other people were doing. It's interesting to see how much cooking in New York has changed in just the last few years.

59

SEARED COPPER RIVER SALMON WITH ONIONS AND RHUBARB | Serves 4

In spring, rhubarb, fava beans, spring onions, and the annual run of wild salmon on the Copper River coincide. The Copper River runs through Washington State and Alaska and is home to what DiSpirito believes to be some of the best wild salmon available. The river produces mostly king salmon, and some cohos in late summer. If you can't get Copper River or other wild salmon, you can use farmed salmon, although the flavor and texture of the farmed fish is quite different from the wild.

FOR THE RHUBARB
1½ cups dry (fino) sherry
¼ cup turbinado, palm, or granulated sugar
½ pound rhubarb, trimmed and sliced on an
    angle into ½-inch pieces

FOR THE ONIONS AND BEANS
3 tablespoons unsalted butter
1 pound spring onions, trimmed and
    thinly sliced
½ cup chicken stock
1 fresh thyme sprig
Kosher salt and freshly ground black pepper
1 pound fava beans, shelled

1 teaspoon fresh lemon juice

FOR THE SALMON
Four 6-ounce Copper River salmon fillets,
    skin-on
Vegetable oil for grilling
Kosher salt and freshly ground black pepper

PREPARE THE RHUBARB: Combine the sherry and sugar in a medium saucepan. Bring to a boil over high heat, stirring occasionally until the sugar is dissolved. Add the rhubarb and cook until just tender, about 1 minute.

Drain in a colander set over a bowl, and set the rhubarb aside. Return the liquid to the saucepan, bring to a boil over high heat, and cook until reduced to ½ cup, about 8 minutes. Set aside.

PREPARE THE ONIONS AND BEANS: Melt the butter in a medium saucepan over low heat. Add the onions, cover, and cook, stirring every now and then, until softened, about 15 minutes. Add the chicken stock, thyme, and a pinch each of salt and pepper. Bring to a boil, reduce the heat to low, and simmer for 6 more minutes.

Meanwhile, bring a medium saucepan of salted water to a boil. Add the shelled fava beans and cook for 2 minutes. Drain and refresh the beans under cold running water; drain again.

Pop the beans out of their jackets, add them to the onion mixture, and simmer for 2 more minutes. Remove from the heat and set aside.

PREPARE THE SALMON: Prepare a medium fire in a grill or heat a grill pan over medium heat.

Lightly oil the salmon fillets and sprinkle with salt and pepper. Put the salmon skin side down on the grill or in the grill pan and grill until the skin is very crisp, about 4 minutes. Turn the salmon and grill until barely cooked through, 3 to 5 more minutes, depending on the thickness of the fillets.

MEANWHILE, FINISH THE REST OF THE DISH: Remove and discard the thyme sprig from the onion mixture. Bring the mixture to a simmer, stir in the lemon juice, and season to taste with salt and pepper.

Bring the sherry-sugar syrup to a boil over high heat. Add the rhubarb and boil to reheat it, about 1 minute.

To serve, divide the rhubarb among four large serving plates. Spoon the onion and bean mixture over the rhubarb and place the salmon fillets on top of the vegetables.

Copper River salmon owes its extraordinary flavor and bright red color to its diet of shrimp.

60

BRAISED BEEF SHORT RIBS WITH TRUFFLED TARO ROOT | Serves 4

These succulent Asian-flavored braised ribs are served with taro root, a starchy, somewhat nutty-tasting root, available in Asian and Latin American markets.

FOR THE SHORT RIBS

3 pieces star anise
1 teaspoon whole cloves
1 teaspoon fennel seeds
2 tablespoons cumin seeds
2 pounds beef short ribs, trimmed to
    4-inch pieces
1½ teaspoons Szechwan peppercorns
Coarse sea salt and freshly ground white pepper
¼ cup corn oil
2 cups diced onions
½ cup sliced leeks (white and light green
    parts only)
½ cup diced carrots
½ cup diced celery
2 cups sliced shallots
2 cups garlic cloves, chopped
¼ cup sliced lemongrass (ivory-colored and
    light green parts only)
2 ounces ginger, peeled and chopped
½ cup diced sweet potatoes
2 cups chopped tomatoes
⅓ cup dried red plums
½ cup Cognac
2 cups red wine
3 quarts chicken stock
3 tablespoons fresh thyme leaves
3 tablespoons coarsely chopped fresh tarragon
3 tablespoons coarsely chopped fresh parsley

FOR THE SAUCE

2 tablespoons corn oil
2 cups diced onions
½ cup diced carrots
½ cup diced celery
½ cup diced parsnips
½ cup diced celery root
½ cup sliced leeks (white and light green
    parts only)
2 ounces fresh ginger, peeled and chopped
2 cups garlic cloves, peeled and crushed
2 cups chopped shallots
2 tablespoons pitted and finely diced dates
½ cup Cognac
2 cups red wine
½ cup sliced lotus root (optional)
Fresh thyme leaves

FOR THE TRUFFLED TARO ROOT

1 pound taro root, peeled and cut into
    2-inch chunks
¾ ounce black truffles, thinly sliced
1½ teaspoons truffle butter
1 tablespoon unsalted butter, softened
Fine sea salt and freshly ground white pepper

4 sprigs each fresh parsley, tarragon, and
    chervil, plus a small handful of fresh chives,
    for garnish

PREPARE THE SHORT RIBS: Tie the star anise, cloves, and fennel and cumin seeds in a square of cheesecloth and set aside.

Season the ribs with the Szechwan pepper and salt and white pepper to taste. Heat the corn oil in a large Dutch oven over medium-high heat. Add the short ribs and brown them all over. Add the onions, leeks, carrots, celery, shallots, garlic, lemongrass, ginger, sweet potatoes, tomatoes, and dried plums and cook, stirring every now and then, until the vegetables are softened and beginning to brown, 8 to 10 minutes. Add the

Cognac and red wine, bring to a boil, and deglaze, scraping up the browned bits from the bottom of the pan with a wooden spoon. Continue cooking until the liquid is reduced by about one-third.

Add the chicken stock, thyme, tarragon, parsley, and the cheesecloth bag of spices. Bring to a boil, reduce the heat, and simmer, covered, until the ribs are tender, about 2 hours. Drain the ribs, reserving the braising liquid for the sauce; set the ribs aside.

PREPARE THE SAUCE. Heat the oil in a large saucepan over medium-high heat. Add the onions, carrots, celery, parsnips, celery root, leeks, ginger, garlic, shallots, and dates and cook until the vegetables are caramelized, 7 to 8 minutes. Add the Cognac, bring to a boil, and deglaze, scraping the browned bits from the bottom of the pan with a wooden spoon. Continue cooking until the pan is almost dry. Add the red wine and simmer to reduce by about one-quarter.

Add the reserved braising liquid and simmer until the liquid is reduced by one-half. Strain the sauce and return it to the pan. Add the short ribs, the lotus root, if using, and the thyme leaves.

MEANWHILE, PREPARE THE TARO ROOT: Bring a saucepan of water to a boil. Add the taro root and cook until tender, about 30 minutes. Drain, transfer to a bowl, and mash with a fork or potato masher. Stir in the black truffle, truffle butter, and butter. Season to taste with salt and white pepper.

To serve, divide the short ribs between four serving plates. Spoon some of the mashed taro root next to the beef and spoon some of the sauce around. Garnish with the sprigs of parsley, tarragon, and chervil, and the chives.

Rocco DiSpirito

Tom Douglas

DAHLIA LOUNGE, ETTA'S SEAFOOD, and PALACE KITCHEN | Seattle

I've always liked to go out to dinner, so I just kind of . . . well, when food is your passion or your hobby, you tend to pick up things. I was eighteen, and moved here from Delaware. I was done with high school and was ready to travel, and I just ended up in Seattle. I turned down a scholarship to cooking school. Me, I'm trained in life. I worked in a lot of restaurants before opening my own. And I honestly didn't want to open my own restaurant. But I had quit my job in a restaurant where I was making a ton of money and thinking I was pretty hot. I thought I would get a lot of offers, because I had been working in the number one–rated restaurant in Seattle at that time, very popular and we were very busy. But I didn't even get one offer. Then it turned out that my wife was pregnant, and there I was, unemployed . . . so we talked her uncle into giving us $50,000 and we opened our restaurant six months later. Five years after that, I finally started making the kind of money I had been making in my previous job.

In New York, the culinary influence is from Europe. Here in Seattle, it is from Asia, Russia, Mexico, the whole Pacific Rim. When we started here in Seattle, you'd only find classic Asian presentation in Japanese or Asian restaurants. American restaurants didn't do it, because they assumed that Americans would never eat this kind of food. What we did here (and it was going on in L.A. and San Francisco, too) was to expose some of the more traditional Asian foods to a mainstream Caucasian population.

Today, we're more about local, regional, sustainable, trying to go more organic, things like that. I think that's happening everywhere.

I'm dreading the day that the *Michelin* comes to try to direct my business. It seems to direct business in Europe, sometimes in unreasonable ways. I hear the hot trend in Europe is to turn a star back in.

63

MAPLE-CURED PORK LOIN WITH BALSAMIC CHERRIES | Serves 4 to 6

At the restaurant, the pork is prepared on a rotisserie over an applewood fire. At home, you can roast the pork in the oven, as in the recipe below, or grill it over indirect heat. Balsamic cherries and maple syrup sweeten the pork loin. The brine flavors the pork and keeps it succulent. Allow for an extra day to marinate the pork.

FOR THE MAPLE-CURE BRINE

5 cups cold water
1 packed cup dark brown sugar
½ cup kosher salt
½ cup pure maple syrup
2 tablespoons molasses
2 bay leaves
½ teaspoon freshly ground black pepper

FOR THE PORK

One 2½- to 3-pound boneless pork loin
2 tablespoons olive oil

FOR THE BALSAMIC CHERRIES AND SAUCE

1½ cups pitted Bing cherries, quartered
½ cup balsamic vinegar
½ cup demi-glace (optional) (see Note)

Freshly ground black pepper

PREPARE THE BRINE: The day before you plan to serve the pork, combine the water, brown sugar, salt, maple syrup, molasses, bay leaves, and pepper in a large nonreactive pan or bowl.

Add the pork loin to the brine, cover, and refrigerate overnight.

ROAST THE PORK: The next day, heat the oven to 350°F. Remove the pork from the brine, set it on a rack over a plate, and let it come to room temperature.

Heat the oil in a large frying pan over medium-high heat. Add the pork and brown it on all sides, adjusting the heat as necessary so that the sugar from the brine doesn't burn.

Place the pork on a rack set in a small roasting pan and roast until the pork registers 140° to 145°F on an instant-read thermometer inserted into the thickest part of the meat, 1 to 1½ hours. Remove the roast from the oven, cover it loosely with foil, and let it rest for 15 minutes.

MEANWHILE, PREPARE THE CHERRIES: Ten minutes before the pork is cooked, toss the cherries with the vinegar in a bowl, then spread them over the bottom of a baking dish and pour the vinegar over. Roast the cherries until they start to crinkle up, about 25 minutes.

FINISH THE DISH: When the pork has rested and the cherries are cooked, cut the pork into thin slices and divide it among four warm serving plates. Remove the cherries from the dish with a slotted spoon and scatter them around the pork. If using demi-glace, heat it in a small saucepan, stir in the juices from the roasted cherries, and spoon over the meat. Or just drizzle some of the cherry juices over the meat. Grind black pepper over the pork and serve immediately.

NOTE: Demi-glace is a highly reduced, syrupy meat stock that is now marketed nationally by some producers, so you are likely to be able to find it at a specialty store. If not, the dish is fine without it.

TASTES FROM THE SEA: ALASKA SPOT PRAWN COCKTAIL, ALBACORE WITH PONZU SAUCE, AND SPICY SCALLOP CEVICHE WITH SHISO | Serves 4

These delicacies are served as part of a seafood tasting at Dahlia Lounge. Each is served in its own tiny ramekin, all three are then set in a shallow bowl of shaved ice. At home, you can serve the three appetizers in ramekins, small bowls, or plates, assembled for each guest on a large dinner plate.

Shiso is a delicious spicy-tasting member of the mint family that really tastes like nothing else but shiso. It is often available fresh at Japanese markets, but if you can't find it, Douglas suggests substituting fresh chives, for a different taste but one that nonetheless is excellent with the fish.

FOR THE PRAWN COURT BOUILLON
4 cups water
1 cup dry white wine
½ leek (white and light green parts only), roughly chopped and washed
1 bouquet garni (1 bay leaf, a few sprigs each fresh thyme, parsley, and tarragon, and a few black peppercorns, in a square of cheesecloth)

8 spot prawns or other large shrimp in the shell

FOR THE COCKTAIL SAUCE
½ cup ketchup
1 tablespoon prepared horseradish
1 tablespoon prepared espresso plus 1 teaspoon "spent" coffee grounds, or 2 teaspoons instant espresso powder dissolved in 1 tablespoon boiling water

FOR THE CEVICHE
4 large sea scallops (about 6 ounces total)
5 tablespoons fresh orange juice
5 tablespoons fresh lime juice
½ teaspoon chopped fresh cilantro
½ teaspoon minced red onion
¼ teaspoon minced jalapeño or serrano chile pepper, or more to taste

FOR THE PONZU SAUCE AND TUNA
2 tablespoons soy sauce
2 tablespoons fresh lime juice
2 teaspoons water
½ teaspoon peeled and minced fresh ginger

4 ounces sashimi-grade albacore or ahi tuna (in one piece)
Kosher salt and freshly ground black pepper
1 tablespoon olive oil
2 shiso leaves, cut into very thin strips, or ½ teaspoon finely sliced fresh chives for garnish

PREPARE THE PRAWN COURT BOUILLON: Combine the water, wine, leek, and bouquet garni in a large saucepan and bring to a boil. Reduce the heat and simmer, covered, for 20 minutes. Strain through a sieve and discard the solids.

POACH THE PRAWNS: Pour the court bouillon back into the saucepan and return to a boil. Add the prawns and cook until firm, 4 to 5 minutes. Scoop out the prawns with a slotted spoon and immediately plunge them into a bowl of ice water. When they are cool, peel them, leaving the tails on. Refrigerate until ready to serve.

PREPARE THE COCKTAIL SAUCE: Combine the ketchup, horseradish, and espresso (and coffee grounds, if using) in a small bowl. Set aside until ready to serve.

PREPARE THE CEVICHE: Cut the scallops horizontally into ¼-inch-thick slices. Combine the remaining ingredients in a small bowl. Add the scallops, cover, and refrigerate for 20 to 30 minutes.

PREPARE THE PONZU SAUCE: Combine the soy sauce, lime juice, water, and ginger in a small bowl and set aside.

PREPARE THE TUNA: Sprinkle the tuna all over with salt and pepper. Heat the oil in a frying pan over high heat. Add the tuna and sear until it is browned on the outside but still raw in the center, about 1 minute on each side.

Slice the tuna as thin as possible and place it in a bowl. Pour over enough ponzu sauce to moisten the slices well. Add the shiso leaves and gently fold in.

ASSEMBLE THE DISH: Spoon a little of the cocktail sauce into each of four ramekins or small bowls and set 2 shrimp into each. Divide the scallop slices among four other ramekins or small bowls and pour some of the marinade into each. Divide the tuna among four more ramekins or small dishes.

Place one ramekin each of shrimp, ceviche, and tuna on each of four large serving plates and serve immediately.

Tom Douglas

Wylie Dufresne

formerly of 71 CLINTON FRESH FOOD | New York

For a small place, we do a lot of different sauces. You might think we'd be able to do only one or two sauces, but we take turns on the stove (there are just three of us in the kitchen), and we're able to get quite a few very intense, flavorful sauces with our dishes. We have a squid dish, for example, that has a really nice, strong, brightly colored, citrusy, blood orange sauce. Citrus fruit goes well with seafood. Lemons, limes, oranges, grapefruits are often paired together with seafood. The blood orange sauce is a nice, concentrated version of something like that.

We make a horseradish oil that goes with our salmon dish. Now, salmon and horseradish have been classically paired for a long time. That's nothing new, but the way we're doing it is with pickled radishes, chopped salmon, lime juice, avocado, and horseradish oil, plus a homemade rice cracker. There's a nice texture to it. I like the textural aspect of food. It is very interesting. It is nice to have a little crunch in your meal. It makes you think while you're eating, "What's going on?" You're not just tasting something, you're experiencing it in a more complete way.

I have a soft spot for cheeseburgers. Yeah, I have a big soft spot for a really good, well-made cheeseburger. There's a great place in the West Village . . . great burger, comes on a paper plate. Simple. Wonderful.

I feel very lucky. My father and I both, independently of each other, had a similar idea of what kind of restaurant we'd like to have. I've worked in all those places in New York with the white gloves, and I've done my training in France. I come from that world, but I thought it would be nice to do that kind of food in a more casual setting, and I think my father believed that even before I did. And our ideas came together, and this is it. There are other investors, and the other owners have a vision, but the food is my idea and my father runs the dining room. He creates the environment that people get when they dine here. He's on the floor every night talking to people. It's nice. There are no pretensions here. But yet you still get the same type of food you'd get if you had to go uptown or at least farther up than here—across Houston Street, at least! I hope that we're giving people a good meal.

LIME-MARINATED SALMON TARTARE WRAPPED IN AVOCADO
WITH CREAMY HORSERADISH OIL | Serves 4

This surprisingly easy recipe makes a stunning first course that is delicious in its simplicity. The avocado provides a creamy backdrop for the lightly piquant salmon mixture and the horseradish oil pulls the two together. The plastic wrap keeps air away from the avocados so that they can be prepared up to an hour ahead of serving without darkening.

You'll need only about half this recipe of horseradish oil: the rest can be refrigerated and served with grilled fish, meats, or vegetables, or on sandwiches. Shake or whisk before using.

At the restaurant, the salmon is served with a homemade rice cracker, made from pureed risotto and baked in a thin layer until crisp.

FOR THE SALMON

12 ounces salmon fillet, skin, pinbones, and
    gray area removed (about 8 ounces
    trimmed salmon)
4 teaspoons minced fresh chives
4 teaspoons minced pickled radish
    or cornichons
2 teaspoons fresh lime juice
2 teaspoons extra-virgin olive oil
¼ teaspoon Tabasco sauce, or to taste
Salt
2 medium-size ripe Hass avocados
Cracked black pepper

FOR THE OIL

3 ounces horseradish, peeled and cut
    into chunks
½ teaspoon rice vinegar
Pinch of salt, or more to taste
About ½ cup grapeseed or other neutral oil

Flaked or coarse sea salt

PREPARE THE SALMON: With a very sharp knife, cut the salmon into thin slices and then chop it to the texture of coarsely ground meat. Place the salmon in a bowl and stir in the chives, radish, lime juice, olive oil, and Tabasco. Season to taste with salt.

Working with 1 avocado at a time, cut each lengthwise in half and twist to separate the 2 halves. Remove and discard the pit. Cut off and discard ½ inch from the top of each half. Carefully peel away and discard the skin, trying not to gouge the flesh with your fingertips. Place the halves pit side down. With a sharp knife, slice each half lengthwise as thin as possible, holding the sides of the avocado half as you work so that it keeps its shape. You should be able to get at least 12 slices from each half.

Lay an 18-by-12-inch sheet of plastic wrap on the work surface. Slide the side of a large knife under a sliced avocado half. Transfer the sliced avocado to the plastic, turning it pit side up. Press lightly on the avocado with an open hand to fan and separate the slices slightly, revealing the dramatic color variation of the fruit. Season with salt and cracked pepper.

Spoon a quarter of the salmon mixture over the center of the avocado half. Lift two opposite corners of the wrap over the fish, then the two remaining corners. Grasping all four corners of the wrap in your left hand, squeeze them together just above the salmon. Then lift the package so that you can cup the avocado in your right hand. Flip the package over as you twist and pull on the wrap to tighten it around the underside of the avocado, pinching the plastic tight over the avocado and gently

forcing the avocado slices into their original shape in your cupped palm. Repeat with the remaining avocado halves and salmon. Refrigerate while you make the horseradish oil.

PREPARE THE OIL: Place the horseradish, vinegar, and salt in a food processor and process, stopping to scrape down sides of bowl several times, until the horseradish is chopped quite fine, 1 to 2 minutes. With the motor running, slowly add the oil through the feed tube in a steady stream and process just until the mixture forms a creamy emulsion; you may not need the entire ½ cup of oil; add just enough to give the mixture the consistency of a sauce. Taste for salt.

ASSEMBLE THE DISH: Lay a wrapped avocado on its side and slice off the twisted portion of the wrap close to the avocado. Turn the avocado so that the salmon filling faces up and gently peel back the plastic wrap. Place a small plate over the avocado, and flip the avocado onto the plate so that the rounded green side faces up. Repeat with the remaining avocado halves. Sprinkle each lightly with coarse salt.

Using about half of the horseradish oil, drizzle oil around the edges of the plates. Serve immediately.

SHRIMP-STUFFED SQUID WITH BLOOD ORANGE EMULSION | Serves 6

Here is another appetizer that is impressive for entertaining but doesn't require a lot of labor. The emulsion can be made a few hours ahead and refrigerated; bring to room temperature before serving. The squid can also be prepared several hours ahead and refrigerated. If the squid is coming straight from the refrigerator, it will need a few more minutes in the oven to warm through.

FOR THE EMULSION
1 cup fresh blood orange juice
½ large egg yolk
Kosher salt
1 teaspoon sherry vinegar
⅓ cup grapeseed or vegetable oil

Blood oranges give the sauce its color.

FOR THE SQUID
2 tablespoons extra-virgin olive oil
2 medium garlic cloves, very finely minced
12 ounces medium shrimp, peeled
    and deveined
2 tablespoons coarse fresh bread crumbs,
    toasted in a dry frying pan until
    golden brown
10 fresh basil leaves, cut into thin strips
Kosher salt to taste
Cayenne pepper to taste
6 cleaned squid bodies, each 5 inches long

2 tablespoons extra-virgin olive oil

PREPARE THE EMULSION: Strain the orange juice into a small saucepan. Bring to a boil, reduce the heat, and simmer until reduced to ¼ cup. Let cool completely.

Whisk the egg yolk and a pinch of salt together in a small bowl. Whisk in the cooled reduced juice and the vinegar. Slowly whisk in the oil until the sauce is emulsified. Taste and add more salt if necessary.

PREPARE THE SQUID: Heat the olive oil in a small frying pan over medium-low heat. Add the garlic and cook until lightly colored, about 2 minutes. Set aside to cool.

Roughly chop each shrimp into 6 or 7 pieces and place in a bowl. Stir in the cooled garlic oil, the bread crumbs, basil, salt, and cayenne. Cover and refrigerate until chilled, at least 30 minutes.

When the stuffing is cool, gently stuff it into the squid, leaving half an inch space at the open end of each squid; don't pack the mixture. Thread a toothpick through the open end of each squid body to seal in the stuffing.

COOK THE SQUID: Preheat the oven to 450°F.

Heat oil in large ovenproof frying pan over medium-high heat. Add the squid and cook for 30 seconds, then turn. Transfer the pan to the oven and roast, turning the squid every 2 minutes, until the squid are opaque and the filling is warm and firm, about 6 minutes; do not overcook. Remove the pan from the oven and let the squid rest in the pan for a minute or two. Remove the toothpicks.

To serve, drizzle the blood orange emulsion over the serving plates and place a squid on each plate.

Wylie Dufresne

Todd English

I was always into food. But I never thought of it as an interesting profession until I started working in restaurants, and somebody suggested that I should try out for cooking school. This was America in 1980, and there were really very few Americans cooking. I wound up going to cooking school, and that's when I started thinking, "I can make a living at it." What a great thought.

I went to work in the French restaurants in New York, got an opportunity to go to Italy, worked for some nice places there, beautiful places, ristorantes and trattorias, and just really fell in love with it all. As much as I love the French countryside and French cooking, the Italian stuff was just in my blood.

When you have a restaurant, you have to do a certain volume to make the economics of it work, and that changes the idea of the restaurant. To me, the ideal restaurant has one seating a night, ten at a table, but it doesn't work that way in reality. So we really have to push it out. But it is also about having fun. We try to have fun here. We don't do tablecloths, we play good music, we have the fans going, there's a lot of action, there's an open kitchen, and there's a lot of energy from the kitchen, so it's an interesting dynamic.

My family on my mother's side is Italian, so I was brought up in that world. I love Italian cooking, and Italian-American cooking. My mother's family came from Calabria and Napoli, the south of Italy, so I grew up on a lot of red sauces, heavy cooked red sauces, the sort of thing now known as Italian American.

At Thanksgiving, we would always start with a huge antipasto. Then we'd go to a pasta, like a big lasagna, or a manicotti, or ziti, or something like that. Then we'd go into the regular turkey. By the time you got to the turkey, you were already thinking, "Come on, forget about it," and then there were pies and cookies and ice cream, gelato. . . . It took us six hours to eat.

OLIVES | Charlestown, Aspen, Las Vegas, New York, Washington, D.C.
FIGS | Boston, Charlestown, Chestnut Hill, Wellesley, New York
KINGFISH HALL | Boston   **MIRAMAR** | Westport
GREG NORMAN'S AUSTRALIAN GRILLE | North Myrtle Beach

TOMATO CAPRESE SALAD | Serves 4

The traditional tomato and mozzarella salad from the island of Capri is translated by English into a whimsical summer salad of overlapping sliced tomatoes pressed so thin as to be almost transparent, topped with a delicious herbed soft goat cheese, enclosed by a "house" of toasted thin bread. Spread the cheese on the toast and eat it with the salad.

At home, you may not be able to slice and press the tomato slices as thin as is possible at the restaurant (and in the photo), but the salad will be tasty anyway.

5 thin slices bread, trimmed to 1½-by-2½-inch rectangles,
    1 rectangle cut diagonally in half
5 teaspoons extra-virgin olive oil plus extra for brushing the bread
3 ounces fresh goat cheese
1 tablespoon chopped fresh basil
Freshly ground black pepper
2 medium tomatoes, cored and sliced as thin as possible into rounds
Kosher or coarse sea salt to taste
3 large fresh basil leaves plus several smaller leaves for garnish
¼ cup loosely packed frisée, cut into 1- to 1½-inch pieces

PREPARE THE TOAST: Preheat the oven to 400°F.

Brush the bread on both sides with olive oil, place on a baking sheet, and toast in the oven until well browned on both sides, about 5 minutes. Set aside.

PREPARE THE GOAT CHEESE: In a small bowl, stir together the goat cheese, 2 teaspoons of the olive oil, the chopped basil, and ⅛ teaspoon pepper until well blended.

PREPARE THE TOMATOES: Lay a 12-inch square of plastic wrap on a work surface. Drizzle 1½ teaspoons of the oil over it and brush or smear with your fingers to make a thin coating. Arrange the tomato slices in an overlapping spiral fashion to make a 9-inch round. Drizzle the remaining 1½ teaspoons olive oil on top. Cover with a second sheet of plastic the same size as the first.

Using a rolling pin, firmly tap and roll over the tomatoes to gently flatten them into a very thin disk. Peel off the top layer of plastic wrap and overturn a 12-inch serving plate on top of the tomatoes. Fold the corners of the plastic wrap up over the bottom of the plate to secure it and then carefully flip the serving plate over so that the tomatoes are now centered on the plate. Peel off the plastic wrap. Sprinkle the tomatoes with salt and pepper. Wipe the edges of the plate clean.

FINISH THE DISH: Spoon the cheese into a mound in the center of the tomatoes. Enclose the cheese with the 4 rectangular pieces of toast to make the walls of the "house." Stick 1 triangular piece, wide end down, in the center of cheese, so that it sticks up through the middle of the house. Place the second triangle on top to make a "roof." Place the large basil leaves on the roof. Scatter the frisée and the smaller basil leaves around the tomatoes and serve.

Herbed goat cheese within a crisp house of toast

72

TUNA LOIN AU POIVRE WITH ANCHOVY AND BLACK OLIVE SLAW | Serves 4

This is a simple and delicious way to cook tuna. The fish is roasted on a bed of whole peppercorns rather than being sautéed in a crust of crushed peppercorns, as in steak *au poivre*. As a result, the tuna is infused with the fragrance of the spice but is not hot with it. The cabbage slaw, redolent with the flavors of the Mediterranean, does away with the need for a sauce.

FOR THE SLAW

3 garlic cloves, unpeeled

½ head cabbage, cored

1 anchovy fillet, rinsed, patted dry, and finely chopped and mashed with the
    side of a large knife

1 tablespoon Dijon mustard

1 tablespoon chopped fresh rosemary

1 tablespoon balsamic vinegar

2 tablespoons chopped pitted black olives, such as Kalamata or Gaeta

½ teaspoon coarse sea or kosher salt

⅛ teaspoon freshly ground black pepper

2 tablespoons olive oil

FOR THE TUNA

One 1½- to 1¾-pound "roast" of tuna loin (in one piece about 3¼ by 2¾ by
    5 inches), trimmed of dark areas (see Note)

Kosher or coarse sea salt

2 tablespoons olive oil

2 cups black peppercorns

Freshly ground black pepper

Preheat the oven to 400°F.

PREPARE THE SLAW: Wrap the garlic in a square of aluminum foil and roast in the oven until soft, about 30 minutes. Remove from the oven and let stand until cool enough to handle. (Leave the oven on.)

Meanwhile, on a vegetable slicer, finely slice enough cabbage to make 6 firmly packed cups; set aside. (Reserve the remaining cabbage for another use.)

Squeeze the cooled garlic out of its skin into a large bowl and mash with a fork. Add the anchovy, mustard, rosemary, vinegar, olives, salt, and pepper and whisk to blend. Gradually add the oil in a steady stream, whisking to emulsify the sauce. Fold the sliced cabbage into the sauce. Set aside at room temperature.

PREPARE THE TUNA: Sprinkle the tuna all over with salt. Heat the olive oil in a 9-inch heavy ovenproof frying pan over high heat. Add the tuna and cook, turning, 1 minute on each side. Remove the tuna from the pan and pour off the fat.

Pour about 1½ cups of the peppercorns into the center of the pan and make a "nest" of them. Set the tuna loin on the nest and press the remaining peppercorns into the top and sides of the tuna. Cover the pan, place it in the oven, and roast until a skewer inserted in the center of the roast for 10 seconds no longer feels cold to the touch, 18 to 20 minutes for rare. (Don't wait until the skewer feels warm—the tuna will be overcooked by then.) Remove the pan from the oven and let the tuna rest for at least 10 minutes.

To serve, brush the peppercorns off the tuna and cut the roast into 4 slices. Place the slices on serving plates and sprinkle with salt and pepper. Spoon the slaw over the tuna.

NOTE: Ask your fish dealer to cut you a piece of tuna from the tail end of the loin and trim it so that it is relatively narrow. A wider cut will overcook on the outside before the inside warms.

Todd English

Bobby Flay

BOLO and MESA GRILL | New York

In the restaurant business, there is no such thing as taking it easy. There are so many details, so many things that have to be fixed, so many things that have to be improved. Luckily, I don't need much sleep.

I hated school. . . . I never saw myself going on to college after finishing high school, so I had to come up with another option. My parents were adamant that if I wasn't going to go to college, I had to go to work. Well, at first I didn't much like that idea, either, but when my father, who was part-owner of a restaurant on the West Side, arranged for me go to work there one day, I agreed. I wasn't crazy about it at first, but six months into it, I began to think, "You know, I do like this." And that was the beginning.

Do I have a love for chilies? Absolutely. They have put me on the culinary map. Chilies are the basis of Southwestern cooking, which is what I'm known for. They have an amazing depth of flavor. They can be sweet, smoky, raisin-like, musty. They are wonderful to work with. People think that they're all heat, but when you learn how to cook them, you realize how much more there is to them than that.

No one on the East Coast was doing what I wanted to do when I started. It is not fusion cuisine. I like to think of [my cooking] as my take on the authentic cuisine of the Southwestern United States. I use ingredients like blue corn and fresh and dried chile peppers, and my dishes are characterized by lots of beautiful colors, big flavors, and vibrant, interesting textures. After so many years [at Mesa Grill], we are just as driven to provide the best. It seems like it would be easy to rest on our laurels, but that doesn't work. We are constantly upgrading. A contemporary style like ours has to be reinvented every day.

Today, food is my life. And not just my own food. Like all chefs, I love to go out to eat. I like to see what the competition is doing, and I like to eat food that is totally different from my own. I love Japanese food, for example. Nobu is at the top of my list when I go out to eat.

NEW MEXICAN CHILE-RUBBED PORK TENDERLOIN WITH BOURBON-ANCHO SAUCE | Serves 4

Here the pleasant bitterness and heat of several ground dried New Mexican chiles are balanced with a bourbon-based sauce sweetened with brown sugar, apple juice, and onion. At Mesa Grill, the chile-rubbed pork is served with a sweet potato tamale, with a spoonful of roasted pecan butter melted on the top, and sautéed spinach.

The recipe for the rub makes more than enough for this dish, but since it will last practically indefinitely in a tightly closed container, make the entire recipe and save the extra to use on chicken or ribs.

FOR THE NEW MEXICAN CHILE RUB
2 tablespoons ancho chile powder (see Note)
2 tablespoons light brown sugar
1 tablespoon ground pasilla chile (see Note)
2 teaspoons ground chile de árbol (see Note)
2 teaspoons ground cinnamon
2 teaspoons ground allspice

FOR THE BOURBON-ANCHO SAUCE
1 ½ ancho chiles
1 tablespoon olive oil
½ large red onion, finely chopped
1 cup plus 1 tablespoon bourbon
3 cups chicken stock
½ cup thawed frozen apple juice concentrate
2 tablespoons light brown sugar
4 black peppercorns
1 teaspoon kosher salt, or to taste

FOR THE PORK TENDERLOIN
2 tablespoons olive oil
Two 1-pound pork tenderloins
Kosher salt

1 tablespoon chopped fresh chives
Fresh cilantro leaves for garnish

PREPARE THE RUB: Combine all of the ingredients in a small bowl; set aside.

PREPARE THE SAUCE: Soak the chiles in warm water to cover until softened; drain, reserving the soaking liquid. Stem and seed the chiles. Transfer to a small food processor and process to a puree, adding a little of the soaking water as needed.

Heat the oil in a large saucepan over medium-high heat. Add the onion and cook, stirring occasionally, until softened, 2 to 3 minutes. Add 1 cup of the bourbon and cook until reduced to a glaze. (Lower the heat at the end of cooking so as not to scorch the sides of the pan.) Add the pureed chiles, the stock, apple juice, brown sugar, and peppercorns and cook until the liquid is reduced by one-half. Strain through a fine-meshed strainer into a clean saucepan. Cook until the mixture thickens to a saucelike consistency. Add the remaining 1 tablespoon bourbon and simmer for 2 more minutes. Stir in the salt and set aside.

PREPARE THE PORK: Preheat the oven to 400°F.

Heat the oil in an ovenproof frying pan or a roasting pan large enough to hold the 2 tenderloins comfortably over medium-high heat. Sprinkle the pork all over with salt. Dredge the pork in the spice rub (using about 2 tablespoons of the rub) and pat off the excess. Add the pork to the pan and sear for 1 to 2 minutes on each side.

Put the pan in the oven and roast for 15 to 18 minutes for medium, 135° to 140°F on an instant-read thermometer. Transfer the pork to a plate, cover loosely, and set aside to rest for 7 to 10 minutes.

FINISH THE DISH: Rewarm the sauce and taste for salt, adding more as needed. Cut the pork into 12 thick slices and divide among four serving plates.

Spoon the hot sauce over the pork and sprinkle with the chives. Garnish the plates with the cilantro leaves and serve.

NOTE: You may be able to find these chile powders at your supermarket. If not, you'll certainly find the whole dried chiles there and you can grind them yourself in a spice or coffee grinder. If the whole chiles are still pliable when you buy them, they aren't dry enough to grind: dry them in a 200°F oven for about 15 minutes, until they get a crackly texture.

Chile-rubbed pork with roasted yellow pepper puree and a bourbon-ancho sauce

BARBECUED SWORDFISH WITH CAPE GOOSEBERRY RELISH

Swordfish steaks are brushed with a smoky Southwestern-style barbecue sauce made by simmering pureed tomatoes with onion and garlic, then seasoning the puree with ketchup, vinegar, Worcestershire sauce, brown sugar, molasses, honey, Dijon mustard, ancho chile powder, and pureed chipotle chiles. The steaks are grilled, then brushed again with the sauce.

The grilled fish is served with a fresh gooseberry relish made by combining raw gooseberries with diced grilled red onion and diced grilled red and yellow peppers, seasoned with olive oil, rice wine vinegar, and chopped fresh cilantro.

Bobby Flay

Claudia Fleming

GRAMERCY TAVERN | New York

What I'm passionate about is flavor and temperature and texture. I'm not so much interested in making structures and erecting things. And I like to eat the stuff I make!

I came to New York to dance, and was a failure at that. I always worked in restaurants to support my career, was very attracted to the creative aspects of working in a kitchen. Eventually I got up the nerve to go to cooking school and start working in a kitchen. I started out cooking and just purely by accident wound up doing pastry. I had left a restaurant where I had been cooking, and when I came back, there were no positions available to cook. So the chef told me that the pastry chef needed an assistant and asked if I wanted to do that, and I said, "Sure." It was love at first bite, so I just kept doing it.

In terms of work and responsibilities, it's very much the same [as cooking]. What differs mostly is technique. I think that's probably what separates cooks from pastry people. Generally, we start very early in the morning, and things are finished very early in the day.

I mean, they are executed for the dinner service, but we don't take raw product and do something with it. Things are preprepared, and then finished.

I work with flour, eggs, butter, cream, chocolate, nuts, and fruits. And I incorporate vegetables on a pretty regular basis into the desserts. I use a lot of cheese. And herbs. The tapioca dessert I make would have to be my favorite of all my desserts. Tapioca is milled cassava, the root of the yuca plant. It looks like tiny marbles or balls, and we cook it in a lot of milk so that it's really frothy and loose, and kind of soupy. The plate looks like a bunch of bubbles. And the texture is amazing. It's all soft and creamy, but it's a little al dente, and then we serve it with sorbet and a crispy coconut wafer, passion fruit caramel, and cilantro syrup.

COCONUT TAPIOCA WITH PASSION FRUIT CARAMEL AND FRESH CILANTRO SYRUP | Serves 6

Brothy coconut-flavored tapioca drizzled with passion fruit caramel and cilantro syrup and served with a coconut wafer and two quenelles of sorbet

This tapioca dessert does not have the traditional consistency of old-fashioned tapioca pudding. It has a lighter consistency—more like a soup than a pudding. Instead of stirring constantly and so breaking up and releasing the starch from the pearls, Fleming whisks the tapioca-milk mixture only occasionally, just enough to keep the pearls from settling and sticking to the bottom of the pan. As a result, the soft pearls are suspended in the thickened sweet milk, giving the effect of something like a tapioca-studded crème anglaise.

The caramel can be made several hours ahead and kept at room temperature until serving time. Leftover caramel can be refrigerated for up to a week, then warmed in a water bath until liquid and served over ice cream. The cilantro syrup should be used within twenty-four hours of being made.

FOR THE TAPIOCA

5½ cups milk
1 cup sugar
¼ cup small pearl tapioca
¼ cup large pearl tapioca
One 14-ounce can coconut milk

FOR THE PASSION FRUIT CARAMEL

1 cup sugar
¼ cup water
2 tablespoons unsalted butter
½ cup unsweetened passion fruit juice or puree
2 ripe passion fruits, halved, seeded, and pulp scooped out (optional)

FOR THE CILANTRO SYRUP

¼ cup tightly packed fresh cilantro leaves
⅓ cup light corn syrup

PREPARE THE TAPIOCA: Combine 2½ cups of the milk and ½ cup of the sugar in a medium saucepan. Combine the remaining 3 cups milk and ½ cup sugar in a second medium saucepan. Place both pans over high heat and bring to a simmer, stirring occasionally to dissolve the sugar. Add the small pearl tapioca to the saucepan with the 2½ cups milk and the large pearl tapioca to the other pan. Reduce the heat under each to medium-low and simmer, whisking occasionally to keep the tapioca from clumping and sticking to the bottoms of the pans, until the tapioca pearls are soft, 35 to 40 minutes for the small pearls, about 50 minutes for the large.

When both mixtures are cooked, combine them in a large bowl. Stir in the coconut milk. Let the mixture cool completely, then cover and chill for at least 8 hours, or, preferably overnight. (The mixture will thicken as it chills.)

PREPARE THE CARAMEL: Combine the sugar and water in a small saucepan. Place over low heat and bring to a simmer, stirring until the sugar dissolves. Raise the heat to high and boil until the caramel turns a medium amber color, 12 to 14 minutes. Immediately remove the saucepan from the heat and whisk in the butter until smooth (stand back—the caramel may splatter). Whisk in the passion fruit juice. Return the pan to low heat and whisk until the caramel is smooth. Remove from heat and let cool to room temperature.

PREPARE THE CILANTRO SYRUP: Bring a small saucepan of water to a boil. Fill a bowl with ice cubes and water. Plunge the cilantro leaves into the boiling water for 15 seconds, then drain and immediately plunge into the ice water. Remove the leaves from the water and pat dry on paper towels.

Combine the corn syrup and cilantro in the bowl of a food processor or blender and puree until smooth. Let the mixture sit for 30 minutes, then strain the syrup and discard the cilantro.

FINISH THE DISH: Just before serving, stir the passion fruit pulp, if using, into the caramel.

To serve, divide the tapioca among six soup plates. Drizzle about 2 tablespoons of the passion fruit caramel in a ring around the tapioca on each plate, and dot each plate with ½ teaspoon of the cilantro syrup.

DESSERT TRIO

A miniature goat cheese cheesecake, a small tarte Tatin, and a green apple napoleon make up a trio of Gramercy Tavern desserts.

For the cheesecake, fresh goat cheese is beaten with cream cheese, sugar, and the seeds of a vanilla bean in an electric mixer until smooth. Then the mascarpone cheese and eggs are beaten in. The mixture is strained and baked in a water bath until set.

For the tarte Tatin, sugar and corn syrup are cooked to a caramel. The caramel is enriched with butter and poured into small ramekins. Cut-up Granny Smith apples are fitted into the ramekins. Rounds of puff pastry are placed on top and the edges tucked in around the apples. The tarts are baked, cooled, and turned out.

For the napoleon, cooked puff pastry is layered with baked apple chips and a green apple sorbet, made with Granny Smith apples sweetened with a sugar syrup and apple cider.

Claudia Fleming

81

Suzanne Goin **LUCQUES** | West Hollywood

We have English peas right now, which you normally think of as being a spring crop, but in L.A. instead of having a once-a-year growing cycle, we have a three-times-a-year cycle. It is really important to be in touch with the farmers, to know what is actually happening in that cycle. Then we base the menu around that. You have to be flexible, but for me it is the best way to cook. Once you've cooked this way, I think it's really hard to switch back. I can't imagine calling a produce company and just ordering something off a list.

When you build a restaurant, you inevitably start running out of money, and there is a lot of pressure to get the place open and, meanwhile, it is not quite ready—the classic restaurant story describes the opening with the paint still drying on the walls. We had a dinner the night before we opened, for all the investors and for our friends, and nothing was finished yet. We had one oven that worked, and when the first order came in and we opened the oven door, it fell off . . . and that was our one oven! So we picked it up and we literally tied it onto the stove with a piece of string, and every time we opened the oven, we had to untie the string and take the door off to check what was inside. And we were doing these chickens in Spanish clay pots; we called it The Devil's Chicken. Well, we had them in the oven, and we had to take them out to put something else in, and this guy I'd just hired took a pizza peel and pulled the chickens out, and he tripped, and they went smashing all over the floor. That was a nice first day. Everybody was wondering, "Where's our food?" It was a little disastrous. And then we had to come back the next day and open.

I love the sweet-salty thing. We have a chicken dish that is made with dandelion greens, and we do it with pancetta and dates and some sherry vinegar. I love sherry vinegar. I like to use old-fashioned and less common products, too, like lamb shanks, suckling pig, and some more unusual kinds of fish. I do a lot with vegetables. I love produce, and I love vegetables, whatever is seasonal. And there are a couple of farmers whom we work with who are really into heirloom Italian greens, cavolo nero, different kinds of broccoli and radicchio. They are bringing back these vegetables that people had kind of forgotten about. The challenge is to see something at the market, or have a farmer bring something in, and think, "Wow, what could we do with that?"

SHELL BEAN SALAD WITH PROSCIUTTO, MINT, AND AÏOLI TOASTS | Serves 6

Fresh shell beans have a velvety, creamy texture and a delicately sweet taste. They are seasoned very simply here with good-quality olive oil, a little lemon juice, shallots, garlic, and fresh herbs, then served as a salad. You should choose at least two different kinds of beans, and you can use more if you like—divide the shallots, garlic, and thyme between however many pots you use. (Each variety of bean needs to be cooked in a separate pot because they all have different cooking times.)

FOR THE AÏOLI

1 large egg yolk
¾ cup extra-virgin olive oil
1 ½ to 2 tablespoons fresh lemon juice
½ garlic clove, pounded to a paste in a mortar
½ teaspoon kosher salt
⅛ teaspoon cayenne pepper

FOR THE BEANS

2 tablespoons extra-virgin olive oil
2 tablespoons minced shallots
2 teaspoons minced garlic
2 teaspoons fresh thyme leaves
3 cups shelled fresh summer shell beans
    such as lima, cranberry, flageolets, and/or
    black-eyed peas—choose two varieties
    (1½ to 2 pounds in the pod)
Kosher salt

FOR THE VINAIGRETTE

1 tablespoon minced shallots
2 tablespoons fresh lemon juice
¼ cup extra-virgin olive oil
½ teaspoon kosher salt

Kosher salt and freshly ground black pepper
1 to 2 teaspoons fresh lemon juice

1 tablespoon chopped fresh flat-leaf parsley
2 tablespoons minced fresh chives
3 scallions, white and pale green parts only,
    thinly sliced on the bias

12 thin slices prosciutto
12 slices rustic bread, toasted or grilled
6 fresh mint leaves, sliced

PREPARE THE AÏOLI: Whisk the egg yolk in a medium bowl until smooth. Slowly drizzle in the oil, whisking constantly to emulsify the sauce. Whisk in the lemon juice, garlic, salt, and cayenne. Refrigerate until ready to serve.

PREPARE THE BEANS: Heat 1 tablespoon of the olive oil in each of two medium saucepans over medium heat. Add half the shallots, garlic, and thyme to each pan and cook until the shallots are translucent, 2 to 3 minutes. Add one variety of shell bean to each pan and cook for 1 minute, then add water to each pan to cover the beans by 1 inch. Bring to a boil, reduce the heat, and cook, partially covered, until the beans are just tender, 20 to 30 minutes, depending on the variety. Ten minutes into the cooking, season each pan of beans with 1½ teaspoons salt.

When the beans are tender, transfer them both to a bowl and let them cool in their cooking liquid.

MEANWHILE, PREPARE THE VINAIGRETTE: Whisk together all of the ingredients in a bowl. Set aside.

FINISH THE SALAD: When the beans are cool, drain them and transfer to a large bowl. Add the vinaigrette and toss. Taste and adjust the seasonings, adding salt and pepper and lemon juice as needed. Gently fold in the parsley, chives, and scallions.

To serve, arrange 2 slices of prosciutto on each of six serving plates, draping them to form a crown. Spoon the bean salad onto the middle of the crowns. Place 2 slices of toast on each plate, at an angle, and spoon about ½ tablespoon of the aïoli over the bottom edge of each piece of toast. Garnish the beans with the mint.

SALT COD–POTATO CAKES WITH ROASTED TOMATOES, ARUGULA, AND FRIED EGGS | Serves 6

Salt cod is cod fillet that has been salted and then dried to preserve it. You'll need to soak it for three days before cooking to soften it and leach out the salt. Its best-known use is probably in the Provençal dish *brandade de morue*, in which the cod is cooked, pureed with lots of raw garlic, cream, and olive oil, and then gratinéed to brown the top. These cakes are substantially less rich than traditional brandade because they are bound with potato and just a few tablespoons of cream and olive oil, yet they are still wonderfully creamy.

Because the cod cakes are soft, they are somewhat tricky to cook. You'll need to use either well-seasoned cast-iron pans, or nonstick pans so that the cakes don't stick. Use two medium pans rather than one large one, so that you have room to get a spatula under each cake without disturbing the others, and turn them carefully.

When buying salt cod, look for the fattest, whitest pieces you can find.

FOR THE SALT COD CAKES
1 pound good-quality salt cod
3 medium Yukon Gold potatoes (about 2 pounds total), peeled and quartered (see Note)
½ small onion
½ small carrot
3 to 4 fresh thyme branches
10 black peppercorns
1 bay leaf
4 to 5 cups milk, or a little more as needed
3 garlic cloves
4 tablespoons extra-virgin olive oil
2 tablespoons heavy cream
¼ teaspoon freshly ground black pepper

FOR THE TOMATOES
½ pint New Jersey, cherry, or Sweet 100 tomatoes (preferably both yellow and red), cut in half
½ teaspoon fresh thyme leaves
1 tablespoon extra-virgin olive oil
Kosher salt and freshly ground black pepper

2 tablespoons olive oil
2 tablespoons unsalted butter
6 large eggs
Kosher salt and freshly ground black pepper
1 bunch arugula, trimmed, washed, and spun-dry

PREPARE THE SALT COD-CAKES: Three days before you want to serve the dish, put the salt cod in a bowl, add water to cover generously, and place in the refrigerator to soak overnight. Change the water the next morning and return the cod to the refrigerator, then change the water that evening as well and refrigerate again. On the third day, when ready to proceed, drain the cod.

Place the cod, potatoes, onion, carrot, thyme, peppercorns, and bay leaf in a stainless steel pot. Pour over the milk, adding more if necessary to cover the cod and potatoes generously. Bring to a simmer and simmer, partially covered, for 15 minutes. Add the garlic and continue cooking until the fish and potatoes are tender, 25 to 30 more minutes. Drain in a colander and discard the milk. Let cool for 10 minutes.

Pick out and discard the onion, carrot, thyme, peppercorns, and bay leaf. Transfer the cod, about three quarters of the potatoes, and the garlic to a stand mixer or a large bowl and beat with the paddle or mash with a potato masher until the mixture comes together but is still a little chunky. Beat or stir in 2 tablespoons of the olive oil and then the cream. Add the pepper and taste for salt—it should be pleasantly but not overly salty. If it is too salty, work more potato into the mixture until the seasoning is to your liking. Let cool.

PREPARE THE TOMATOES: Preheat the oven to 400°F.

Toss the tomatoes with the thyme and olive oil on a baking sheet. Season with salt and pepper and roast until the tomatoes are a little blistered but still juicy, 8 to 10 minutes. Set aside.

SAUTÉ THE COD CAKES: Shape the cod mixture into 6 cakes, each about 3½ inches in diameter. Heat 1 tablespoon of the remaining 2 tablespoons of olive oil in each of two well-seasoned or nonstick medium frying pans over medium-high heat. Add 3 cod cakes to each pan and cook, carefully turning once, until golden brown and crisp on both sides, 3 to 5 minutes per side.

MEANWHILE, PREPARE THE EGGS: When the cod cakes are almost cooked, melt 1 tablespoon of butter in each of 2 medium frying pans over medium-high heat. Crack the eggs into the pans, season with salt and pepper, cover, and cook until the whites are set but the yolks are still runny, 3 to 4 minutes.

To serve, place a cod cake in the center of each of six dinner plates. Set an egg on the side of each. Spoon the warm tomatoes around the cod cakes and scatter the arugula leaves over. Serve hot.

NOTE: The potato in this mixture acts to balance the salt of the salt cod. But because the cod can vary in saltiness, it's difficult to predict exactly how much potato you'll need. Start by adding about three quarters of the potato, and then adding more until the seasoning is correct.

Suzanne Goin

Christine Keff

FLYING FISH and FANDANGO | Seattle

Early in my career, I did an apprenticeship under a Swiss chef at the Four Seasons in New York. I kept saying to him, "I need to go to France, I need to go to France," and he kept saying to me that almost everyone was over here in New York, so I decided to save my money and stay. There were—and are—a lot of good people in New York, that's for sure.

I had always had it in the back of my mind that I wanted to have my own restaurant. I think every cook does. I'd been cooking for some twenty-five years when I opened this restaurant, and it was just time for me to go out on my own. It was also a way of creating a place for myself here in Seattle. I wasn't really enjoying working for other people anymore.

Most of the existing restaurants [in Seattle] were based on the East Coast seafood-house tradition. Very conservative. Good, but conservative. I became convinced that there was a niche for an innovative seafood restaurant. People come here for seafood, yet nobody was doing anything interesting with it. I had traveled a lot in Southeast Asia and Indonesia and had come to believe that Asian flavors go better with fish and seafood than any others do. I use acids, like lime juice. And soy sauce, maybe a little sugar, or hot chiles—sometimes searingly hot. Lemongrass is great, as is fish sauce. I have a wonderful fish sauce that I make from fried

anchovies. All of these things are terrific. They work really well with the fish, not masking its flavor but enhancing it.

We have the luxury of not being rooted in tradition in this country, and sometimes that's a problem because you can get way off the track. But often it's freeing to try new things and see how they work.

When we opened here, things took off quickly. It was good timing. I kept hearing people saying things like, "Oh, this reminds me of New York," or, "This reminds me of San Francisco." It's funny. I now think of what we do as being pure Seattle.

I've been cooking seafood for such a long time, that when we opened Fandango, where we cook a lot of meat, we weren't sure we could remember how. But we did.

WHOLE FRIED SNAPPER WITH PINEAPPLE DIPPING SAUCE | Serves 3 to 4

A deep-fried whole fish is the sort of food one really doesn't expect to eat outside of a restaurant. But this superb Southeast Asian–inspired dish is, in fact, very practical for home cooking. It's much simpler to make than you might expect, and deep-frying is an excellent way to keep the fish moist. A 16-inch wok is a necessity for cooking the fish and a large wire spider will make it easier to remove it from the oil.

The fish is eaten in rice paper wrappers stuffed with bean sprouts and whole basil and cilantro leaves.

FOR THE DIPPING SAUCE

2 anchovy fillets
2 small garlic cloves
½ teaspoon Asian or other chile paste
¼ pineapple, peeled, cored, and
    coarsely chopped
¼ cup chopped fresh mint
2 tablespoons fresh lime juice
1½ teaspoons fish sauce

FOR THE SNAPPER

¼ cup fish sauce
¼ cup fresh lime juice
4 Thai green or other hot chiles, coarsely
    chopped
2 garlic cloves, chopped
1 stalk lemongrass, trimmed to the ivory-
    colored core and coarsely chopped
One 2-pound red snapper, gutted and scaled
6 cups peanut oil for deep-frying
1 to 2 tablespoons cornstarch

FOR THE GARNISH

1 cup loosely packed fresh basil leaves
1 cup loosely packed fresh cilantro sprigs
2 cups bean sprouts, rinsed and dried
Rice paper wrappers, dipped in hot water for a
    few seconds to make them pliable, or several
    red leaf lettuce leaves rinsed and dried
    (optional) (see Note)

PREPARE THE DIPPING SAUCE: Combine the anchovies, garlic, and chile paste in a small food processor and blend until smooth, scraping down the sides as needed. Add the pineapple and pulse to coarsely chop. Add the mint, lime juice, and fish sauce and pulse to mix. Refrigerate until ready to serve.

PREPARE THE SNAPPER: Combine the fish sauce, lime juice, chiles, garlic, and lemongrass in a blender and blend to a smooth paste. Transfer to a small bowl.

Rinse the snapper under cold running water until the water runs clear. Scrape off any remaining scales if necessary. Make 4 or 5 crosswise slits in the flesh on both sides of the fish. Fill the slits with the lemongrass paste, using a spoon to spoon up the paste and leaving the liquid behind in the bowl. Cover and refrigerate for at least 15 and up to 30 minutes.

Pour the oil into a 16-inch wok and heat to 350°F on a deep-frying thermometer. Using a fine-meshed sieve for even coating, dust the entire fish with the cornstarch. Slide the fish into the hot oil and fry, spooning the oil over the top of the fish every now and then for even

cooking, until just cooked, 6 to 7 minutes. You can check on the progress of the cooking by gently peeking at the flesh where it was slit; the fish should still be translucent at the bone. (It will continue cooking out of the oil.) Using a large wire spider or two kitchen spoons or spatulas, carefully transfer the fish to a large platter.

To serve, arrange the fresh herbs and bean sprouts around the fish. Remove the fish from the bones with two spoons. Let diners wrap the fish with the herbs and sprouts in the rice papers or lettuce leaves, if using. Serve with the dipping sauce.

NOTE: Rice papers, also used to wrap fresh spring rolls, are available at Asian markets. If you can't find them, you can wrap the fish in red-leaf lettuce leaves instead.

Guests bundle crispy fried snapper with fresh herbs and sprouts in rice paper wrappers.

SOFT-SHELL CRABS WITH THAI CURRY | Serves 4

Soft-shell crabs, dredged in cornstarch as they are here, become wonderfully crispy when sautéed.

The curry paste calls for galangal and fresh turmeric. Both rhizomes are available fresh or frozen in Asian markets. Galangal is similar in taste to ginger.

This recipe makes more curry paste than you'll need for the crabs. Freeze it and use it to sauce other sautéed seafood or chicken.

FOR THE CURRY PASTE

2 ounces fresh galangal, peeled
2 ounces fresh ginger, peeled
2 ounces fresh turmeric root, peeled
4 ounces shallots, peeled
½ head garlic, separated into cloves and
    peeled
½ bunch fresh cilantro
Juice of 1 lime
5 Thai dried chiles, soaked in hot water
    to soften
8 teaspoons peanut oil

FOR THE CRABS

3 tablespoons sambal chile paste with garlic
1 tablespoon fresh lime juice
1 tablespoon fish sauce
1 teaspoon kosher salt
½ teaspoon freshly ground black pepper
8 medium soft-shell crabs, cleaned (see Note)

1 cup cornstarch
½ cup canola oil

FOR THE GREEN PAPAYA SALAD

1 green (unripe) papaya, peeled, seeded, and
    cut into fine julienne or shredded

½ zucchini, cut into fine julienne or shredded
½ yellow squash, cut into fine julienne
    or shredded
½ carrot, peeled and cut into fine julienne
    or shredded
¼ cup fresh lime juice
3 tablespoons fish sauce

⅔ cup chicken stock
½ cup coconut milk

PREPARE THE CURRY PASTE: Place all of the ingredients except the peanut oil in the bowl of a food processor and process until well ground. Add the oil and process to a smooth paste. Set aside.

MARINATE THE CRABS: Stir together the sambal, lime juice, fish sauce, salt, and pepper. Pour over the crabs in a baking dish and marinate in the refrigerator for 30 minutes to 1 hour.

MEANWHILE, PREPARE THE SALAD: Toss together the papaya and vegetables. Add the lime juice and fish sauce and toss. Let the salad marinate at room temperature until you are ready to eat.

COOK THE CRABS: Measure the cornstarch onto a deep plate. Dredge the crabs in the cornstarch and pat off the excess.

Heat ¼ cup of the oil in each of two large frying pans over high heat. Add 4 crabs to each pan and sauté until the crabs turn a reddish-orange color and are crisp, 3 to 5 minutes on each side. Remove the crabs to a warm platter. Pour off the oil from the pans.

FINISH THE DISH: Add 3 tablespoons of the curry paste to each of the pans and cook, stirring, for 1 minute. Then add ⅓ cup of the chicken stock to each pan and simmer to reduce by one-half. Combine the contents of both pans in one, add the coconut milk, and simmer until the sauce is reduced and thick enough to coat a spoon. Pour the sauce over the crabs and serve hot, with the papaya salad.

NOTE: Soft-shell crabs are blue crabs that are harvested just after they have molted, before their shells have hardened, so that the entire crab is edible. Like a lot of shellfish, the crabs must be alive when you buy them.

Soft-shell crab with Thai-inspired curry sauce and green papaya salad on a shiso leaf

Christine Keff

Thomas Keller **FRENCH LAUNDRY** | Yountville

For me, it's the satisfaction of cooking every day: tournéing a carrot, or cutting salmon, or portioning foie gras—the mechanical jobs I do daily, year after year. That's what cooking is all about. This is the great challenge: to maintain passion for the everyday routine and the endlessly repeated act, to derive deep gratification from the mundane.

When you take the braising pan out of the oven to see the rich color of the liquid and the slow thick bubble of the deepening sauce, the beautiful clear layer of fat on top, when you really see it, smell it, you've connected yourself to generations and generations of people who have done the same thing for hundreds of years in exactly the same way. My mentor, Roland Henin, told me something long ago that changed the way I thought about cooking: "If you're a really good cook," he said, "you can go back in time."

93

SADDLE OF LAMB NAVARIN

A saddle of lamb is boned and cut in half, so that each half includes a sirloin and a tenderloin. Working with one half, the tenderloin is removed and set aside. The layer of fat that covers the saddle is trimmed from the meat in one sheet and left connected on one long side of the sirloin; it is a flap that can be opened out from the sirloin like the cover of a book. The sirloin itself is left covered with a thin layer of fat as well. The sirloin and the tenderloin are seasoned with salt and pepper, and the tenderloin is pressed back against the loin. The flap of fat is folded over the meat so that the meat is formed into a roulade, covered with a thin layer of fat. The roulade is tied at ½-inch intervals with kitchen twine, seasoned, and browned on top of the stove.

A quick lamb jus is made by browning the bones from the saddle, moistening with chicken stock, and simmering with a caramelized mirepoix of carrot, onion, and leek, along with fresh thyme, tomato, and garlic. The jus is bolstered with veal stock, then the whole thing is strained and reduced.

The lamb roulade is cut into medallions that are seasoned and sautéed until medium-rare. The lamb medallion is served in a pool of sauce, seasoned with fresh *fines herbes*. The plate is garnished with braised slices of Yukon Gold potatoes and glazed brussel sprouts, fava beans, pearl onions, Tokyo turnips, and carrots, also seasoned with fresh *fines herbes*.

My style is sort of conservative. We don't do a lot of weirdness on our plates, no architectural constructions, no stuff on the rims. It's pretty straightforward.

Bob Kinkead

Bob Kinkead

KINKEAD'S | Washington, D.C.
COLVIN RUN TAVERN | Tyson's Corner

I'm self-taught. I've worked in restaurants since I was fifteen, when I started washing dishes on Cape Cod. I've worked in a lot of different types of restaurants. Then I went to college and did different kinds of odd jobs there. I sold insurance, I was a disk jockey for some discotheques, I did some strange stuff. But I kept gravitating back to the restaurant business. I always enjoyed it, and anyone who is in the business will tell you that once it is in your blood, it is hard to get away from it. So I thought, "Well, this seems to be what I like to do, so I better get good at it." I decided that I really needed to learn the craft, so I worked in some good places, and taught myself a lot, bought a lot of cookbooks, traveled, ate in a lot of good restaurants, and basically that was it.

In France, I spent some time working, but mostly spent my time there eating. I always felt I got a lot more out of eating in the restaurants of France than working in them. It isn't just the food on the plate. It's the service, the ambience, the whole style that the owner and the chef want to present to the diner. When I went there, I had already worked as a chef in a couple of places, so I knew the basics. I just wanted to see . . . well, they are the best in the world, and I wanted to see where they were taking it. I'm not as impressed in my recent travels to Paris with a lot of the new guys. I think they're doing a lot of "Emperor's New Clothes." I think London, on the other hand, has really come around. I was there a couple of times recently, and was knocked out by the work they were doing over there. In the United States, the caliber of cooking has certainly gotten much better. People are doing a lot of interesting stuff right now.

My style is sort of conservative. We don't do a lot of weirdness on our plates, no architectural constructions, no stuff on the rims. It's pretty straightforward. We do classic flavor combinations, tweaked a little bit. One of my dishes is a version of a dish that my grandmother used to make. It is a New England version of a succotash. When I was growing up, my father would make it for my family in August, using fresh shell beans and fresh corn. I took that as a base and embellished it a little bit. I also do a beet sauce where the beets are juiced and then the sauce is finished with horseradish. . . . It's a borscht flavor thing, done in a different way. It is a very pretty plate, a lot of vibrant color to it.

WALNUT-AND-HORSERADISH-CRUSTED ROCKFISH WITH SHERRY-BEET SAUCE | Serves 6

Although a great number of white-fleshed, snapperlike fish caught off the Pacific coast of North America are called rockfish, in this case, *rockfish* is the colloquial name used throughout the southern part of the Eastern Seaboard to refer to wild striped bass. The bass is dusted with a toasted walnut–bread crumb mixture flavored with horseradish and sauced with a sweet and tart sauce made from a base of reduced fresh beet juice. At the restaurant, this dish is garnished with a cauliflower flan.

If you have a juicer, you can make beet juice from whole beets. If not, a health-food store that makes its own vegetable juices can sell you beet juice.

FOR THE WALNUT-HORSERADISH CRUST

1½ cups walnut pieces, toasted

1 cup fresh bread crumbs

2 tablespoons grated fresh or prepared horseradish

2 tablespoons unsalted butter, melted and cooled

¾ teaspoon kosher salt

¼ teaspoon freshly ground black pepper

FOR THE FISH

½ cup buttermilk

Six 5-ounce striped bass, mahi-mahi, or snapper fillets

Kosher salt and freshly ground black pepper

2 tablespoons peanut oil

2 tablespoons walnut oil (or an additional 2 tablespoons peanut oil)

FOR THE HORSERADISH CRÈME FRAÎCHE

2 teaspoons prepared horseradish

1 teaspoon fresh lemon juice

¼ cup crème fraîche

Kosher salt and freshly ground black pepper

FOR THE SHERRY-BEET SAUCE

6 tablespoons dry sherry

6 tablespoons dry white wine

¼ cup sherry vinegar

3 large shiitake mushroom caps, sliced

2 garlic cloves, minced

1 medium shallot, minced

½ teaspoon fresh thyme leaves

½ teaspoon black peppercorns

3 cups fresh beet juice

6 tablespoons (¾ stick) unsalted butter, cut into pieces

¼ teaspoon kosher salt

⅛ teaspoon freshly ground black pepper

FOR THE SPINACH

1 tablespoon unsalted butter

8 ounces spinach, stemmed and washed

¼ teaspoon kosher salt

⅛ teaspoon freshly ground black pepper

PREPARE THE CRUST: Put the walnuts in the bowl of a food processor and pulse to coarsely chop. Add the bread crumbs and horseradish and pulse until you have a coarse puree. Add the melted butter, salt, and pepper and pulse to incorporate. Transfer to a bread pan.

BREAD THE FISH: Pour the buttermilk into a deep plate. Sprinkle the fish with salt and pepper. Dip each fillet top side down into the buttermilk and then into the walnut mixture, pressing the mixture onto the fish. Place the fillets breaded side up in a single layer on two plates and refrigerate while you make the sauces.

PREPARE THE HORSERADISH CRÈME FRAÎCHE: Stir the horseradish and lemon juice into the crème fraîche and season to taste with salt and pepper. Refrigerate until ready to serve.

Preheat the oven to 400°F.

PREPARE THE SHERRY-BEET SAUCE: Combine the sherry, white wine, sherry vinegar, shiitakes, garlic, shallot, thyme, and peppercorns in a large nonreactive saucepan. Bring to a boil, reduce the heat, and simmer over low heat until reduced by one-half. Strain through a fine-meshed strainer and return to the saucepan.

Add the beet juice and return to a boil, then reduce the heat and simmer to reduce again by one-half. Pour the sauce into a blender, add the butter, and blend until smooth. Return to the saucepan and season with the salt and pepper. Set aside while you cook the fish.

Rockfish on a beet juice-sherry reduction drizzled with horseradish cream, served with a cauliflower flan and sautéed greens

98

COOK THE FISH: Combine the peanut and walnut oils. Heat two large ovenproof frying pans over medium-high heat. Add 2 tablespoons of the oil mixture (or 2 tablespoons of peanut oil) to each pan and heat until shimmering. Add the fillets, breaded sides down, and sauté until browned and crisp, 2 to 3 minutes. Carefully turn the fillets over, place the pan in the oven, and bake until the fish is cooked through, 3 to 5 minutes, depending on the thickness of the fillets.

MEANWHILE, PREPARE THE SPINACH: Melt the butter in a large frying pan over medium-high heat. Add the spinach and about 1 tablespoon water and toss the spinach in the butter. Cover the pan and steam the spinach until wilted, about 2 minutes. Drain well and season with the salt and pepper.

To serve, return the sherry-beet sauce to a simmer. Divide the spinach among six serving plates. Place a piece of fish next to the spinach on each plate. Spoon some of the sherry-beet sauce next to the fish and drizzle with the horseradish crème fraîche.

LOBSTER AND SHELL BEAN SUCCOTASH

This is the chef's version of a traditional New England dish that his grandmother used to make. New England cooks use cranberry or other shell beans in place of the lima or butter beans that are standard in southern-style succotash. Salt pork is also typical of New England cookery. The finished succotash should be the consistency of a soup rather than a vegetable side dish.

Lobsters are steamed whole and shelled; the tail meat is cut into large pieces. Salt pork is cooked in a saucepan until its fat is rendered. Shelled cranberry beans and onions are added to the pan along with some of the lobster cooking water, and the beans are simmered until they are nearly tender. Then corn and a little sugar are added, and the mixture is cooked until corn and beans are tender. The lobster is folded in, and the succotash is served in bowls with plenty of cracked black pepper and a little butter on top and a corn flan alongside.

Bob Kinkead

Jean-Marie Lacroix

I was fourteen when I first knew I wanted to be a chef . . . no, a cook, really. You start out being a cook, and you become a chef after that.

A chef's style is a personal thing. Every chef is different. What I emphasize a lot is team. Teamwork is very important. We can serve something like three thousand covers in a day, if you count everything from sandwiches to burgers to lobster to whatever. So I need to have a strong team. They definitely make it happen. We do everything from one kitchen, and it is a very small kitchen.

I hope this is a nice place to work. Sometimes it is. Sometimes it is not so nice, I'm sure of that! Yes, well, I think I have mellowed a bit. I used to be stricter. I used to be more demanding, and everything had to be done in one way. Now there are two ways, and I like that better. I learned that in America. People ask a lot of questions, they always challenge you, which is nice in a way. In the kitchens of France, you never ask questions. No, you never do. Oh my God! You are supposed to know everything, even if you don't!

Some days you are going to be perfect, some other days you are going to be less so. When it comes to taste, yes, you strive for perfection all the time. And when you do reach perfection, that's it. You know it. And then again, sometimes you are very happy with something, and you get a person complaining out front . . . he didn't like it! But in this job, things change all the time. Nothing is black or white. It's exciting, it's hard work, it's a lot of movement, it's a lot of sweat, but at the end of the day you have achieved something. Everybody achieves something. I like my guys, from the top to the bottom, to be a part of that. They need to achieve something and feel it.

In the kitchen, we talk, probe, ask questions. Somebody will come one day and say, "What do you think of this and that?" And we'll try it, look at it, change it, and we love it, or we don't. And that's it.

101

formerly of FOUNTAIN RESTAURANT | Philadelphia

SASHIMI TUNA CARPACCIO WITH POTATO RISOTTO AND TOMATO-INFUSED OIL | Serves 4

Here's a twist on risotto in which the rice is replaced with tiny cubes of potato, cooked in chicken stock and flavored with Parmigiano. Slice the potatoes on a vegetable slicer, then julienne and cube them by hand. Yukon Gold potatoes have a creamy texture and won't fall apart when cooked, as baking potatoes would.

The recipe makes more of the tomato-infused oil than you'll need for this dish. It keeps for two to three weeks in the refrigerator. Bring it to room temperature and then use it in salads or as a sauce for fish, chicken, or vegetables.

FOR THE OIL
1 cup extra-virgin olive oil
1 medium shallot, finely chopped
2 ripe tomatoes, peeled, seeded, and cut into ⅛-inch dice

FOR THE POTATO RISOTTO
2 large Yukon Gold potatoes (1½ to 1¾ pounds total)
2 cups chicken stock
Kosher salt and freshly ground black pepper
1 tablespoon olive oil
½ small onion, chopped
½ medium carrot, chopped
½ celery stalk, peeled and chopped
8 tablespoons (1 stick) unsalted butter, cut into cubes
½ cup finely grated Parmigiano-Reggiano

FOR THE FISH
4 large thin 4-ounce slices very fresh sushi-quality tuna
¼ cup chopped fresh chives for garnish

PREPARE THE OIL: Heat 1 tablespoon of the oil in a small saucepan over low heat. Add the shallot and cook until translucent, about 2 minutes. Add the remainder of the oil and bring to a boil. Add the tomatoes, remove the pan from the heat, and allow the oil to cool. Cover and refrigerate until cold.

PREPARE THE RISOTTO: Peel the potatoes and cut them into ¼-inch cubes. As you prepare the potatoes, put them into a bowl of cold water to keep them from darkening. Set the potatoes aside.

Put the stock in a small saucepan and season with 2 teaspoons salt and ⅛ teaspoon pepper. Bring to a boil and reduce the heat to low.

Heat the oil in a deep, straight-sided medium frying pan or large saucepan over low heat. Add the onion, carrot, and celery and cook until tender but not colored, 4 to 5 minutes. Drain the potatoes, add to the pan, and raise the heat to medium-high. Add 1½ cups of the chicken stock and simmer briskly, stirring constantly, until the potatoes are just beginning to get tender and the stock has reduced to a saucelike consistency, 8 to 10 minutes.

Stir in the butter and cheese. Season to taste with salt and pepper and remove from the heat.

ASSEMBLE THE DISH: Divide the risotto among four large white serving plates. Drape a slice of tuna over each mound. Drizzle a tablespoon of the tomato-infused oil over each slice of the fish. Sprinkle the chives on top of the tuna and around the plates. Serve immediately.

SAUTÉED VENISON CHOP WITH EXOTIC MUSHROOM TOWER AND CABERNET SAUCE

For the sauce, venison bones are roasted with a mirepoix of celery, onion, and carrot until well browned. The bones and vegetables are covered with Cabernet Sauvignon, port, and demi-glace and simmered for 2 hours. The sauce is strained and then reduced and enriched with butter to make an intensely flavored glaze.

A mousseline mixture of chicken breast and sautéed diced shiitake, cremini, and portobello mushrooms, bound with cream, is shaped into cylindrical "towers" that are wrapped in plastic wrap and steamed until firm.

To serve, the bases of the towers are trimmed so that they will stand upright on the plates. Sautéed spinach is placed next to each tower and roasted venison chops are balanced between them. The red wine sauce is drizzled with a white wine–mushroom cream reduction and the plates are garnished with whole sprigs of fresh thyme and a crisp potato flower.

103

Jean-Marie Lacroix

I was born and grew up in Japan, and that is where I started training. I also worked in Peru, Argentina, and Anchorage, Alaska. The restaurant in Anchorage burned down after fifty days. It was very hard, very hard. That's when I came here, to L.A. That was about twenty-three years ago. You know, what can I say? . . . Was the fire lucky? Unlucky? I'm here now, and I'm happy, and if we hadn't been burned out of the Alaskan restaurant, maybe I'd still be there, but you never know. There is always something happening.

Nobuyuki Matsuhisa

NOBU | New York, Malibu, Las Vegas, Tokyo, London, Paris

NOBU NEXT DOOR | New York

MATSUHISA | Beverly Hills, Aspen

UBON | Los Angeles

My customers are international travelers. One day, I am here in L.A., and the next day when I am in London, I see my customers there, from New York or L.A. Even in the airplane I see somebody, all the time. I have to fly a lot. Every month I go to Japan for five days, then from Japan I go to London, and from London to Italy. Every month it is a cycle. Then I go to New York and Las Vegas. . . . The travel and the jet lag are hard. Many times I wake up in the middle of the night and I don't know where I am. One time, I really got scared. I was on a flight, in the airplane, and I forgot where I was going. It has only happened once, but it was very scary! I stay a week to a maximum of ten days in Los Angeles. The other twenty or so days of the month I am always traveling. My wife travels with me.

Basically, my food is prepared in the Japanese style, but to me food is just like a fashion. . . . I find there is a lot of influence from Peru in the dishes I make. And every season has new dishes, new fashions, different styles, different colors . . . every year these things are different, right? So the food is always growing, changing, like a person.

Thin slices of snapper and a rosette of cucumber slices dotted with chile paste and seasoned with yuzu juice

UNAGI WITH SHIITAKE MUSHROOM AND FOIE GRAS SAUCE | Serves 4

Unagi is barbecued freshwater eel, a soft, rich-fleshed fish that the Japanese eat coated with a dark, salty-sweet glaze; you'll find it in Japanese markets already cooked and glazed. A slice of daikon, steamed but still crisp, is placed underneath each portion of eel for textural contrast. The eel and daikon are served with a mirin–soy sauce reduction flavored with shiitake mushrooms, white truffle oil, and foie gras.

Kosher salt
½ teaspoon all-purpose flour
4 big slices peeled daikon, each about ¼ inch thick
2 cups fish stock or bottled clam juice

FOR THE SAUCE
6 ounces raw foie gras, cut into ⅓-inch slices
4 shiitake mushrooms
¾ cup mirin
¼ cup soy sauce
1 teaspoon white truffle oil

Four 2- to 3-ounce pieces unagi
4 sansyo leaves (optional) (see Note)
Eel spine (optional)

PREPARE THE DAIKON: Bring 2 cups of salted water to a boil in a large saucepan with the flour. Add the daikon slices and boil for 2 minutes. Drain. Bring the fish stock to a boil in the same saucepan. Add the daikon and boil until softened, about 5 minutes. Drain the daikon and set aside. Discard the stock or reserve for another use, such as soup.

PREPARE THE SAUCE: Heat a large frying pan over medium-high heat until hot. Add the foie gras and sauté for 1 minute. Turn the slices, then add the mushrooms and cook until the foie gras and the mushrooms are lightly browned and softened, 1 to 2 more minutes. Then add the mirin and soy sauce, bring to a boil, and boil until the sauce is reduced and thickened, about 3 minutes. Remove the mushrooms and foie gras from the pan and reserve. Stir in the truffle oil.

PREPARE THE UNAGI: Put the unagi on a piece of aluminum foil and place in a toaster oven. Set the oven to medium-dark and toast to warm the eel through. (Or broil the eel for about 30 seconds, or until warm.)

To serve, put a daikon slice on each of four serving plates, and then a slice of foie gras, and then the mushrooms. Set the hot unagi on top. Pour the hot sauce around each and garnish with the sansyo and eel spine, if using.

NOTE: Sansyo leaves, also called kinome, are the leaves of the prickly ash tree, from which the spice sansho comes.

106

JAPANESE RED SNAPPER TIRADITO | Serves 4

A plate of pure white, impeccably fresh raw Japanese red snapper is seasoned with cilantro and a dab of chile paste and brightened with citrus. Japanese red snapper is hard to find and isn't anything like the snapper marketed here. It's better to substitute tilefish or grouper.

Yuzu is a very sour type of citrus fruit about the size of a tangerine, common in Japan. You may be able to find the juice fresh or bottled in Japanese markets. And although nothing is really similar to the lovely and distinctive fragrance of yuzu, lime juice is an acceptable substitute, as it recalls something of the floral quality of the fruit. Rocoto paste is a red chile paste from Peru; any chile paste can be substituted.

At the restaurant, the snapper is served with a sliced cucumber salad.

One 1½-pound very fresh Japanese red snapper, filleted and skinned, or 10
    ounces skinless tilefish or grouper fillet
40 fresh cilantro leaves
2 teaspoons Rocoto paste or other red chile paste
½ to 1 teaspoon kosher salt
4 teaspoons fresh or bottled yuzu juice or fresh lime juice
4 teaspoons fresh lemon juice

Cut the fish fillets into 40 thin slices, cutting on a shallow angle in order to get wide slices (*escalopes*).

Arrange 10 slices in an overlapping spiral fashion on each of four serving plates. Place a cilantro leaf in the center of each slice and dab each leaf with chile paste. Sprinkle the fish with the salt, yuzu juice, and lemon juice. Serve immediately.

Nobu Matsuhisa

Discussing or pinpointing the creative process is, I think, a bit difficult because you are sort of one with your creative process and you rarely observe it objectively. But I would say that the ingredients are the inspiration, and often people are the inspiration. The trends are always interesting and you look at them, but I think that what we do here is a bit more intuitive.

Nancy Oakes

Nancy Oakes

Nancy: Pam [Pamela Mazzola, Boulevard's co-chef de cuisine] and I have worked together here for seven years, and before that we had another small restaurant—forty-eight seats—for five years. I had a restaurant for ten years prior to that, and I worked in the front of the house for ten years prior to that. Pam and I work well together. I generally take care of dinner, and Pam takes care of lunch, although we do interact. Pam has three children, and it is a difficult combination. We both put an enormous amount of energy into this place, keeping it fresh, keeping it new.

Discussing or pinpointing the creative process is, I think, a bit difficult because you are sort of one with your creative process and you rarely observe it objectively. So it is difficult to paint a pretty picture of it and explain it to other people. But I would say that the ingredients are the inspiration, and often people are the inspiration. The trends are always interesting and you have to look at them, but I think that what Pam and I have done here is a bit more intuitive. We cook what we like to eat, and it's always subjective and not always conceptual. I know that there are a lot of restaurants out there [that] try to get a concept and roll it out, you know, you find a bowl of noodles, and then roll out fifty thousand of them. And although we've both traveled a lot and lived in other countries, we try to avoid souvenir cooking, which

I think is a dangerous thing. You know, you go to Vietnam and bring home a noodle dish. Instead of a postcard, you bring home a cuisine. So, while we are influenced by things that we see and try, ultimately it all comes back to what works for us, and what we like to eat, and what looks delicious to us.

Pamela: We change the menu seasonally, and whenever we feel that we have a solid idea. A new product might inspire us, or we'll think, "Well, we've been running this dish for a couple of weeks and we're tired of it, let's think of something else." But it's always based on a solid idea. We don't change just to change. Being in California, we are really blessed with every kind of product you can imagine. We probably have some of the best produce and meats in the world. Nancy and I bounce ideas off each other. I think it helps to have someone to talk to about what you want to do. I'll say, "Let's do this with a dish," and then Nancy will say, "Well, yeah, that's a good way to start, but why don't we try putting another ingredient with it?" or, "Let's not do it with duck, let's do it with squab." It is very collaborative.

109

BOULEVARD | San Francisco

Nancy Oakes

PAN-ROASTED HALIBUT WITH CONFIT CREAMER POTATOES, MAINE BOUCHOT MUSSELS, ARTICHOKES, SAFFRON SAUCE, AND LEMON SALSA

Mussels are steamed in white wine flavored with shallots and garlic. Then the mussel cooking liquid is reduced, lightly creamed, and flavored with saffron and a little tomato paste. The shelled mussels are combined with roasted potatoes, sautéed artichokes, and garlicky spinach and arranged in the center of the plates. A sautéed halibut fillet is set on top of each and the mussel-saffron sauce spooned around. A lemon salsa, made by microwaving strips of Meyer lemon zest with olive oil, then combining the drained zest with Meyer lemon sections, capers, ground coriander, and tiny croutons, is served spooned on top of the halibut.

TUNA TARTARE

Very fresh tuna is cut into ¼-inch cubes, mixed with a tiny dice of jalapeño pepper and young, pink ginger, and seasoned with Vietnamese red chile sauce, soy sauce, Asian sesame oil, and fresh lime juice. The tartare is pressed into individual molds and then turned out onto a serving plate.

Each plate is garnished with potato gaufrettes, avocado slices drizzled with lime juice, and a toasted rice mixture made by mixing Rice Krispies with white and black sesame seeds, dried red pepper flakes, julienned nori, and Asian sesame oil that are baked until crisp and arranged in 3 small mounds around the tartare. The tartare is served with two sauces: soy sauce seasoned with ginger, mirin, and sliced shallot and thickened with cornstarch, and a mayonnaise flavored with fresh wasabi root and wasabi tobiko, rice wine vinegar, fine dice of cucumber, tomatillo, and jalapeño. Thin strips of nori are scattered over the plate before serving.

I had studied theater, wanted to be an actor, was particularly
interested in film. I received an acting scholarship and went to college,
but I never found it as interesting as the restaurants I was working in.
All through high school and college, I worked in restaurants and fell in
love with restaurant people. It was a little bit like belonging to the circus.
They were so eccentric and unusual and fascinating. And abnormal.

Patrick O'Connell

Patrick O'Connell

THE INN AT LITTLE WASHINGTON | Washington, Va.

My partner and I bought an old rundown farm and brandy distillery about twenty miles from here, and I began cooking on an old wood-burning cookstove in the farmhouse, and people began visiting us. We had a big garden and we raised lots of vegetables. It was the seventies, and it was perfectly acceptable to retire early. . . . I think it is an excellent concept to retire when you are young and work when you are old.

It took us about six years to find this building, which had been an old garage and gas station at one time, then a Ford Motor Company [building], then a little store, and we rented half of it for two hundred dollars a month, which was a very stiff price at the time. Fortunately, we also had an option to purchase the premises at the end of the first year. On opening weekend, we had about seventy-eight guests, and I had one helper in the kitchen. A fantastic review came out in the Washington, D.C., newspapers, calling us the best restaurant in a radius of a hundred fifty miles of Washington. It took about ten years before we were able to come up for air, really. It was nonstop madness.

From the early days, we still kept the farm, had chickens and goats and a large garden, and all of our neighbors had gardens, and people began bringing us supplies. We now have a network of about fifty local farmers, and they each raise certain things for us. In the spring, they'll come to us to decide what they should plant and how much of everything we'll be using, so it is kind of a network of custom growers that has evolved over the years.

Originally, no deliveries were made here. The only thing we could have brought to the door was milk. So if we wanted fish or caviar or lobster, we had to, each day, drive into the city and pick it up. We had an old Dodge that we bought for a hundred fifty dollars, and my partner would leave the restaurant at midnight and bring back the provisions for the next day. It was pretty wacky. So, out of necessity, we had to get as many local ingredients as we could. Each year, we could find more and more of the menu items right in this local county. And now, it is like the best of both worlds—anything we want that exists in the world we can have in two hours, and we can have all the custom things grown here as well.

PISTACHIO-CRUSTED RACK OF LAMB WITH CARROT ESSENCE | Serves 6

A pistachio-crusted rack of lamb is sauced with a very lightly creamed carrot juice reduction. An Asian-inspired dressing seasons the quickly sautéed watercress served with the lamb.

FOR THE DRESSING

1 tablespoon rice wine vinegar

7 tablespoons fish sauce

2 tablespoons sugar

½ cup cold water

Juice of 1 lime

2 tablespoons finely julienned carrot

¼ cup minced fresh cilantro

2 large garlic cloves, minced

2 jalapeño peppers, stemmed, seeds and ribs removed, and finely chopped

FOR THE CARROT ESSENCE

1½ cups fresh carrot juice

2 tablespoons crème fraîche

Kosher salt

FOR THE GLAZE

1 packed cup brown sugar

1 cup Dijon mustard

FOR THE LAMB

3 racks of lamb (1½ pounds each), frenched (have the butcher do this)

Kosher salt and freshly ground black pepper

2½ cups pistachios, toasted and coarsely chopped

FOR THE WATERCRESS

1 tablespoon vegetable oil

4 firmly packed cups watercress, washed and thoroughly dried

¼ cup toasted pistachios for garnish

PREPARE THE DRESSING: Combine all of the ingredients in a small bowl and stir to dissolve the sugar. Set aside.

PREPARE THE CARROT ESSENCE: Bring the carrot juice to a boil in a small nonaluminum saucepan over medium heat and simmer until reduced by one-half. Remove the pan from the heat and whisk in the crème fraîche. Season to taste with salt. Strain and set the sauce aside.

PREPARE THE GLAZE: Whisk together the brown sugar and mustard in a medium bowl until there are no lumps of sugar. Set aside.

PREPARE THE LAMB: Preheat the broiler.

Sprinkle the lamb all over with salt and pepper. Wrap the bones with aluminum foil to prevent them from burning.

Place the lamb on a broiling pan or baking sheet and broil the lamb until lightly charred 1 to 2 minutes on each side. Remove the lamb from oven. Lower the oven heat to 400°F.

Place the lamb in a single layer in a baking dish or small roasting pan. Brush the racks on all sides with the glaze and roast until medium-rare, 8 to 10 minutes. Roll the racks in the pistachios so that the entire surface of the meat is coated. Set the racks on a cutting board and let rest for 5 minutes.

MEANWHILE, PREPARE THE WATERCRESS: Place a large frying pan over high heat. Add the oil and heat to the smoking point. Add the watercress, toss once or twice, and cook until just slightly wilted, 2 to 3 seconds. Sprinkle with the dressing and toss to coat. Remove the watercress from the heat and drain in a colander.

To serve, rewarm the carrot essence over medium heat. Cut each rack into chops and divide the chops among six serving plates. Arrange the watercress around the chops like a wreath. Ladle the carrot essence around the perimeter of the plates and sprinkle each plate with 5 or 6 pistachios.

Lamb on a root vegetable roesti bound with grated cooked potatoes and sautéed until very crisp

PINEAPPLE UPSIDE-DOWN CRÊPES | Serves 10 to 12

Partly cooked crêpes are covered with triangles of pineapple, sprinkled with sugar, and then turned over in the pan so that the sugar and pineapple caramelize like the pineapple in an upside-down cake. This is a good dessert for entertaining, because the crêpes can be made up to 4 hours ahead and then reheated in the oven.

FOR THE BATTER

2 cups all-purpose flour
6 tablespoons (¾ stick) unsalted butter, melted and cooled
¼ cup sugar
3 large eggs
Pinch of kosher salt
1 cup milk, or as needed

FOR THE CRÊPES

About 1 tablespoon unsalted butter
1 cup toasted and coarsely ground macadamia nuts
2 large ripe pineapples, peeled, cored, quartered, and cut crosswise into ⅛-inch-thick slices
About ½ cup sugar
6 tablespoons (¾ stick) cold unsalted butter, cut into bits

¾ cup heavy cream

½ cup 151-proof rum
1 quart vanilla, buttermilk, or coconut ice cream

PREPARE THE BATTER: Combine the flour, melted butter, sugar, eggs, and salt in the bowl of a food processor or blender. With the motor running, add enough milk to make a fluid batter.

PREPARE THE CRÊPES: Line a large baking sheet with parchment paper and set aside.

Melt about ¼ teaspoon of the butter in a 7-inch nonstick crêpe pan or frying pan over medium heat, spreading the butter over the bottom with a spatula. Remove the pan from the heat and allow it to cool slightly. With the pan off the heat, ladle about 3 tablespoons of the batter into the pan and tilt the pan until the bottom is evenly coated. Sprinkle with 1 tablespoon of the macadamia nuts. Return the pan to the heat and cook until the crêpe is almost set but still wet on top (the crêpe must be wet in order for the pineapple slices to stick to it when the crêpe is flipped). Remove the pan from the heat and arrange 12 to 16 pineapple slices in an overlapping circular pattern, completely covering the crêpe. Shake the pan slightly every now and then to keep the crêpe from sticking.

Return the pan to the heat. Sprinkle the pineapple with 2 teaspoons sugar and about ½ tablespoon cold butter bits. Use a rubber spatula to loosen the edge of the crêpe to check the underside. When the bottom is golden brown, loosen the crêpe from the pan by running the spatula around its edges and carefully flip the crêpe. Then drizzle 1 tablespoon of the cream around the perimeter of the crêpe and tilt the pan so that the cream runs under it.

Spray a flat metal surface (like the bottom of a cake pan or the removable bottom of a tart pan) with nonstick cooking spray. Place the sprayed side over the crêpe, invert the pan so that the crêpe falls onto the surface, and slide the crêpe onto the prepared baking sheet. Repeat the process with the remaining batter, wiping the pan clean after each crêpe. Cover the crêpes and refrigerate until you're ready to serve.

FINISH THE DISH: Preheat the oven to 350°F.

Reheat the crêpes on the baking sheet until they are hot all the way through, about 4 minutes. Use a spatula to transfer the crêpes to serving plates.

Meanwhile, pour the rum into a small saucepan and heat over medium heat. When the rum is hot, carefully hold a lighted match to one side of the pan so that the alcohol ignites. Carefully spoon the flaming rum over the crêpes and garnish each with a miniature scoop of ice cream.

Patrick O'Connell

Tadashi Ono   **SONO** | New York

Soy sauce has a great flavor. It comes from a neutral source, the soybean, rather than from meat or fish, and just the right amount will enhance the flavor of an ingredient rather than covering it.

I began cooking in Japan, and I wasn't really sure that it was my passion. My friend had introduced me to it. . . . I just wanted to work. I was a student at that time, and I worked part-time in the restaurant. I wasn't very interested in it. Then I started working for an export-import company, and they sent me to Los Angeles. I really liked it there. When they wanted to move me back to Japan, I said, "No, I want to stay." But they didn't need me anymore in the Los Angeles office, so I looked for a job and wound up in a restaurant.

I think that where chefs come from influences their cooking. I have been to France many times, but I am not French and I have not cooked there. What I have gained from the French tradition is technique. French technique is very broad. In the main, of course, my approach to cooking is based on a mentality that is Japanese. To me, the inner nature of an ingredient is very beautiful. I want to bring that nature out. The first step in this process is to determine what the nature of the ingredient is. Lobster, for example, is characterized by a taste of the ocean, a natural sweetness, a springy texture. These are the qualities I want people to recognize, and I use sharp and crispy things like yuzu, a Japanese citrus, and ginger and scallions to enhance them.

I think the California approach to cooking is more free minded, free spirited. They are famous for their produce, and so they are more conscious of how things grow. Here in New York, we are more about concept, technique, idea, combining. We care more about skill.

When I was looking for the ceramics to use at Sono, I couldn't find what I really wanted, so during the building delays before the opening, I put a kiln in the basement and started making my own ceramics. I am always thinking about what kind of plates my food should be served on. If I am cooking something from the sea, I want to serve it on a plate that evokes a feeling of the sea. And when I am designing that sea plate, thinking about what will be served on it helps me to establish its form. My plates are often very rustic, natural, rough textured. Wavy and bumpy, the way nature is. I want to feel the natural environment, water or mountains, for example, in the plate. The earthy character of my plates helps the fundamental nature of foods to shine.

SHIITAKE-DUXELLES TOFU "POUCHES" WITH WILD MUSHROOM CONSOMMÉ | Serves 4

In a dish that shows clear influences of both France and Japan, pureed tofu is used to make a tender, delicately flavored "pouch" to hold a filling of shiitake mushroom duxelles. The consommé is based on an infusion of dried shiitakes and kombu, a variety of dried seaweed used in the classic Japanese soup stock, *dashi*. The consommé is flavored and garnished with several varieties of Japanese mushrooms, all of which are available at specialty food stores and even in many supermarkets. You may find hon-shimeji mushrooms sold as beech mushrooms, and maitake are also called hen o' the woods.

FOR THE CONSOMMÉ

½ pound dried shiitake mushrooms
4 quarts water
2 ounces dried kombu

2 tablespoons soy sauce
1 tablespoon sake
4 ounces shimeji mushrooms
4 ounces maitake mushrooms
4 ounces nameko mushrooms
4 ounces enoki mushrooms
1 ounce mitsuba (see Note)

FOR THE TOFU POUCHES

1 block firm tofu (15 to 16 ounces)
1½ teaspoons olive oil
1 tablespoon minced shallots
½ garlic clove, minced
¼ pound shiitake mushrooms, stemmed and minced
2 tablespoons dry white wine
¼ teaspoon kosher salt
⅛ teaspoon freshly ground black pepper

PREPARE THE CONSOMMÉ: The day before you plan to serve the dish, put the dried shiitakes in the water in a large pot and let soak overnight.

The next day, add the kombu to the pot and bring to a boil. Immediately remove and discard the kombu. Lower the heat and simmer until the broth has reduced by three-quarters. (This will take about 2 hours.)

MEANWHILE, PREPARE THE TOFU POUCHES: Place the tofu in a fine-meshed sieve and press to drain out as much water as possible. Transfer to a food processor and process until smooth. Turn out onto a large plate and divide into 4 equal parts. Set aside.

Heat the oil in a small saucepan over low heat. Add the shallots and garlic and cook until translucent, about 1 minute. Add the shiitakes and cook until soft, about 3 minutes. Raise the heat to medium, add the wine, and cook until the pan is dry. Stir in the salt and pepper. Spread the mixture out on a plate and refrigerate until cool.

Cut four 5-inch squares of tripled cheesecloth. Spoon one-quarter of the tofu puree into the center of one of the cheesecloth squares and spread it out to a 3-inch circle. Put one-quarter of the cooled mushroom mixture in the center of the tofu round. Bring the four corners of the cheesecloth up over the mushrooms and grasp them in your right hand. Then lift the pouch, cup your left hand under the bottom, and twist the cheesecloth so that it tightens just above the mushrooms. The tofu will enclose the mushrooms in a rounded pouch shape. Tie the pouch with kitchen twine to close tightly. Repeat to make 3 more pouches. Refrigerate while you finish the consommé.

FINISH THE CONSOMMÉ: Strain the broth through a fine-meshed strainer, discard the shiitakes, and return the broth to the pot. Add the soy sauce and sake and bring to a simmer. Add the shimeji, maitake, nameko, and enoki mushrooms and the tofu pouches. Simmer until the tofu has heated through and firmed, 7 to 8 minutes.

To serve, remove the pouches from the consommé with a slotted spoon, and remove the cheesecloth. Place 1 pouch in the center of each of four soup bowls. Use the slotted spoon to spoon out and divide the mushrooms among the bowls. Pour over the consommé and garnish with the mitsuba.

NOTE: Mitsuba, an herb that is usually called trefoil in the United States, has a light green leaf that looks like celery leaf or parsley.

ROASTED DUCK BREAST WITH WASABI-WATERCRESS SAUCE AND STEAMED BUCKWHEAT

Buckwheat groats, the same grain from which flour is milled for Japanese soba noodles, are steamed until al dente and then tossed with watercress sprigs, and fresh ginger and soy sauce to season. The buckwheat is centered on the plates and Pekin duck breast, roasted to medium-rare, is sliced and fanned around the buckwheat. A bright green sauce of watercress leaves pureed with duck stock, soy sauce, wasabi powder, and a little olive oil is spooned around the duck.

Tadashi Ono

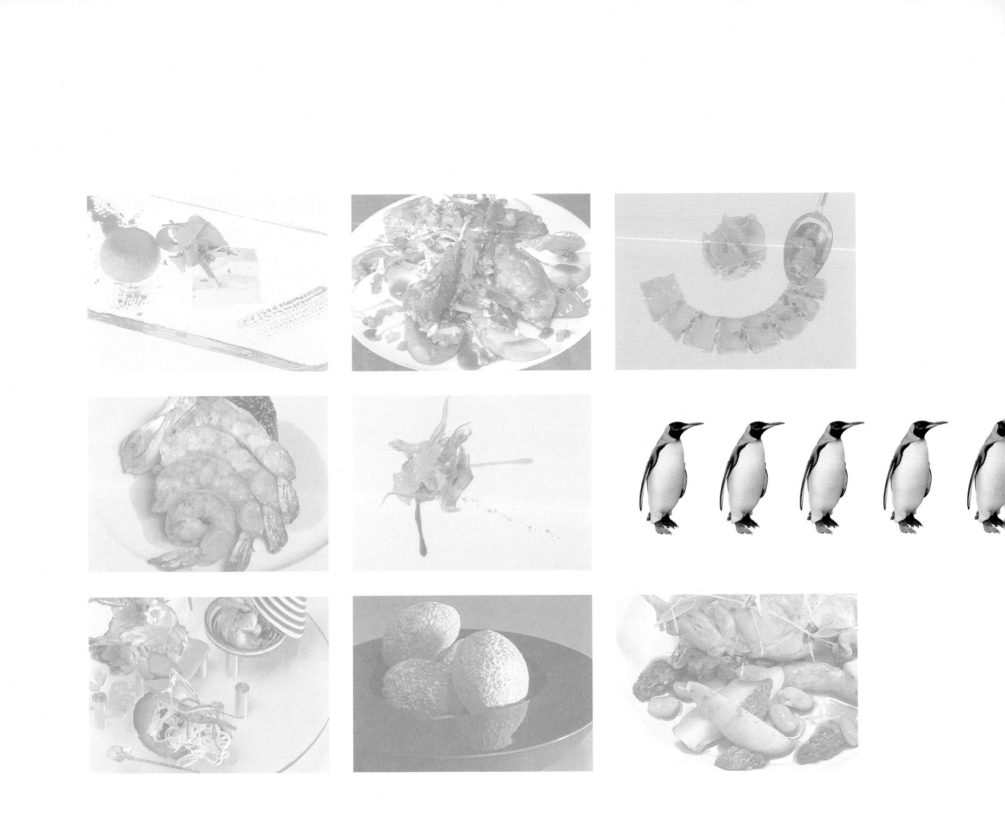

Sometimes I think I was lucky to have grown up in a poor family. If I had been rich, I might have become a lawyer . . . then, too bad, world, no chef Michel Richard! But I was poor, and God made me to be a chef. I smell like a chef, I feel like a chef, I look like a chef. I am a chef. Thank God. I could have been born a millionaire . . . what a disaster.

Michel Richard

Michel Richard

Highlights of my life? The best thing . . . let me see . . . is to be a chef. It is a religion. When I was a kid, a friend of mine took me to his father's restaurant. I was eight or nine years old, a small boy. And after meeting his father, I was amazed, I felt like I was in paradise. I fell in love with the kitchen, I fell in love with the restaurant. I was supposed to spend two weeks with my friend, but instead of spending two weeks with the kid, I spent two weeks in the kitchen. And I fell in love with food. After that, at school, when the teacher asked me what I wanted to be when I grew up, I said, "I want to be a chef! I want to be a chef!" and everybody was laughing. It was not a very glamorous profession then.

Before I became a chef, I was an *artiste*. I used to paint in Paris, in Montmartre, la Place du Tertre. That was twenty years ago, but I was not selling too many of my paintings. When I did sell one, we would drink the whole evening . . . drink the money. We were *artistes,* and we were like that. Maybe one day, when I am tired, when I am not strong enough to be a chef anymore, I will become an *artiste* again. I gave it up when I was twenty, twenty-two years old. You know, I would paint all night . . . and you hate yourself because what you did was not good, and it is tough, because that is what you are thinking.

After that I worked in a restaurant, and I didn't like it in those days. We were not able to create our own recipes. But then I worked for a very famous pastry chef, and he sent me to another pastry chef in New York. And that was a very special time in my life. To be a young man who had chosen to go to New York, . . . that was exciting. I had no money, but it wasn't long before I did start making money. At twenty-six years old, I was making a lot of money. And I started to go back to France and to go to the three-star restaurants and eat good food, and I fell in love with food again, and with the system of the restaurant.

Being a chef is very wonderful. But it has its ups and downs. Sometimes I feel like I can't cook, like I am the worst chef in the world, and the next day, I wake up and think, "Let's forget about yesterday. Let's do something new today." I love that.

125

CITRONELLE | Washington, D.C., Santa Barbara

CAVIAR CRAZY EGGS | Serves 6

For this appetizer of softly scrambled eggs presented in their shells, the eggs are scrambled in traditional French style—that is, over low heat so that they don't develop a hard curd—and enriched, as is traditional, with crème fraîche and butter. (This version is notable for its restrained use of both.) A handful of chives and a spoon of Beluga caviar on top of each adds a contrasting crunch to the silken, luscious eggs.

6 large eggs
¼ cup crème fraîche
1 tablespoon minced shallot
1 teaspoon fresh lemon juice
½ teaspoon kosher salt
⅛ teaspoon freshly ground black pepper
1 tablespoon unsalted butter
¼ cup chopped fresh chives
2 tablespoons Beluga caviar

PREPARE THE EGGSHELLS: Preheat the oven to 250°F.

Cut off the top ½ inch of each egg with an egg-cutter or by tapping firmly around the top with a small knife. Discard the tops. Empty the eggs into a bowl, cover, and refrigerate. Rinse the eggshells under cold running water and pull out the membranes that line the shells. Place the shells cut sides down on a baking sheet and bake for 5 minutes to dry.

Glue the dried eggshells onto six small plates, or make a small mound of coarse sea salt in the center of each plate to hold them upright and set the eggshells in the salt.

PREPARE THE EGGS: Beat the eggs with a whisk. Strain through a fine-meshed sieve, to remove any shells, into a small heavy saucepan. Add the crème fraîche, place over low heat, and cook, whisking constantly, until the eggs are set with small curds but still soft. (If the eggs start to set too quickly, remove the pan from the heat and whisk for a minute to cool, then return to the heat.) Just before the eggs are completely cooked, whisk in the shallot and lemon juice and season with the salt and pepper. Remove the pan from the heat and stir in the butter and chives.

To serve, carefully spoon the scrambled egg into the shells and top each with 1 teaspoon caviar.

SUGARED BEIGNETS

Individual wonton skins are brushed with egg wash, then each is topped with a second wonton skin. The doubled skins are cut into rounds (whatever size you like) with a cookie cutter, then deep-fried in 375°F oil until each round puffs into a ball and turns golden brown. The beignets are drained on paper towels, sprinkled with confectioners' sugar, and served hot, with ice cream.

Michel Richard

Eric Ripert

LE BERNARDIN | New York

I was born in Antibes and grew up in Andorra. I am a Mediterranean guy. I think you have to cook, reminding yourself of where you come from, and you cannot forget your origins, because it's where you are the best.

There is a renaissance in cooking happening now. You know, we are living a real revolution here. Today, New York attracts the best chefs in the world. You have great celebrated chefs from Asia, celebrated chefs from South America, from Europe. . . . It is a capital of food, and everybody is into reinventing "*la cuisine*," his cuisine. Then you get interaction between all the chefs, and the influences of some flavors, some spices, and it is very exciting to be here. We don't feel any pressure on our shoulders from people who say, "No, you cannot do that, it is not correct." If you feel like you want to play with it, and if you have the talent and you are good, you will get the recognition. That is the way it works.

If you say to me, "rosemary," not only do I see the plant, I also taste the flavor in my head. If you say to me, "carrot and rosemary," I can automatically hear in my head whether it will work or not to combine those two things, and what we have to do to make it work. So when I create a dish, the first work is intellectual. Then I put it down on paper, and after that I go into production here with my sous-chefs and we try to make it happen. From the theory, we go to *practique*. This is a critical moment.

I think there are two types of cooking, and it is very important to know the difference between them. There is *cooking with* and *cooking for*. If you take a piece of turbot, for example, and you are *cooking with* the turbot, you are going to serve what you want with the turbot—you might have some artichokes, and some tomatoes and some string beans, chervil, mushroom sauce. You are not elevating the turbot above these other ingredients. If you are *cooking for* the turbot, the turbot is the main product. In this case, you say, "I'm going to do my best to make this turbot better than any other turbot." Then, everything you are going to add in your dish will be to elevate the turbot. And I think that is very important.

SEARED YELLOWTAIL WITH BABY ARUGULA, BASIL-TAPENADE PASTA SALAD, AND PINE NUT SAUCE VIERGE | Serves 4

This thin-sliced rare tuna was inspired by a Vietnamese beef salad that the chef often orders from a restaurant near his home. In that salad, the beef is cooked very rare and sliced thin. *Sauce vierge* is a classic French sauce of tomato, basil, shallots, capers, and olive oil that is traditionally served with poached fish. This version is embellished with toasted pine nuts and Parmigiano. The recipe for the sauce makes more than you'll need for this dish. Refrigerate the remainder and use it within two days on other sautéed or grilled fish. (Bring the refrigerated sauce to room temperature before serving.)

FOR THE PASTA SALAD

1 cup cooked penne
1 tablespoon prepared pesto
1 tablespoon prepared tapenade (black olive paste)
1 teaspoon chopped capers
2 tablespoons diced (¼-inch) peeled and seeded tomato
¼ teaspoon Tabasco sauce
1 teaspoon fresh lemon juice
Fine sea salt and freshly ground white pepper

FOR THE SAUCE

½ cup extra-virgin olive oil
1 tablespoon freshly grated Parmigiano-Reggiano
1 tablespoon diced (¼-inch) fresh basil
¼ cup diced (¼-inch) peeled and seeded tomatoes
1 tablespoon toasted pine nuts
1 tablespoon fresh lemon juice
1 teaspoon chopped capers
1 teaspoon minced shallot
Fine sea salt and freshly ground black pepper to taste

FOR THE TUNA

Two 4-ounce pieces (each 2 by 4 by 1 inch thick) yellowtail tuna
2 tablespoons fresh thyme leaves
Fine sea salt and freshly ground white pepper
¼ cup extra-virgin olive oil

FOR THE ARUGULA SALAD

¼ teaspoon Dijon mustard
1½ teaspoons sherry vinegar
Pinch of fine sea salt
Pinch of freshly ground white pepper
1½ tablespoons canola oil
1 cup baby arugula, washed

Thin slices of barely cooked tuna drizzled with a fresh tomato sauce, accompanied by an arugula salad and pasta tossed with basil tapenade

PREPARE THE PASTA SALAD: Combine the penne, pesto, tapenade, capers, tomatoes, Tabasco sauce, and lemon juice in a bowl. Season to taste with salt and pepper. Cover and refrigerate.

PREPARE THE SAUCE: Combine all the ingredients in a bowl. Set aside at room temperature.

PREPARE THE TUNA: Sprinkle both sides of each piece of tuna with the thyme and a pinch each of salt and pepper. Drizzle 2 tablespoons of the olive oil over each and rub the oil into the tuna.

Heat a large nonstick frying pan over high heat until smoking. Put the tuna in the pan and sear until browned on all four sides (top, bottom, and long sides) and rare but warm in the center, about 1 minute on each side. Remove from the pan and slice ¼ inch thick.

PREPARE THE ARUGULA SALAD: Whisk together the mustard, vinegar, salt, and pepper in a bowl. Whisk in the oil. Add the arugula and toss.

To serve, place a 2- to 2½-inch ring mold near the top of each of four serving plates and spoon one-quarter of the pasta salad into each mold. Top each pasta salad with one-quarter of the arugula salad and then carefully remove the molds. Fan one-quarter of the sliced yellowtail below each pasta salad. Spoon 2 tablespoons of the sauce over each serving of tuna.

PAN-ROASTED MONKFISH "AUX CAROTTES" WITH MINT PESTO | Serves 4

This recipe shows Moroccan influence in its use of cumin, ground ginger, harissa, lemon juice, and mint. The chef likes Moroccan food for the way in which the cuisine plays with spices and brings sour and sweet flavors together.

FOR THE PESTO
½ cup fresh peppermint leaves
¼ cup extra-virgin olive oil
4 tablespoons (½ stick) unsalted butter, melted

FOR THE CARROTS AND SAUCE
2 tablespoons extra-virgin olive oil
1 tablespoon thinly sliced garlic
2 cups sliced (¼-inch-thick) carrots
½ cup sliced onions
½ teaspoon ground cumin, or to taste
½ teaspoon harissa, or to taste (see Note)
Grated zest of 1 lemon
8 cups chicken stock, boiled until reduced to 4 cups
Kosher salt and freshly ground black pepper to taste
1 tablespoon fresh lemon juice

FOR THE MONKFISH
Large pinch of curry powder
Large pinch of ground ginger
Large pinch of cayenne pepper
Pinch of freshly ground white pepper
¼ teaspoon fine sea salt
1 bone-in monkfish tail (about 3 pounds), dark skin and fat removed,
    cut into 1-inch slices
2 tablespoons corn oil

4 fresh peppermint sprigs, for garnish

PREPARE THE PESTO: Puree the mint with the olive oil in a blender. Blend in the melted butter. Put the pesto into a serving bowl and set aside at room temperature.

PREPARE THE CARROTS AND SAUCE: Combine the olive oil, garlic, carrots, onions, cumin, harissa, and lemon zest in a medium heavy saucepan. Place over medium heat and cook slowly, stirring every now and then, until the carrots are tender, about 20 minutes.

Meanwhile, preheat the oven to 500°F.

Add the chicken stock and continue cooking until the stock is reduced by one-half. Strain the liquid into a saucepan and reserve; this is the sauce. Return the carrot mixture to the pan and mash with a fork to make a coarse puree, with pieces of carrot still visible in it. Season with salt and pepper and add more cumin and/or harissa if you like. Set aside.

PREPARE THE MONKFISH: Combine the curry powder, ginger, cayenne, white pepper, and salt in a bowl. Lay the monkfish slices on a work surface and, holding your hand about 6 inches above the fish, sprinkle half the spice mixture over the fish. Then turn the slices and repeat.

Heat 1 tablespoon of the corn oil in each of two large ovenproof nonstick frying pans over high heat until the oil is just smoking. Add half of the fish slices to each pan and sauté until browned on the bottom, about 3 minutes. Flip the slices, put the pans in the oven, and roast the fish until a skewer inserted into the slices for 5 seconds is warm when removed, 3 to 5 minutes.

FINISH THE DISH: Reheat the carrot mixture over medium heat. Bring the sauce to a boil and add the lemon juice.

To serve, spread the carrot mixture in a line down the center of each of four dinnner plates. Lay 3 pieces (2 if the pieces are large) of the monkfish across the puree. Spoon some of the sauce over the fish and carrots. Decorate the plates with the peppermint sprigs, and pass the pesto at the table.

NOTE: Harissa is a very hot sauce made from chile peppers, usually served with couscous, that is sold canned or jarred at specialty food shops.

Eric Ripert

Marcus Samuelsson

AQUAVIT | New York, Minneapolis

I was born in Ethiopia, raised in Sweden, I've traveled through Asia, and I cook in the United States. All of these influences come out in my food. When you are from Sweden, you can't just cook Swedish food. It doesn't make any sense. For me, it has to be a reflection of all the things I've done in the past.

You ask if salmon was invented in Sweden? I think you would start a war with Norway if you said that, so I'm not going to say that.

I've been cooking all my life. I started out as my grandmother's apprentice, baking cookies and bread and learning her secrets of the Swedish kitchen. And just in the course of my everyday life, I spent a lot of time learning about food. In Sweden, children regularly go mushroom and berry picking. Actually, whether they want to or not, all Swedish kids go strawberry picking in early summer. And then you have the lingonberries in August, and the blueberries, and then the mushrooms start coming. . . . I learned a lot from these foraging activities. And when you've gone out mushroom hunting, for example, with your family, you can be sure that the mushrooms you bring home will be the best-tasting mushrooms in the world. You make your mushroom stew and you serve it with a nice, crusty bread and maybe some tea; such meals belong to the category of "best you can ever eat."

I trained in France, which is rich in tradition. I could never do all of this beautiful, funky food without having learned French cooking technique. I don't try to force cool flavors, cool ideas. I work with unique products, but it always comes back to a very basic, grandmother's-style or French-cooking approach. I would never say that American cooking is better than European cooking. There are simply two different approaches right now: In Europe, it is about protecting beautiful techniques and traditions, and it is great that we have that. In America, it is more about breaking rules.

CURRIED HERRING SALAD | Serves 6

This sweet, spicy, crunchy salad starts with pickled herring that you make at home with a "1-2-3 vinegar," so called because it is made of one cup of vinegar, two cups of sugar, and three cups of water. The herring is mixed with crisp diced apple and creamy boiled potato and seasoned with an innovative Southeast Asian-and-Swedish spiced curry paste. If you cannot find fresh herring, substitute mackerel and skin it after pickling. The fish must remain in the brine for at least twenty-four hours, but it won't suffer from several days of brining if that's how it works out in your kitchen.

FOR THE PICKLED HERRING

1 cup Swedish or white wine vinegar

2 cups sugar

3 cups water

2 bay leaves

2 black peppercorns

1 carrot, peeled and sliced

1 red onion, sliced

½ leek, sliced

6 herring or mackerel fillets (about 1 pound total)

FOR THE CURRY PASTE

1 stalk lemongrass, trimmed to the ivory core and roughly chopped

5 kaffir lime leaves

¾ teaspoon shrimp paste

2 dried chiles

1½ teaspoons coriander seeds

1¼ teaspoons ground cumin

2 small garlic cloves

1½ teaspoons fennel seeds

¾ teaspoon yellow mustard seeds

¾ teaspoon brown mustard seeds

1 black cardamom pod

½ cinnamon stick

2 cloves

½-inch piece fresh ginger, peeled

1 tablespoon dill seeds

1 tablespoon ground turmeric

5 tablespoons vegetable oil

Juice of 1 lime

3 tablespoons sour cream

1 teaspoon kosher salt

1 Yukon Gold potato, peeled, boiled until tender, cooled, and cut into small dice

1 Fuji apple, peeled, cored, and cut into small dice

PREPARE THE PICKLED HERRING: Combine the vinegar, sugar, water, bay leaves, peppercorns, carrot, and onion in a large saucepan. Bring to a boil, reduce the heat, and simmer for 3 minutes. Add the leek, remove the pan from the heat, and let the brine cool completely.

Transfer the brine to a bowl, add the herring (or mackerel) to the brine, and refrigerate overnight, or for several days.

PREPARE THE CURRY PASTE: Combine all of the ingredients in a blender and blend until smooth.

FINISH THE DISH: Remove the herring from the brine and pat the fillets dry on paper towels. (If using mackerel, skin it.) Cut the fillets crosswise into thin strips.

Combine 1 tablespoon of the curry paste, the lime juice, sour cream, and salt in a medium bowl and stir until smooth. Add the fish, potato, and apple and gently fold all of the ingredients together. Serve cold.

HERRING SUSHI WITH BLACK MUSTARD | Serves 4

This is a spin on traditional Japanese sushi, combining elements of both Swedish and Japanese cuisines. The ingredients are Swedish—pickled herring and potatoes—but the technique for rolling the sushi is strictly Japanese. The sushi is served as part of a herring plate that also includes Curried Herring Salad (page 134) and a herring taco with black mustard.

If you can't find fresh herring, mackerel is a fine substitute but, unlike herring, it must be skinned after pickling.

FOR THE BLACK MUSTARD

1 tablespoon Swedish or other mild yellow mustard, such as
   honey mustard or Gulden's
1½ teaspoons Chinese mustard
1 teaspoon black mustard seeds
¾ teaspoon mild red miso
¾ teaspoon black bean paste
¼ teaspoon squid ink
1½ teaspoons mustard oil
1½ teaspoons olive oil

FOR THE HERRING SUSHI

1½ pounds fingerling or Yukon Gold potatoes
1 tablespoon mustard oil
1 teaspoon rice wine vinegar
½ teaspoon prepared wasabi
½ teaspoon kosher salt
2 pickled herring (or mackerel) fillets (see page 134),
   (5 to 6 ounces total)

PREPARE THE BLACK MUSTARD: Combine the prepared mustards, the mustard seeds, miso, black bean paste, and squid ink in a mini-food processor or mortar and pestle and process or grind until smooth. Add the mustard and olive oils and blend again until smooth.

PREPARE THE SUSHI: Cook the potatoes in boiling salted water until tender, 15 to 20 minutes depending on size. Let cool slightly, then peel and mash the potatoes with a fork. Add the mustard oil, 1 teaspoon of the black mustard, the rice wine vinegar, wasabi, and salt and stir until smooth. Set aside.

Pat the herring (or mackerel) fillets dry on paper towels. (Skin the fillets if using mackerel.) Cut the fillets lengthwise in half and then slice crosswise into thin strips.

Lay a sushi mat on a work surface with one long side facing you. Wrap the mat (both sides) in a long sheet of plastic wrap. Place about 3 tablespoons of the still-warm mashed potatoes in the center of the mat and press with your fingers into a 4-by-5-inch rectangle, the longer side running parallel to the bottom of the mat. Arrange a line of 6 to 8 strips of herring across the rectangle, about 1½ inches up from the bottom.

Now bring the bottom of the mat up and over the top half of the mat so that the mashed potatoes fold over on themselves and the herring is in the center. With your palms down, curl your fingertips around the top edge of the roll and set your thumbs at the bottom edge, and gently squeeze the potatoes into a roll. Unfold the mat and check the roll; you should have a neat cylinder with the herring completely enclosed. If necessary, fold the mat back over the roll and squeeze it again. Unfold the mat, remove the sushi roll, and set it on a plate. Repeat the process to make 3 more rolls.

To serve, cut each roll crosswise into 4 pieces and stand 4 pieces on end on each of four serving plates.

135

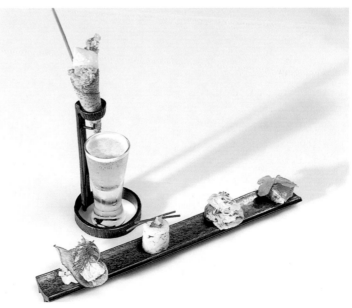

Left to right on the herring plate appetizer: Pickled Herring Taco with Black Mustard; Herring Sushi (seasoned with dill); Sour Cream, Garlic and Herb Herring; and Matjes Herring, a herring that has been cured in sandalwood with lime and spices

Marcus Samuelsson

Lydia Shire

BIBA and PIGNOLI | Boston

If you do something a little unusual, people will notice you. I once baked a seven-layer cake and brought It to a job interview at a restaurant, and they hired me on the spot. I brought the cake to them in an air-conditioned cab—it was the middle of summer and the cake had a buttercream frosting—and that was how I started working in restaurants.

My sous-chef, Susan Regis, and I have been cooking together for seventeen years. We have never lost our enthusiasm for what we do, or our sense of fun. We figure you only go once through this world, and you might as well have fun. But we do respect tradition. We take liberties, but we do it in a respectful way. We do not do what I call "bad fusion." For instance, if we do a dish that has its beginnings in Japan and that has wasabi in it, I'm not going to put cumin seed in the dish. If I'm going to be cooking something from Spain or South America, I stay true to its roots. I may have to use an American fish, but I'll also make something like a tamale with it. I wouldn't start mixing wasabi with tamales. To me, that's confusing, and in the end you don't know what you're eating. Biba is an eclectic American restaurant. We take liberties, but we don't stray too far, because we want to respect the country we're cooking in.

My father, who was Irish, was a wonderful cook. He used to cut recipes out of *The New York Times*. He had an innate understanding of things like heat—knew that you have to get a pan really hot if you are going to sear a steak and get a crust on the outside. I remember him putting newspapers down on the floor to catch the splatters, but he didn't care if he messed up the kitchen a little. What was important to him was that the steak be correctly seared, and served rare and juicy. I learned a lot about cooking from him.

I write seasonal menus. Biba does not serve asparagus unless it is spring. In the winter, we'll have oxtails on the menu, in autumn, we'll try to get truffles and porcini, and do some bean dishes. In summer, we do lots of corn and tomatoes and lobster. One recipe that I love is a soft-shell lobster dish. Soft-shell lobster is actually the most flavorful kind of lobster. In the summer when a lobster molts, its meat doesn't fill the new shell, and that space fills up with a liquid from the lobster. There is a certain sweetness to that lobster . . . its flavor is incomparable. I like to make a stack of soft-shell lobsters.

When we were designing the inside of Biba, I told the architect that I wanted lots of color. I showed him some kilim rugs that I have at home, and we looked at a book of Albanian rug designs that he had. The result is that the ceiling of the dining room is filled with canvases painted to represent the traditional patterns of Albanian rugs. It gives the restaurant an Adriatic or Mediterranean feel, a little bit Moroccan, a little bit Middle Eastern, a little bit Italian, southern French, Spanish. It is a very warm atmosphere.

STACKED SUMMER SOFT-SHELL LOBSTERS WITH GREEN BEANS, SHELL BEANS, AND A SHOT OF ICED VODKA | Serves 2

New England summers offer young lobsters that have just molted. Their shells are still soft and their flesh especially tender. Here soft-shell lobsters are served with green beans and shell beans, such as flageolets and cranberry beans, which are harvested in the summer as well.

If you're making this out of season, substitute hard-shell lobsters for the soft-shells.

FOR THE LOBSTERS

Six 1-pound soft-shell lobsters or two 1½- to
1¾-pound hard-shell lobsters

FOR THE SAUCE

3 tablespoons unsalted butter
2 shallots, minced
3 garlic cloves, minced
¼ cup olive oil
The reserved lobster bodies
1 cup dry white wine
½ cup brandy
2 cups water
8 cherry tomatoes
1 stalk lemongrass, trimmed to the ivory core
    and roughly chopped
⅓ cup heavy cream
½ teaspoon kosher salt
¼ teaspoon freshly ground black pepper
1 teaspoon fresh lime juice

FOR THE SHELL BEANS

¼ cup extra-virgin olive oil
1 small onion, diced
1 pound fresh flageolets or other shell beans,
    such as cranberry, shelled (about 1½ cups)
½ teaspoon fine sea salt
¼ teaspoon freshly ground black pepper

FOR THE GREEN BEANS

1 cup peanut or grapeseed oil
½ pound green beans, stems ends trimmed
2 thin slices fresh ginger
2 garlic cloves, sliced
½ scallion, sliced
¼ jalapeño pepper, stemmed and slivered
1 tablespoon oyster sauce
1 tablespoon soy sauce
Small handful of fresh cilantro sprigs
½ teaspoon kosher salt
¼ teaspoon freshly ground black pepper

2 tablespoons clarified butter
2 fresh tarragon sprigs for garnish
2 tablespoons ice-cold vodka

PREPARE THE LOBSTERS: Bring a large pot of salted water to a boil. Add the lobsters, return to a boil, cover, and simmer until just cooked through, 6 to 7 minutes for soft-shell lobsters, about 10 minutes for hard-shell lobsters. Let cool completely, then shell the lobsters. Reserve the bodies for the sauce. Cover and refrigerate the tail meat; reserve the claw meat for another meal.

Lobster and twice-fried beans served with a chilled shot glass of vodka

PREPARE THE SAUCE: Melt 2 tablespoons of the butter in a medium saucepan over low heat. Add the shallots and garlic and cook until translucent, 2 to 3 minutes. Set the pan aside.

Heat the oil in a large frying pan over high heat. Add the lobster bodies and cook until they turn bright red. Add the wine and brandy, bring to a boil, and reduce by one-half. Add the water, cherry tomatoes, and lemongrass and simmer for 20 minutes.

Strain into the saucepan with the shallots and garlic, pressing down on the lobster bodies to extract all of the flavor. (You should have about ½ cup sauce.) Add the cream, salt, and pepper. Whisk in the remaining 1 tablespoon butter and the lime juice. Set the sauce aside.

PREPARE THE SHELL BEANS: Heat the oil in a medium saucepan over medium heat. Add the onion and cook until translucent, 3 to 4 minutes. Add the beans and cook for 1 more minute. Add water to barely cover the beans, partially cover the pan, and simmer until the beans are tender, 25 to 40 minutes, depending on the type. Season with the salt and pepper.

MEANWHILE, PREPARE THE GREEN BEANS: Heat the oil in a large frying pan over medium-high heat until shimmering. Add the beans and cook until they blister, 1 to 1½ minutes. Transfer the beans to a serving plate.

Pour off and discard all but about 2 tablespoons of the oil from the pan. Add the ginger, garlic, scallion, and chile and cook over medium-high heat until the garlic turns a pale golden color, about 1 minute. Return the beans to the pan. Add the oyster sauce, soy sauce, cilantro sprigs, salt, and pepper and toss to coat the beans. Transfer the contents of the pan to a plate and loosely cover to keep warm.

FINISH THE DISH: Bring the sauce to a simmer; remove from the heat and cover to keep warm.

Heat the 2 tablespoons clarified butter over medium-high heat in a frying pan large enough to hold the lobster tails. Add the lobster tails and cook until they turn a very bright red, 2 to 3 minutes. For soft-shell lobsters, stack 3 tails on each of two serving plates, skewering each stack with a wooden skewer to keep it upright.

For hard-shells, place 1 tail in the center of each plate. Spoon some of the sauce over and around the lobster. Arrange the beans in separate piles around the lobster. Garnish each plate with a sprig of fresh tarragon, pour 1 tablespoon vodka over each serving of lobster, and serve hot.

139

RAVIOLI WITH BITTER GREENS AND PARMIGIANO | Serves 4 or 8

This is a dish that is easy to make at home. Sheets of delicate spinach pasta are stuffed with Parmigiano and garlic-flavored bitter greens, subtly flavored with fresh chile, and cut into ravioli shapes. The raviolis are sauced simply with melted butter and a sprinkling of cheese.

This will feed 4 people comfortably as a main course, or 8 people as an appetizer or side dish.

FOR THE PASTA DOUGH

10 ounces spinach, stemmed and washed
¼ cup cold water
2 cups all-purpose flour, plus extra
    for kneading
1½ teaspoons olive oil
½ teaspoon kosher salt
1 large egg, lightly beaten
1 large egg beaten with 1 tablespoon water,
    for egg wash
Semolina flour or cornmeal

FOR THE FILLING

½ cup olive oil
6 garlic cloves, chopped
1 red chile pepper, stemmed, seeded, and
    thinly sliced
1 bunch broccoli rabe, trimmed, washed,
    stems minced, and leaves and florets sliced
    into chiffonade
2 cups firmly packed stemmed mustard
    greens, sliced into chiffonade
Kosher salt and freshly ground black pepper
1 tablespoon unsalted butter
2 tablespoons freshly grated Parmigiano-
    Reggiano
2 tablespoons unsalted butter, melted and
    still hot
Kosher salt and freshly ground black pepper
¼ cup freshly grated Parmigiano-Reggiano

PREPARE THE PASTA DOUGH: Bring a large pot of salted water to a boil. Add the spinach and cook until tender, about 1 minute. Drain the spinach and refresh under cold running water to set the bright green color; drain again. Squeeze the spinach between the palms of your hands to remove as much water as possible.

Combine the spinach and the ¼ cup water in a blender and puree until smooth. Scrape the puree into a large mixing bowl. Add the flour, olive oil, salt, and egg. Mix with a wooden spoon until combined.

Turn the dough out onto a lightly floured work surface and knead for 10 minutes, or until satiny-smooth. Cover loosely with plastic wrap and let rest at room temperature for at least 1 hour.

PREPARE THE FILLING: Heat the oil in a large frying pan over medium-high heat. Add the garlic and chile and cook until the garlic begins to turn golden brown, about 45 seconds. Add the broccoli rabe and mustard greens and stir to stop the garlic from browning further. Sprinkle with salt and pepper to taste, cover, and let the greens steam until tender, stirring from time to time, 5 to 6 minutes. Remove the cover, turn the heat to high, and cook, stirring every now and then, until the greens are dry, 8 to 10 minutes. Stir in the butter and cheese and taste for seasoning. Let cool completely.

ROLL OUT THE DOUGH: Divide the dough into 8 equal balls. Roll each one out through a pasta machine to the second-thinnest setting. Let the pasta sheets dry for 15 minutes.

FILL THE RAVIOLI: On a lightly floured work surface, lay out one sheet of pasta so that a long edge is facing you. (Trim the sheets to 10 inches if necessary.) Using about 1 tablespoon of filling per ravioli and starting about 1 inch in from either end, evenly space 4 spoonfuls of the filling mixture in a row across the top half of the sheet of pasta. Brush all around the filling with the egg wash. Then fold the bottom half of the sheet up over the filling so that the bottom edge meets the top edge. Gently press all around the mounds of filling to seal the dough. Using a fluted cutter or a knife, cut between the ravioli to separate them. You'll have 4 ravioli, each about 2½ inches square. Place the ravioli on a baking sheet sprinkled with semolina and continue with the remaining sheets of dough and filling, to make a total of 32 ravioli.

COOK THE RAVIOLI: Bring a large pot of salted water to a boil. Carefully place the ravioli into the water one by one (they are very delicate) and boil until tender, about 4 minutes. Use a spider to remove and drain the ravioli one by one.

FINISH THE DISH: Divide the ravioli among four plates. Drizzle one-quarter of the melted butter over each plate of pasta. Season with salt and pepper to taste and sprinkle with the Parmigiano. Serve immediately.

Lydia Shire

140

Cooking is a macho business. It is like a sport. In the back of the house, people are very driven. They get hooked on the adrenaline, and it can be very rough-and-tumble. Some people think women don't have the drive to compete in that way, night after night after night. But I do.

Katy Sparks

Katy Sparks

QUILTY'S | New York

My cooking is simple, but layered. I like to use interesting ingredients to surprise the palate a little bit. But I'm not interested in offering surprise for the mere sake of surprising. There is nothing arbitrary in the combinations I make. The ingredients I use have to make sense in the dishes I prepare, and those dishes have to work on the same level that any classical cuisine does. For example, I have one dish that is made with tuna and umeboshi [pickled Japanese plum] coulis. I pepper-sear the tuna, and the tangy, cooling quality of the umeboshi brings the dish into balance. The umeboshi functions in the same way that the more traditional lemon, lime, or soy would function in a more classical version of the dish, counterbalancing the richness of the tuna and cooling the peppery crust. But, unlike the traditional condiments, umeboshi adds an element of surprise to the dish. I like that.

Female chefs are in the minority. There's a special burden on women bosses. A male chef yelling at people is almost humorous. You get people afterward saying, "Hey, that was a good one. Let's go have a beer." But if a woman were to yell like that, people might feel belittled, humiliated in front of their peers.

The competition can be tough when you're working on the line with a lot of guys, but I'm strong, 5'10", not a little girl. Small women might have to fight to keep up, and that can be difficult. Especially when you start from the ground up, like I did.

143

The chef makes her appetizers, such as this plate of grilled sardines and deep-fried squid, somewhat more ornate than her main dishes; with an appetizer, you only get a few bites to excite the diners' palates. She likes the contrast between the texture and flavor of the sardines and squid: The sardines have a nice, rich oiliness that works well when grilled. The lighter flavor of the squid is captured by breading and frying.

FOR THE DIPPING SAUCE

1 garlic clove, minced
½ red bell pepper, cored, seeded, and cut into fine dice
½ yellow bell pepper, cored, seeded, and cut into fine dice
1 large poblano pepper, stemmed, seeded, and cut into fine dice
¼ fennel bulb, cut into fine dice
½ small red onion, cut into fine dice
¼ cup fresh lime juice
¼ cup fresh lemon juice
¼ cup Thai fish sauce
1 teaspoon honey
1 tablespoon minced fresh mint
1 tablespoon minced fresh cilantro
1 tablespoon minced fresh basil

FOR THE SARDINE MARINADE

1 garlic clove, thinly sliced
½ teaspoon minced fresh rosemary
1 tablespoon balsamic vinegar
1 teaspoon soy sauce
2 tablespoons finely diced peeled and seeded tomato
3 tablespoons extra-virgin olive oil

FOR THE SQUID

1 cup milk
1 pound squid (preferably medium-sized), cleaned, bodies cut into ¼-inch-thick rings
1 quart canola oil
1 cup Wondra flour
1 cup finely ground unblanched almonds
Kosher salt and freshly ground black pepper

FOR THE ALMONDS

2 tablespoons clarified butter
¼ cup sliced unblanched almonds
1 to 2 teaspoons ancho chile powder
Kosher salt and freshly ground black pepper

FOR THE SARDINES

8 fresh sardines, gutted, heads removed, bodies butterflied, and backbones removed
2 tablespoons extra-virgin olive oil
Kosher salt and freshly ground black pepper

2 cups firmly packed bitter greens, such as frisée or mustard greens
Fresh sage leaves for garnish

PREPARE THE DIPPING SAUCE: Combine all the ingredients in a bowl. Set aside at room temperature for 2 hours.

PREPARE THE SARDINE MARINADE: Combine all the ingredients in a large bowl. Set aside at room temperature for 2 hours.

MARINATE THE SQUID: Pour the milk over the squid in a bowl and refrigerate.

PREPARE THE ALMONDS: Heat the clarified butter in a medium frying pan over medium heat. Add the almonds and sauté until golden, 1 to 2 minutes. Drain on paper towels, then dust with the ancho powder and sprinkle with salt and pepper.

GRILL THE SARDINES: Prepare a medium fire in a grill or heat a grill pan over medium heat. Brush the sardines on both sides with the olive oil and sprinkle lightly with salt and pepper. Place the sardines skin side down on the grill and grill until the flesh is opaque and firm, 3 to 4 minutes. Transfer the sardines to a platter and spoon the marinade over them. Set aside.

FRY THE SQUID: Heat the canola oil in a large deep heavy pot, preferably cast iron, until it registers 350°F on a deep-frying thermometer. Meanwhile, combine the Wondra flour and ground almonds on a large plate and season to taste with salt and pepper.

Drain the squid, allowing some of the milk to cling to it. Working in four batches, toss a handful of squid in flour mixture to evenly coat it, then put the squid in a sieve and shake it over the plate to remove the excess flour. Add the squid to the oil and fry until crisp, about 45 seconds. Use a spider to transfer the squid to a plate lined with paper towels.

To serve, place a small handful of the bitter greens in the center of each of four shallow pasta bowls. Place 2 sardines each, skin side up, on top of the greens. Mound the squid on top of the sardines. Ladle the dipping sauce around the fish and garnish the plates with the almonds and sage leaves.

144

Katy Sparks

BRAISED RABBIT WITH MORELS, FAVA BEANS, AND SPRING POTATOES AND A LEMON AND SAGE GREMOLATA

Rabbit legs are dusted with flour and browned all over. Then a mirepoix of onion, carrot, celery, garlic, and tomato is added to the pan, along with fresh thyme and rosemary and ancho chile powder. The pan is deglazed with white wine. Then a rabbit stock (made from the forelegs and carcasses of the rabbit), juniper berries, coriander seeds, peppercorns, and lemon zest are added and simmered until the legs are tender. The braising liquid is strained and reduced to a saucy consistency, then returned to the pan with the legs.

To finish the dish, fresh morels are sautéed in butter with shallots. Spring new potatoes are boiled in their skins. The potatoes and morels are added to the braise and the whole thing is gently warmed to infuse the sauce with the flavor of the morels. The dish is garnished with fresh fava beans, warmed in butter and seasoned with mint, and a sprinkling of a garlic, parsley, sage, and lemon zest gremolata.

NOTE: Because the saddles cook much more quickly than the legs, they are less suitable for braising; the chef reserves them for another dish.

Susan Spicer **BAYONA** | New Orleans

I always said that if I was going to have a restaurant in New Orleans, it had to have a courtyard; you had to be able to eat outside. And this place is a hidden mystery of the French Quarter . . . the gridiron all over is beautiful, and you kind of peek through it as you go past and wonder what's back here.

I didn't really have a grand cooking epiphany until I started cooking professionally. That was when I was twenty-six, and I realized that this was something I'd been looking for for a long time, and that it satisfied many, many requirements. . . . It is very challenging, physically, emotionally, and mentally, and I really love that. I have little food epiphanies, though . . . discoveries, certain ingredients, going to Thailand to cook, for example, and discovering how they use flowers. I walked into the kitchen one morning and I could smell them—there were flowers everywhere. I was following my nose and they were making a beef stock and they had big trays of jasmine flowers and they were dumping them into the stock, and it was gorgeous.

Because my family was not from the Louisiana area, Cajun food was not a very big part of my upbringing. I grew up on naval stations, and we didn't go to restaurants. . . . I didn't get exposed to the local Creole or Cajun food until much later. But if you have an innate ability and an appreciation and a respect for the culture—if you understand a little bit about what goes into the creation of its cuisine, how it uses ingredients and why—then you can learn that cuisine. If you look at my menu, you'll see that I am influenced by many cuisines—Louisiana's as much as anything else. I make a good gumbo, and jambalaya, and all those kinds of things, but I am not at all a Cajun chef. My cuisine is really just representative of my life, I think, a life spent traveling. New Orleans has great seafood, the shellfish, the crabs, the oysters, the crawfish, the shrimp—all those kinds of things. That is really the heart and soul, I think, of Louisiana cuisine. And they are so versatile; you can do anything with them. I make a crawfish curry that's really good. And we make all the condiments that go with it. It's a traditional ingredient used in a nontraditional way.

147

CRISPY SMOKED QUAIL SALAD

Quail is marinated in peanut oil flavored with honey, bourbon, and
Indonesian sweet soy sauce, then cold-smoked. After smoking, the
quail are coated in a rice flour batter and deep-fried, which makes
them very crisp. The quail are quartered and served on a bed of
spinach leaves mixed with sliced ripe pear, pickled red onion, and
celery hearts and leaves. This salad is seasoned with a dressing
based on an emulsion of olive oil and highly reduced brown chicken
stock, flavored with molasses, cider and walnut vinegar, shallots,
and bourbon.

Susan Spicer

I believe that if you are focused and you deliver quality and consistency, that will bring the people in. I don't know if I'd say that is my motto, but I've always believed this. If you do something right, people will come back.

Joachim Splichal

Joachim Splichal

My parents had a *gasthaus* in Germany, an inn, so I was exposed to the restaurant life very early on. I went to Switzerland to go to hotel school; I was supposed to be a general manager, working the front desk, but I didn't really like that, so I left and went to work in Chalet Suisse in The Hague. That's where everything started. Eventually, I came to the United States. I found this location, and my wife and I and thirty-eight employees opened the door, and we were full the first day, and since then we are full. Slowly we got good reviews and better reviews and got known all over the United States and Europe. Then, two years later, I wanted to do something new. That was during the recession, and I wanted to do a bistro. I bought a restaurant in Studio City, went to France and picked up all the antiques, and I moved one of the Patina chefs there to do the food, and Pinot was born. And we started a catering company and became the biggest catering company in town. We did the Democratic Convention, fifty thousand people, we do the Emmys, the Grammys, we do anybody from two people up to fifty thousand. Meanwhile, the food is still good here.

PATINA RESTAURANT | Hollywood
PINOT BISTRO | Studio City
PINOT PROVENCE | Costa Mesa
CAFÉ PINOT | Los Angeles
PINOT BRASSERIE | Las Vegas
PINOT BLANC | St. Helena
NICK & STEF'S | Los Angeles, Washington, D.C., New York

150

There was no plan. There was never a plan. But at the end of the day, it is negative to say you have twenty-one restaurants, [as though] you don't have control, your quality goes down the drain, etc. So when they come here, they see Patina, that's it. When they go somewhere else, they don't see the postcards of our other restaurants. Each individual restaurant has its own clientele. . . . In a bistro you can eat for thirty dollars, while here you eat for a hundred, in a café you eat for eight. So each segment of our group delivers food to a different customer. We do one point eight million meals a year. And you try to make everybody feel like he or she is really the only person you care about. You also have to hire good people. It is a team effort. You cannot do it all yourself.

I believe that if you are focused and you deliver quality and consistency, that will bring the people in. I don't know if I'd say that is my motto, but I've always believed this. If you do something right, people will come back.

QUARTET OF THE SEA

Here is an appetizer comprised of tiny tastes of yellowtail, lobster, sea scallop, and tuna.

For the yellowtail, sliced hon-shimeji (beech) mushrooms are sautéed in olive oil with ginger and garlic. The pan is deglazed with soy sauce, yuzu juice, and rice wine vinegar. A tablespoon of extra-virgin olive oil is swirled into the pan sauce and the mushrooms and sauce are spooned over thin slices of raw hamachi (yellowtail).

Lobster is parboiled and then shelled; the tail is cut into medallions and the claws and knuckles cut in half. The lobster is seasoned with salt and pepper, lemon juice, and a vanilla oil made by warming a split vanilla bean in grapeseed oil. The lobster is garnished with diced mango, a fresh mango coulis, and a bouquet of frisée lettuce dressed with lemon juice, chervil, and vanilla oil.

Thin slices of raw sea scallop are seasoned with salt and pepper, lemon juice, and extra-virgin olive oil and topped with a spoonful of osetra caviar and minced fresh chives.

Center-cut yellowfin tuna is cut into ½-inch cubes and seasoned with salt, pepper, and a few drops of extra-virgin olive oil. The tuna is garnished with a mixture of finely shaved celery hearts and leaves and shaved white truffle, seasoned with salt and pepper, lemon juice, white truffle oil, and julienned parsley.

152

ROCKY ROAD REVISITED

A marshmallow mixture is made by first dissolving gelatin in water with a little coffee added, then bringing sugar, corn syrup, water, and a pinch of salt to hard-ball stage and whipping this cooked syrup into the gelatin mixture until it is white and fluffy; the mixture is flavored with vanilla. Then chocolate ice cream flavored with rum is shaped into a quenelle and placed on a cooked triangle of sablé pastry. Chopped caramelized almonds are sprinkled over the ice cream. The warm marshmallow mixture is spooned over the ice cream. The plate is garnished with two types of cookies—a thin caramel cookie and a pulled chocolate confection—and chocolate and caramel sauces.

Below left, clockwise from top left: Thin slices of raw yellowtail are sauced with beech mushrooms; vanilla-scented lobster is served with mango and a mango coulis; raw scallops are seasoned with lemon and osetra caviar; tuna is garnished with celery, white truffle oil and shaved white truffles. Below right: Rum-flavored chocolate ice cream is topped with a warm "marshmallow" cream, crisp cookies, and chocolate and caramel sauces.

Joachim Splichal

Allen Susser

CHEF ALLEN'S | North Miami Beach

Though I grew up in my grandmother's kitchen, cooking her food, Eastern European food, I had no plans to travel the culinary path. But then I went to Paris and I loved the food there—the preparation, presentation, the focus on detail, on cuisine. The French took their time to eat and enjoy. There was a whole different attitude toward food in Europe than we had here, and this was twenty-five years ago. At that time, the American public was not yet ready to dine, but they are today.

Today it's a new era. Southeast Asian, Indian, North African, and Mediterranean influences are strong. Instead of being limited by doing a regional cuisine, I've branched out in my grasp for flavors, for spice combinations, for historical antecedents, for depth, and have started to incorporate a lot of "world" flavors that aren't native to the U.S.

I also learned how other countries use ingredients there. When I wrote a book about citrus, I really started to see the ways of the world in an unlimited way. I became acquainted with some of the flavors of the Japanese, who use citrus, and with Chinese, Southeast Asian, and Mediterranean citrus. In all of these places, they use just as much citrus as we do here in Florida.

And, of course, I'm the mango guy. I've written a book on mangoes. India has been using mangoes for four thousand years. I'm deeply interested in how they use them, from green mangoes to mango chutneys to amchoor [green mango powder] to sweet mango to mango ice cream. And they use them very differently in Southeast Asia. They are sold on street corners, green mangoes with hot chiles and peanut sauce . . . really very interesting to see. There is a real cultural passion for the mango. You don't see this type of thing going on in the United States very much, but there, the love for mangoes is a great driving force.

In Florida, a lot of people have mangoes growing in their backyards, and I encourage them to bring me their mangoes. I trade mangoes for dinners, and I get to see lots of different varieties. Homegrown mangoes are beautiful and delicious.

155

FIRE-ROASTED SHRIMP WITH BLACK OLIVE COUSCOUS AND LEMON FRIES | Serves 4

These lovely North African–inspired shrimp are seasoned with garlic and olive oil, which makes them sweet, then grilled and served with an herbed olive couscous. Because the couscous is instant and the shrimp are so quick to cook, this is a dish that takes almost no time to put together and is exceptionally practical for home cooks. In the restaurant, the lemon fries are deep-fried, but they can be panfried at home.

FOR THE SHRIMP

16 jumbo shrimp (about 1¼ pounds), peeled and deveined
2 teaspoons chopped garlic
2 teaspoons olive oil
½ teaspoon kosher salt

FOR THE COUSCOUS

2 cups chicken stock
2 cups instant couscous
½ teaspoon ground cumin
¼ teaspoon dried red pepper flakes
½ teaspoon kosher salt
16 dry-cured black olives, chopped
2 tablespoons olive oil
¼ cup chopped fresh cilantro
2 tablespoons chopped fresh mint

FOR THE LEMON FRIES

¼ cup vegetable oil
8 thin lemon slices
About ¼ cup all-purpose flour for dredging

PREPARE THE SHRIMP: Light a charcoal grill or preheat a gas grill to medium-high.

Put the shrimp in a bowl and add the garlic, olive oil, and salt. Mix well to coat the shrimp. Line up 4 shrimp, back to belly, and thread them onto two parallel skewers, to hold them flat. Repeat with the remaining 12 shrimp. Refrigerate the shrimp until you are ready to grill.

PREPARE THE COUSCOUS: Bring the stock to a boil and remove from the heat. Stir in the couscous, cumin, red pepper flakes, and salt. Cover and let steep for 15 minutes.

Uncover and fluff the couscous with a fork. Stir in the olives, the olive oil, and fresh herbs.

PREPARE THE LEMON FRIES: Heat the vegetable oil in a medium frying pan over medium-high heat until it shimmers. Dredge the lemon slices in the flour and fry, turning once, until golden brown on both sides, 1 to 1½ minutes on each side. Drain on paper towels.

MEANWHILE, GRILL THE SHRIMP: Place the shrimp on the fire and cook, turning once, until they turn bright pink, 2 to 3 minutes on each side.

To serve, spoon a mound of couscous into the center of each of four serving plates. Remove the shrimp from the skewers. Arrange the shrimp on top of each mound of coucous and garnish with the lemon slices.

156

RED SNAPPER WITH FENNEL, ENDIVE, AND TOMATO COMPOTE | Serves 4

This very fresh tomato, fennel, and endive compote is a subtle balance of sweet, acid, and bitter: the tomato is both sweet and acidic, the fennel is sweet, the endive pleasantly bitter. The compote is particularly good with snapper, whose mild flavor is easily overwhelmed by assertive sauces. But it is equally good on other fish, such as wild striped bass or even salmon.

Crush the fennel seeds by pulsing them in a spice grinder or clean coffee grinder.

4 large plum tomatoes, peeled, cut in half, and seeded
1 garlic clove
⅔ cup olive oil

½ large fennel bulb, cut into ¼-inch dice
¾ teaspoon kosher salt
1 large endive
¼ teaspoon freshly ground black pepper

Four 6-ounce red snapper fillets, skin on
Kosher salt and freshly ground black pepper
2 teaspoons crushed fennel seeds

2 tablespoons sliced fresh basil leaves

PREPARE THE TOMATO CONFIT AND OIL: Put the tomatoes, garlic, and oil in a small saucepan and heat over low heat until the tomatoes are soft, about 20 minutes. With a slotted spoon, spoon the tomatoes into a bowl. Reserve the oil.

PREPARE THE COMPOTE: Heat 1 tablespoon of the tomato oil in a medium heavy frying pan over medium-high heat. Add the fennel, sprinkle with ¼ teaspoon of the salt, and cook, stirring every now and then, until the fennel loses its raw crunch, about 3 minutes. Meanwhile, cut the endive crosswise into thin slices.

Add the endive to the pan. Cook, stirring every now and then, for 2 minutes. Stir in 1 more tablespoon of the tomato oil, the tomato confit, the remaining ½ teaspoon salt, and the pepper. Transfer to a bowl and cover to keep warm.

PREPARE THE SNAPPER: Wipe the frying pan. Add 2 tablespoons of the tomato oil to the pan, and add 2 tablespoons more oil to a second heavy frying pan. Heat both over medium-high heat until the oil shimmers. Meanwhile, sprinkle the snapper on both sides with salt, pepper, and the crushed fennel seeds.

Place 2 fillets, skin side down, in each of the pans and cook until the skin is lightly browned and crisp, 4 to 5 minutes. Carefully turn the fillets with a spatula and cook until just cooked through, 1 to 2 more minutes.

To serve, spoon one-quarter of the compote into the center of each of four serving plates. Place a snapper fillet skin side up on top. Garnish with the sliced basil.

Allen Susser

157

Rick Tramonto **TRU** | Chicago

I think our food is really modern, so I wanted to have a white restaurant, a white palette almost, to show it off. I didn't want a lot of traditionalism. The idea was to keep it very simple and very clean, very clean lines, the only things in the room being some beautiful artwork and the food.

I think a lot of the American chefs are taught early on that it doesn't matter how good your food is if you can't make money, because if you can't stay in business, you can't do your food. But it doesn't matter how good you are at making money if your food isn't good because people won't come, and you won't make money. So the balance has to be there.

I left school when I was 16. When I started in this business, it was very blue collar, as they say. There was no such thing as the celebrity chef. I worked at a fast-food restaurant, a steakhouse, and a hotel before going to Manhattan, where I spent about five years trying to capture the essence of the business. This was during the mid-eighties, and Jonathan Waxman and Larry Forgione, Alice Waters, Jeremiah Towers, and all those guys were just starting to explode. "California cuisine" was beginning to evolve. Then I moved to Chicago and started to work at "Lettuce Entertain You." It was almost like going to college for a business degree. I learned about food costs and labor costs and all that stuff. After that I became chef at a country-house hotel in Stapleford Park in Leicestershire, England. While I was there, we earned a Michelin star—we were the first Americans in eight years to do so. And that opened a lot of doors. All these wonderful chefs started to come up to Leicestershire to see what we were doing—a "Who are these young Americans?" kind of thing. We became friends with a lot of chefs in London, and it became a wonderful networking situation.

I spend a lot of time in the kitchen. I'm here five or six nights a week. I'm at the pass, I coordinate, and I do all the menus, but I have a chef de cuisine and two sous-chefs who execute the day-to-day stuff, the butchering and all. In order to grow, I could never be tied down to a station. I love being here every day, thinking about things like fois gras and caviar and wild presentations, seeing the food and touching the food and tasting the food to make sure that it's right. But I believe in my heart that if a chef is really good, he needs to be able to pass on his knowledge. If you can't teach somebody and instill your passion and the knowledge, if you keep secrets, what good is that? You need to be able to spread the wealth. You want the young guys coming up to be able to be successful, and you want to be able to do other things yourself, whether it's writing books or having a kid, or whatever. In the old days, chefs stayed in their restaurants forever. That was what they did; it was a lifestyle. Things are different now.

PORCINI CAPPUCCINO | Serves 6

At Tru, this soup is served with a froth of steamed milk on top, though it is quite sublime on its own.

To make porcini powder, further dehydrate dried sliced porcini mushrooms on a baking sheet in a 200°F oven for 10 minutes, then grind to a powder in a spice or coffee grinder.

The recipe for vegetable stock makes more than you'll need for the soup. Freeze the leftover stock and use it for another soup.

FOR THE VEGETABLE STOCK
4 teaspoons olive oil
1 medium onion, sliced
4 celery stalks, sliced
3 medium carrots, sliced
1 head garlic, cut in half
4 ounces mushrooms (a selection of cultivated varieties plus morels, if available), trimmed and sliced
2 tomatoes, cored and chopped
1 cup dry white wine
4 large fresh thyme sprigs
1 small fresh rosemary sprig
1 large bay leaf
15 black peppercorns
3 quarts water

FOR THE SOUP
2 tablespoons clarified butter
1 shallot, sliced
½ medium onion, chopped
2 ounces stemmed portobello mushrooms, cut into medium dice
4 ounces fresh or thawed frozen porcini mushrooms, cut into medium dice
1 teaspoon porcini powder
½ cup dry white wine
¾ teaspoon chopped fresh rosemary
¾ teaspoon chopped fresh thyme
2 teaspoons kosher salt, or to taste
⅛ teaspoon freshly ground black pepper, or to taste

PREPARE THE STOCK: Heat the oil in a large soup pot over medium heat. Add the onion, celery, carrots, garlic, and mushrooms and cook, stirring every now and then, for 10 minutes. Add the tomatoes, turn the heat to medium-high, and cook for 2 more minutes. Add the wine, bring to a boil, and cook until reduced by about one-half.

Add the herbs, peppercorns, and water. Bring to a boil, reduce the heat, cover, and simmer, skimming the foam that rises to the top, for 40 minutes. Let the stock cool completely, then strain.

PREPARE THE SOUP: Melt the butter in a large saucepan over medium heat. Add the shallot and onion and cook until softened, 2 to 3 minutes. Add the mushrooms and porcini powder and cook until the mushrooms are tender, 4 to 5 minutes. Add the wine, bring to a boil, and simmer until it has almost evaporated.

Add the herbs, 6 cups of the vegetable stock, the salt, and pepper. Bring to a boil, reduce the heat, and simmer until the liquid has reduced by about one-quarter.

Working in several batches, transfer the soup to a blender and blend until smooth. Strain through a fine-meshed sieve and return to the saucepan. Bring to a simmer over medium heat. Taste and reseason the soup as needed.

To serve, ladle the soup into cups or small bowls.

Porcini soup served with a froth of steamed milk. It can also be topped with stiffly whipped cream seasoned with salt and pepper and a little truffle oil.

SWEET CORN SOUP WITH SWEET AND HOT PEPPERS | Serves 4 to 6

This silky-smooth corn soup, sweetened with honey, is served as part of a quartet of soups to offer diners the experience of a progression of tastes: from light to heavy, for example, as in the lighter flavors of vegetable soups such as this one and Porcini Cappuccino (page 162), to the heavier flavors of seafood and meat-based soups. The vegetable stock gives the soup a fuller flavor, but if you don't have the time to make it, water works fine.

4 ears corn, shucked

1 tablespoon olive oil

½ medium onion, chopped

2 celery stalks, chopped

½ yellow bell pepper, cored, seeds and ribs
    removed, and chopped

½ serrano chile, stemmed, seeded, and
    chopped

¼ cup dry white wine

6 cups Vegetable Stock (page 162) or water

1 cup heavy cream

2 teaspoons kosher salt, or to taste

5 to 6 teaspoons honey

¼ teaspoon freshly ground black pepper

PREPARE THE CORN: Stand an ear of corn in a large bowl and, with a knife, shave the kernels off into the bowl. Reserve the corncob and do the same with the other 3 ears corn; set the bowl aside. One at a time, stand the corncobs in a second bowl and scrape with the knife to remove the "cream of corn." Set aside.

PREPARE THE SOUP: Heat the oil in a large saucepan over medium heat. Add the onion, celery, and bell and serrano peppers and cook until softened, 3 to 4 minutes. Add the corn kernels and cook for 5 minutes. Add the wine, bring to a boil, and cook for 1 minute. Then add the stock, heavy cream, cream of corn, and salt. Bring to a boil, reduce the heat, and simmer until the liquid is reduced by about one-third.

Stir in the honey and pepper. Taste for salt. Working in several batches, transfer the soup to a blender and blend until smooth. Strain through a fine-meshed sieve and return to the saucepan. Bring to a simmer over medium heat.

To serve, ladle into cups or small bowls.

Rick Tramonto

163

Charlie Trotter

CHARLIE TROTTER'S | Chicago

I think you find that the people who are drawn to this field, in this country, come from all sorts of different backgrounds. They don't necessarily start when they're fourteen and that's all they know. Maybe they've even gone to universities and have advanced degrees, and they are bringing a different intellectual sort of rigor to it. They are studying it differently. They are looking at the history and culture and anthropology of different societies, different countries, and saying, "I can apply this, I can do that," and it's a different thing. There is definitely more freedom. We are not restricted.

If we were to take this restaurant, literally pick it up with a large helicopter, and take it along with the entire staff and drop it down in Manhattan or London, or Paris or Hong Kong, or Sydney or L.A., I don't really think we would have to change anything that we do. I believe there is a certain universality that exists in the service, the cuisine, the ambience, the wine program that would allow the restaurant to be accepted and understood in all of these different cultures and different parts of the world. The food is essentially rooted in the Western European tradition, French and Italian, putting together certain time-honored combinations, literally centuries-old combinations. But at the same time, I'm not French, no one who works here is French, we serve only just a few French clients each night or each week. And I find myself, personally, drawn to an Asian minimalist aesthetic, that is, eliminating the use of cream except for maybe a little ice cream at the end of the meal, eliminating or greatly reducing the use of butter, other than maybe to finish a sauce, just a touch.

I am drawn to pristine seafood products, whether they are raw, or marinated, or barely cooked. I like using a lot of vegetable elements for texture, for flavor, for color, vegetable juices for sauces, vegetable broths. You might say we use a light Asian touch, yet employ techniques that come from Western Europe. And we are putting these things together in a way that isn't just contrived. There is even a seamlessness to it.

A dish or a meal is successful if it is delightful or appealing to the very, very sophisticated diner and the "lay diner" or uninitiated diner alike. Equally. For me, a perfect plate of food is one that invites the connoisseur to marvel at its nuance and subtlety and at the skill involved in bringing it all together. But the inexperienced diner should also be able to marvel at how delicious that same plate of food tastes, even if he might not totally understand what it is about. That's really what we're trying to do. We're not trying to blow people out of the water with some sort of ultra–avant-garde cuisine, but at the same time, we do want to make food that will appeal to someone who has been around the world, who has been to some of the great restaurants, understands how things have been done, and understands that we are doing things differently, challenging the paradigm.

ROASTED ROOT VEGETABLE TERRINE WITH A FROMAGE BLANC FLAN STUFFED WITH CHANTERELLES

Leeks are braised in butter with a little chicken stock. At the same time, carrots, radishes, yellow beets, and turnips are roasted whole, then peeled and cut into pieces. All of the vegetables are dipped into cold chicken stock, then layered in a plastic wrap-lined terrine mold. A small board, about the size of the opening of the terrine, is pressed down onto the vegetables to pack them together. (The gelatin in the chicken stock will "glue" the vegetables together.) The terrine is refrigerated for several hours until thoroughly chilled. Then it is turned out of the mold and—still wrapped in plastic wrap—cut into slices. (The plastic keeps the terrine from falling apart.) The plastic is removed and the slices are placed on serving plates.

Each plate is garnished with a small flan of fromage blanc bound with a little gelatin and stuffed with hot-and-sour chanterelle mushrooms. Sautéed chanterelles are strewn around the plate. Two purees—one made from arugula and one from chanterelle mushrooms—serve as sauces. The plate is drizzled with both an arugula and an herb oil (infused with parsley, spinach, and basil). Finally, the plate is garnished with micro-parsley, a parsley that is grown for its tiny leaves.

166

Charlie Trotter

Ming Tsai
BLUE GINGER | Wellesley

When I was growing up, my mom had a Mandarin restaurant. We cooked in small batches and turned the food around really quickly, as, during the lunch rush, we had lines of thirty to forty people. From the time that I was four or so, I was always hanging out in the kitchen. Either my parents or my grandparents were cooking, making noodles or scallion cakes. I was fascinated by it, and, a little more pragmatically, I was hungry. . . . I was always hungry, and I still am. I haven't grown out of it.

My parents were gourmets/gourmands. And they were travelers as well. My first "fine French dining" experience was in Den Haag [The Hague], in a French restaurant called Papillon. They served me wine—diluted with water. I was thoroughly amazed by the quality of the food and the fact that these guys in bow ties and immaculate suits were serving me. I was ten, and I was just blown away. I think I was very lucky to have parents who put an emphasis on food. When we traveled, we never paid for first class or fancy hotels . . . we always saved our money for the food.

When I was halfway through my mechanical engineering degree, I started going to France for the summers to shore up my French. I started doing apprenticeships . . . *stages*. I attended the Cordon Bleu one summer, and that really turned my life around. I thought, "Wow, this is really what I want to do." Two days after graduating, I was on my way to Paris to cook. I ended up working at Fauchon under Pierre Hermé, the master pastry chef. I was an unusual kind of person at Fauchon. They had a lot of Asians working there, but I was Chinese American, and I could speak French. When they made fun of me, which they did quite a lot, I could understand. I would make a pear out of sugar, and they'd say, "Oh, what a beautiful eggplant." And I'd say, "*Non, c'est une poire!*" And they'd say, "*Mais non, mon ami, c'est une aubergine!*"

I call my food "East meets West" cuisine. In a nutshell, it is a blending of Eastern and Western ingredients and techniques that produce a food that is bold in flavor. I don't believe in putting a nuance of ginger in a dish such that you can barely taste it. If you say there is ginger in the sauce, you should really be able to taste it. This is my Chinese background. You need to be able to taste the heat or the pepper, or whatever it is. I also love textural differences, crunchy and smooth, things like that. And I love temperature differences. Quite often I'll garnish hot soups with cold salads, a gazpacho with a hot shrimp toast. Most of my plates have hot and cold, or hot and room temperature on them. I love color; I think it is important that a plate be beautiful.

There is a taste sensation that the Japanese call *umami*. It is beyond the sensations that we know, like salty, sweet, tangy. *Umami* is something that naturally occurs in things like uni [sea urchin] and seaweed. It is beyond salty. The best way to describe it is to say that it is like tasting the sea. It is characterized by a slightly drying sensation. This is something that fascinates me.

LOMI-STYLE SALMON TARTARE WITH LILIKOI BROWN-BUTTER VINAIGRETTE | Serves 4

This appetizer was inspired by a traditional Hawaiian preparation called "lomi-lomi" in which fish is cubed or cut up and then salted. (Although originally used exclusively for fish, the term is now used to refer to cut-up, salted beef as well.) Raw salmon is cut into tiny dice and seasoned with salt, lime, and Tabasco sauce. The salmon is sauced with a brown butter vinaigrette. The passion fruit juice (*lilikoi,* in Hawaiian) recipe makes more than you will need—use the leftover sauce on fish.

FOR THE RICE CAKES
1 cup short-grain rice
1½ cups water
½ teaspoon kosher salt

One 7½-by-8-inch sheet toasted nori, coarsely ground in a spice or coffee grinder
1½ teaspoons toasted sesame seeds
2 tablespoons canola oil

FOR THE VINAIGRETTE
8 tablespoons (1 stick) unsalted butter
¼ cup fresh orange juice
3 tablespoons passion fruit juice
1 tablespoon minced shallot
1 teaspoon minced fresh ginger
1 tablespoon Dijon mustard
1 teaspoon sugar
Kosher salt
Pinch of freshly ground black pepper

FOR THE TARTARE
8 ounces very fresh skinned salmon fillet, cut into ¼-inch dice
¼ cup diced (¼-inch) red tomato
¼ cup diced (¼-inch) yellow tomato
¼ cup thinly sliced scallion greens
Juice of 1 lime

1 to 2 dashes Tabasco sauce
1 teaspoon canola oil
½ teaspoon coarse pink Hawaiian sea salt or fleur de sel
¼ teaspoon freshly ground black pepper

FOR THE GARNISH
2 cups vegetable oil for deep-frying
1 cup finely julienned taro root
Kosher salt
1 tablespoon Chinese black vinegar
1 teaspoon mirin
½ teaspoon canola oil
½ teaspoon Asian sesame oil
½ teaspoon salt
Pinch of freshly ground black pepper
1 cup mâche or mesclun

PREPARE THE RICE CAKES FOR COOKING:
Place the rice in a large bowl and add water to cover generously. Swirl the rice around with your hand until the water becomes cloudy. Pour off the water. Repeat two or three more times, until the water is almost clear. Place the rice in a medium-heavy saucepan, add the 1½ cups water, and bring to a boil. Reduce the heat to very low, cover, and simmer until tender, about 15 minutes. Remove from the heat and let stand, covered, for 15 minutes.

Stir the salt into the rice and let stand until cool enough to handle. Then lightly oil four ring molds, each about 3½ inches in diameter and 1½ inches tall, place molds on a plate or tray, and firmly press one quarter of the rice into each mold.

PREPARE THE VINAIGRETTE: Heat the butter in a small frying pan over low heat until it turns golden brown and has a nutty fragrance, about 10 minutes. (Watch carefully—the butter can

Salmon tartare tops a round of nori-coated rice cake, sauced with a brown butter–passion fruit vinaigrette.

burn quickly.) Pour into a measuring cup.

In a blender, combine the fruit juices, shallot, ginger, mustard, and sugar and blend to puree. While the machine is running, slowly add the brown butter and blend to emulsify. Season with the salt and pepper and set aside.

PREPARE THE TARTARE: No more than 15 minutes before serving, combine the salmon, tomatoes, scallion greens, lime juice, Tabasco sauce, and oil in a bowl and toss gently to mix. Season with the salt and pepper and refrigerate until ready to serve.

FINISH THE RICE CAKES: Heat the oil in a large skillet over medium heat. Combine the ground nori and sesame seeds in a bowl and sprinkle the bottom of each rice cake with about 1 teaspoon of the nori mixture, pressing it gently into the rice. Place the rice cakes (still in the molds) in the skillet, nori-sprinkled sides down, and cook until the bottoms are browned and crisp, 6 to 8 minutes. Set the cakes aside, without removing the molds. Reserve the remaining nori mixture.

PREPARE THE GARNISH: While the rice cakes are cooking, in a large saucepan, heat the vegetable oil to 320°F on a deep-frying thermometer. Add the taro and cook, stirring to separate the strands, until lightly browned and crisp, about 2 minutes. With a wire spider or slotted spoon, transfer to a plate lined with paper towels and sprinkle with salt.

In a small bowl, whisk together the vinegar, mirin, and canola and sesame oils. Season with ½ teaspoon salt and the pepper. Drizzle over the mâche and toss.

ASSEMBLE THE DISH: Place a ring mold in the center of each of four large serving plates. Run a small knife around the inside of each mold to loosen the rice (do not remove the molds yet). Spoon an equal amount of the salmon tartare onto each of the rice cakes and smooth the top. Carefully remove each ring mold. Gently set the mâche on top of the salmon tartare. Sprinkle the fried taro on top.

Drizzle about 2 tablespoons of the vinaigrette around each cake, sprinkle the reserved nori mixture over, and serve immediately.

LEMONGRASS FRIED RICE | Serves 4

2 tablespoons canola oil
1 yellow onion, finely diced
1½ teaspoons minced garlic
1½ teaspoons minced fresh ginger
3 stalks lemongrass, trimmed to the ivory core
    and minced
1 teaspoon kosher salt, or to taste
¼ teaspoon freshly ground black pepper,
    or to taste
4 cups cooked cold jasmine rice
2 tablespoons fresh lemon juice

Heat the oil in a large saucepan over high heat. Add the onion, garlic, ginger, and lemongrass and cook, stirring, until the onion is translucent, 2 to 3 minutes. Season with the salt and pepper. Add the rice and sauté, stirring, until hot, 3 to 5 minutes.

Stir in the lemon juice and taste for seasoning. Serve hot.

Ming Tsai and Tom Berry

Lobster stir-fried with garlic, scallions, and lots of black pepper, then sauced with a reduction of chicken stock, fish sauce, and tomatoes. For presentation, reserved lobster heads are stuffed with lemongrass fried rice.

Norman Van Aken **NORMAN'S** | Coral Gables

When I was ten, my mother went back to work in the restaurant business. And from that time on, I had a restaurant family, made up of the extended family that restaurant people always have. I was a busboy and dishwasher by the time I was thirteen, although that didn't last very long, actually. By the time I was twenty-one, I had worked in a carnival, in the roofing business, in factories, and then, finally, when I got fired from a job for laughing and had to go find yet another job, I found a listing in the paper for a short-order cook. They hired me. So I started cooking then. Now, you don't go into a situation, especially at the age of twenty-two, and say, "I'm going to create New World Cuisine. I'm going to try to have my work embody Florida." You don't make those sorts of sweeping statements, unless you're Alexander the Great. It was more day by day, week by week, month by month, restaurant by restaurant that I began to define [a particular] type of food for myself. Living in Key West, Florida, in 1971, was magical. I loved it. It ended up becoming my home for twenty years. It gave me a background in tropically inspired cooking. And I grew up there, in that very funky, kind of pretourist fishing town. It was very wonderful.

When I was a little boy, I wanted to be a writer, and I write a lot today. Collecting books, having books, reading books, being surrounded by books . . . makes me comfortable, makes me happy. Books and kitchens, yeah. One of my favorite writers is Annie Dillard. She was teaching a class on writing and one of her students said, "I really want to be a great writer, like you." Dillard said, "Well, do you like making sentences? It you don't like making sentences, you'll never be a very good writer." And that is the way I feel about cooking, and making up plates. People often ask me, "Why do you like cooking? Is it because you make money, or because you are on television, or because your name is in a magazine?" I say, "No, I just like making plates." I like the very simple Zen process of putting something on a plate.

173

POULET CREOLE | Serves 4

This *poulet Creole,* or chicken curry, is predominantly inspired by Caribbean cuisine, but it combines elements of other cultures as well: Scotch bonnet chiles are native to the Caribbean; curry powder is Indian, although many Caribbean cultures also cook with a particular curry mixture; coconut milk is used in both Asian and Caribbean cuisines; and saffron is a Mediterranean spice.

FOR THE HOT-FRY FLOUR

½ cup all-purpose flour
2 teaspoons kosher salt
1½ teaspoons freshly ground black pepper
1 tablespoon dried red pepper flakes
1 teaspoon cayenne pepper

FOR THE CHICKEN

One 4-pound chicken, cut into 6 to 8 pieces
3 tablespoons canola oil
2 ounces slab bacon, cut crosswise,
   ¼ inch thick

FOR THE SAUCE

4 garlic cloves, thinly sliced
1 Scotch bonnet chile, stemmed, seeded,
   and minced
1 red onion, chopped
2 tablespoons curry powder
1 cup fresh orange juice
2 star anise
Large pinch of saffron threads
1 cup chicken stock
1 vanilla bean, split lengthwise
1 bay leaf
1½ cups coconut milk

2 tomatoes, peeled, seeded, and diced
   (optional)
Kosher salt and freshly ground black pepper

FOR THE GARNISH

1 European (hothouse) cucumber
1 tablespoon kosher salt
1½ cups pineapple, cut into ¼-inch dice

PREPARE THE HOT-FRY FLOUR: Stir together all of the ingredients in a small bowl, then spread on a large plate.

PREPARE THE CHICKEN: Preheat the oven to 350°F.

Dredge the chicken pieces in the hot-fry flour and pat off the excess. Heat the oil over medium heat in a frying pan large enough to hold the chicken in a single layer. Add the bacon and cook until most of the fat is rendered, 2 to 3 minutes. Add the chicken and cook, turning, until browned all over, 10 to 15 minutes. Transfer the chicken to a baking dish large enough to hold it in a single layer; reserve the frying pan with the bacon for the sauce.

Put the chicken in the oven and bake until cooked through, 25 to 35 minutes. Remove the chicken from the oven and cover the dish loosely with aluminum foil to keep warm until ready to serve.

MEANWHILE, PREPARE THE SAUCE: Combine the garlic, chile, and red onion in the pan you used to brown the chicken and stir to coat with the oil. Place the pan over medium heat and cook, stirring every now and then, until the vegetables are caramelized, about 10 minutes. Add the curry powder and cook, stirring, for 30 seconds, until aromatic. Add the orange juice, star anise, and saffron, bring to a boil, reduce the heat, and simmer for 2 minutes. Add the stock, vanilla bean, bay leaf, and coconut milk. Bring to a boil, reduce the heat, and simmer for 20 minutes.

PREPARE THE CUCUMBER: While the sauce is simmering, peel the cucumber and cut it lengthwise in half. Scoop out and discard the seeds. Cut each half crosswise into 8 chunks. Cut the chunks lengthwise into strips about ¼ inch thick. Put the cucumber in a colander, sprinkle with the salt, and let stand for 20 minutes, stirring every now and then to distribute the salt. Rinse the cucumber under cold running water. Drain and blot dry on paper towels.

FINISH THE SAUCE: When the sauce has cooked for 20 minutes, strain it through a fine-meshed strainer into a small saucepan. Place over medium heat, stir in the tomatoes, if using, and cook for 1 minute. Season to taste with salt and pepper.

To serve, place 1 or 2 pieces of chicken in the center of each of four serving plates. Ladle some of the sauce around the chicken and sprinkle with the cucumber and pineapple.

Chicken served with rice seasoned with annatto and wrapped in a thin slice of blanched cucumber. The sauce is finished with a drizzle of sour cream.

Norman Van Aken

174

I want it to be fun to come and eat here. You are supposed to relax and enjoy yourself. You don't want to hear some chef yelling in the back, flipping out because the olive should be one centimeter over to the left.

Marc Vetri

Marc Vetri VETRI | Philadelphia

I worked for Wolfgang Puck for four years, and I liked it there, but I didn't really like that Asian/fusion-style food. My family is from Italy, and I was raised on the foods of Italy, and traditional Italian fare was what interested me. And then the owner of Valentino's in Los Angeles sent me to Italy, to a restaurant in Bergamo. I started working there as a *stagiaire*, and then went to about seven different restaurants all over Italy. It was great. Now I have this little thirty-five-seat restaurant and we try to live our lives a lot like it's lived in Europe. We're not open for lunch, we're not open Sundays, we shut down three weeks in August and one week over New Year's. I've never had so much fun working in a restaurant. Of course, they've all been fun . . . but here, even though we're very serious about our food, we also try to be very relaxed and have some fun.

It is all about the product now. That is the most important thing—the ingredients. If you start out with nothing, you're going to make nothing. But if you start out with something nice, something really fresh, with a wonderful flavor, then you can go somewhere with it.

I wouldn't say that, as a chef, you actually make up new things. It is more that the dishes you make remind you of certain other dishes you've encountered. For example, when summertime rolls around, I think about the vegetables of summer, and the fruits, and then I sort of reminisce. "When I was in Sicily that summer, we used a lot of this . . ." and "When I worked in that restaurant, we prepared [a particular ingredient] that way. . . ." And then I go on to make those things. But maybe instead of using exactly the same ingredients, you use something else. You switch it around and make it your own. I might hear a song that reminds me of a European restaurant I once ate in, and I'll think about what I was eating as I listened to that song in that restaurant, and I'll try making it.

ROASTED TURBOT ON A CRISP POTATO CAKE WITH TEARDROP TOMATOES AND GAETA OLIVES | Serves 2

The turbot is roasted on a thin cake of overlapping potato slices and then sauced with a simple pan sauce, garnished with tomatoes and black olives. Turbot is rarely available in the United States, but another flatfish such as a fluke or flounder makes a good substitute.

You will need a mandoline or other vegetable slicer to slice the potatoes very thin. Ovenproof nonstick frying pans work best here, so the potato cakes don't stick, but if necessary you can use other 8-inch frying pans or cake pans; line them with rounds of parchment paper.

One 1½-pound whole turbot or fluke, gutted and scaled
2 medium Yukon Gold potatoes (about 1 pound total)
Leaves from 2 fresh thyme sprigs (about 1 teaspoon)
½ teaspoon kosher salt
Freshly ground black pepper
2 tablespoons extra-virgin olive oil

FOR THE SAUCE
10 pear or cherry tomatoes (preferably small)
½ cup dry white wine
1 tablespoon white wine vinegar
1 tablespoon unsalted butter
¼ cup pitted Gaeta olives
2 tablespoons extra-virgin olive oil
Kosher salt and freshly ground black pepper

2 fresh rosemary sprigs

PREPARE THE TURBOT: Rinse the fish under cold running water until the water runs clear and no trace of blood remains. Cut off the head and tail with a large knife or cleaver. Use a pair of scissors to cut off the fins, including the two lines of fins that run along the sides of the fish. Cut the fish crosswise in half through the backbone and set aside.

Preheat the oven to 450°F.

PREPARE THE POTATO CAKES: Peel 1 of the potatoes and slice very thin on a mandoline. As you slice the potato, arrange the slices in a single layer in a spiral fashion, starting in the center of the pan in an ovenproof 8-inch nonstick frying pan, covering the bottom of the pan. Sprinkle with half the thyme, ¼ teaspoon of the salt, and pepper to taste and drizzle with 1 tablespoon of the olive oil. Repeat to make a second potato cake in a second pan.

ROAST THE FISH: Place one piece of the fish in the center of each potato cake. Put the pans in the oven and roast until the fish is cooked through, about 15 minutes. Transfer the fish to a cutting board.

Return the cakes to the oven to brown, about 5 more minutes. Turn the potato cakes out onto two serving plates.

MEANWHILE, PREPARE THE SAUCE: Combine the tomatoes, wine, and vinegar in another medium frying pan and bring to a boil on top of the stove. Reduce the heat and simmer until the liquid is reduced by one-half and the tomatoes are softened, about 5 minutes. Add the butter, olives, and olive oil and whisk to emulsify. Season to taste with salt and pepper.

ASSEMBLE THE DISH: Remove the skin and lift the fish fillets from the bones. Place the 2 halves of each fillet on top of each other, in the center of each cake. Arrange 5 tomatoes around each potato cake. Pour the sauce over the fish and scatter the olives around. Garnish each plate with a sprig of rosemary and serve immediately.

VERY SPINACH GNOCCHI | Serves 8

These tender dark green gnocchi are made from a spinach puree with a little flour and bread crumb to bind it, so they are very delicate and softer than the gnocchi we're used to. You'll find the dough to be very loose, and that's correct—it needs to be loose enough to be piped from a pastry bag. Use just enough flour on the baking sheet and the raw gnocchi so that your hands don't stick when you pick the gnocchi up; if you use too much, the flour will not wash away during cooking.

FOR THE GNOCCHI

5 pounds flat-leaf spinach, stemmed and washed
1 large egg
¼ cup milk
1 cup all-purpose flour
1 cup fresh bread crumbs
1 cup freshly grated grana padano or Parmigiano-Reggiano
5 teaspoons kosher salt
½ teaspoon freshly grated nutmeg
½ teaspoon freshly ground black pepper

8 tablespoons (1 stick) unsalted butter
Freshly grated grana padano or Parmigiano-Reggiano for serving
One 3- to 4-ounce piece ricotta salata

PREPARE THE SPINACH: Bring a very large stockpot of water to a boil. Working in three batches, blanch the spinach for about 2 minutes in the boiling water; use a spider to transfer the spinach to a bowl. Place a grate (such as a cooling rack) on top of the bowl to keep the spinach from escaping and set it under a thin stream of cold running water to refresh. Then drain and squeeze the spinach between your hands to remove most of the water.

Again working in three batches, put the spinach in a food processor and process until very finely pureed, 4 to 5 minutes for each batch.

PREPARE THE GNOCCHI: Put the spinach in a large bowl. Stir in the egg and milk with a large rubber spatula. Add the flour, bread crumbs, and cheese and stir until smooth. Season with the salt, nutmeg, and pepper.

Sprinkle two baking sheets with flour. Fill a pastry bag without a tip with the gnocchi mixture. Pipe 1-inch mounds of the gnocchi mixture onto the baking sheets. (You should have about 80 gnocchi.) Sprinkle the gnocchi lightly with more flour, enough so that the gnocchi don't stick to your hands when you pick them up.

COOK THE GNOCCHI: Bring two large pots of salted water to a boil. Set out eight serving plates.

Working in batches, add the gnocchi to the boiling water and cook until they firm slightly, about 1½ minutes. Use a spider to remove the gnocchi, draining them well over the pots, and divide them among the plates.

FINISH THE DISH: While the gnocchi cook, melt the butter in a large frying pan over medium heat and cook until it turns a light brown color and smells nutty.

Spoon the butter over the gnocchi. Sprinkle 1 to 2 teaspoons grated cheese over each plate of gnocchi, grate some ricotta salata over each, and serve immediately.

Marc Vetri

Jean-Georges Vongerichten

My parents nicknamed me "The Palate" because I was always in the kitchen, helping to cook, going through the refrigerator. When it came to tasting the food, I always had my five cents to put in.

When I first arrived in New York, I was doing very French food. Then I noticed that most New Yorkers eat out almost every night, so I took a look at things and decided to do food you could eat every day. I threw the traditional stocks and creams and butters out and started cooking with vegetable juices, particurlarly carrot juice, and with flavored oils, spices, and fragrant herbs. The spiced carrot juice became one of my signature dishes—it made my name in the beginning. The idea was to minimize food to its bare essence. I wanted to make the food lighter, and to keep a quicker pace in the kitchen. Also, there is a wonderful Chinatown in New York, so I was able to get and use ingredients that I came to love while working in Asia. Of course, these things were all new, and putting them into practice earned me the nickmane of *l'enfant terrible* of modern French cooking.

The United States was just at the beginning of a new movement in food when I first arrived in 1985, and it has been changing ever since. The variety of food continues to grow more diverse. The quality and resources are improving, and young chefs are pushing for better ingredients and getting involved with local farmers. The openness of New Yorkers encourages you to do groundbreaking food. I feel that New York is the best place to be. I consider myself a New Yorker—with a heavy French accent that I have been trying to get rid of for the past sixteen years.

I try to maintain a very Zen kitchen—clean, quiet, smokeless. And I like to call what we do nonaggressive cooking—slow baking, delicate broths, exposing flavors.

Of the dishes currently on my menu, I'd say the spice-crusted sea bass with a mushroom, honey, soy sauce, and vinegar broth is a favorite. The broth, combined with the spice crust, results in a dish that you want to have every other day. This is what food is about, creating cravings. When I'm making a new dish, my first inspiration comes from seasonal cravings, such as for asparagus, strawberries, and rhubarb in the spring. After that, things take a turn to become either a little more French or Asian. The markets, the traveling, visiting different countries—these things inspire me. The people I work with inspire me. Life inspires me.

181

LIPSTICK CAFÉ, THE MERCER KITCHEN, and JEAN GEORGES | New York

VONG | New York, Chicago, Hong Kong, London   **PRIME STEAKHOUSE** | Las Vegas

RHUBARB TART | Makes one 9½-inch tart, Serves 8

At Jean Georges, you are served an individual tartlet, one of four tastes on a plate of rhubarb desserts that also includes a rhubarb compote (see page 183), rhubarb ice cream, and rhubarb soup. The pastry is like a wonderfully rich cookie dough. Roll it out fairly thick (about ⅛ to ¼ inch), and don't worry if it tears. It's easy to patch.

The recipe makes slightly more dough than you'll need for the tart. Once you've rolled and fitted the dough for the crust, gather up the scraps, then reroll and cut the dough into cookies. Bake them at 350°F for about 15 minutes.

FOR THE PASTRY
8 tablespoons (1 stick) unsalted butter, sliced
1¼ cups confectioners' sugar
4 large egg yolks
1 vanilla bean
⅓ cup finely ground almonds
1½ cups all-purpose flour, plus extra for
    kneading and rolling
¼ teaspoon kosher salt

FOR THE FILLING
2 large egg yolks
2½ tablespoons granulated sugar
⅔ cup crème fraîche
⅓ cup heavy cream
10 ounces rhubarb, trimmed and cut into
    1-by-¼-inch bâtonnets

Confectioners' sugar for dusting

PREPARE THE PASTRY: Combine the butter, ¾ cup of the confectioners' sugar, and 2 of the egg yolks in the bowl of a food processor. Split the vanilla bean lengthwise in half and use a small knife to scrape the tiny black seeds inside the bean into the processor bowl. Process the mixture until smooth. Add the almond powder, flour, salt, and the remaining ½ cup confectioners' sugar and process to combine. Add the remaining 2 yolks and process until the mixture comes together.

Turn the dough out onto a lightly floured work surface and gather it into a ball. Then, with the heel of one hand, starting at the edge of the ball that is farthest away from you, push the dough away from you so that it smears across the board. Keep doing this, moving your hand toward you as you go, until the entire ball of dough has been smeared onto the board. Gather the dough back into a ball and repeat once or twice, until the dough is smooth and thoroughly blended. Wrap in plastic and refrigerate for 1 hour. (If you need to refrigerate longer than that, let the dough warm up a bit at room temperature before rolling.)

On a lightly floured work surface, roll out the dough to a round about ⅛ to ¼ inch thick. Fit it into a 9½-inch fluted tart pan with a removable bottom, patching tears where necessary. Chill the tart shell until very cold, about 15 minutes.

Meanwhile, preheat the oven to 375°F.

BLIND BAKE THE PASTRY: Line the chilled tart shell with aluminum foil or parchment paper and fill with dried beans or rice. Bake the pastry until it begins to brown around on the edges, about 15 minutes. Remove the foil or parchment and beans or rice. Return the shell to the oven and bake for 5 more minutes until cooked. Let cool slightly.

FILL AND BAKE THE TART: Whisk together the egg yolks, sugar, crème fraîche, and heavy cream until smooth. Scatter the rhubarb bâtonnets over the bottom of the tart shell and pour the filling mixture over.

Bake the tart until the filling is just set, 30 to 35 minutes. Halfway through the baking time, cover the edges of the crust with strips of aluminum foil to keep the pastry from browning too much. Let the tart cool to room temperature.

To serve, sift confectioners' sugar over the tart and cut into wedges.

182

RHUBARB AND STRAWBERRY COMPOTE | Serves 4

At the restaurant, this compote is served with yogurt pancakes, as one of four elements on a rhubarb dessert plate including a rhubarb tart (see page 182), rhubarb soup with *oeufs à la neige,* and rhubarb ice cream. You can serve the compote as is, or with vanilla ice cream.

1 cup water

¼ cup sugar

1 vanilla bean, split lengthwise

10 ounces rhubarb, trimmed

10 ounces strawberries, hulled and cut in half
    or quarters, depending on size

Combine the water, sugar, and vanilla bean in a saucepan and bring to a boil.

Meanwhile, slice the rhubarb crosswise about ⅛ inch thick (don't slice it too thin, or it will fall apart). Add it to the sugar syrup. Simmer, uncovered, until the rhubarb is tender, about 3 minutes. Let the compote cool to room temperature, then remove the vanilla bean and fold in the strawberries.

Serve at room temperature or chilled.

183

A selection of rhubarb desserts (clockwise from top left): rhubarb soup with *oeufs à la neige;* yogurt pancake with rhubarb and strawberry compote; rhubarb tartlet, and rhubarb ice cream.

Jean-Georges Vongerichten

Bob Waggoner **CHARLESTON GRILL** | Charleston

I think the old way, the old-school way is great. You can't learn that in school. You don't see it. The appreciation of the product. Here, we've got baby carrots on this and zucchini blossoms on that, whereas, my gosh, in France, if you can even afford to get baby carrots, you've got them peeled and arranged in a row and nestled in a little napkin and kept in the refrigerator. I am truly grateful that I had that kind of training.

In the toughest kitchen I ever worked in, the chef would sometimes get so pissed off in the middle of the service that he'd ask one of the apprentices to go and get him a flat of eggs and he'd just start throwing eggs around the kitchen, just heaving them around the kitchen. Or he'd call you up to the table as you were putting out dishes and he'd say, "Does that smell the way it is supposed to smell?" and you'd say, "Well, it looks like it is supposed to . . ." and you'd put your head over the plate to smell it and he'd crack an egg onto your head. He'd just be heaving things all over the kitchen, even during a busy service. Ruining things . . . he didn't care.

In the two- and three-star French restaurants . . . even the one-stars, you've got a lot of great guys working in the kitchen. I thought, "Wow, these guys are gods; they must be really passionate about food," but I don't think anyone had as much passion as I did or was as excited about it. I didn't even care that I wasn't getting paid—I was so into it. That helped to move me along. Here I was from Hollywood, and the chefs were amazed that I knew who all the great chefs of France were, while their apprentices didn't have a clue. I wanted to stay longer. I said, "What an opportunity, I'd love to come back next year—I'll work for room and board." I didn't care. And the chef replied, "Well, let's try getting you into a three-star Michelin restaurant. We're going to one for dinner, so we'll wait until the chef comes out in the middle of the dining room, and then we'll ask him. We'll be spending two thousand dollars for dinner, so he can't say no." So we were all there, and the chef came out, and my friend said, "Hey, this kid wants to come and work for you for six months, what do you think?" The chef said, "Sure. And I'll just pay him like this . . ." and he made a motion as if he were shooting a slingshot.

Bob Waggoner

QUAIL BREAST OVER A FOIE GRAS, SHALLOT, AND BRAISED BEEF TONGUE RAGOUT IN A SMOKED BACON AND FRESH TRUFFLE REDUCTION

First, quail breasts are sautéed in butter and removed from the pan. Then, sautéed shallots, sautéed beef tongue, and sautéed foie gras are added to the pan and cooked together briefly into a ragout.

To serve, the ragout is gently pressed into ring molds on serving plates. Four spoonfuls of mashed potatoes are arranged around each portion of ragout. A quail breast is set on top of each spoonful of potato. While blanched pencil-thin white asparagus and baby carrots are warmed in butter, a quail stock, made from the quail legs and carcasses, is finished with cooked diced bacon and truffles. The sauce is spooned over the quail breasts and the vegetables are scattered over all.

About the Chefs

Julia Child

FAVORITE COOKING TOOL: My ten-inch, nonstick, Wearever frying pan

FAVORITE INGREDIENT: Besides butter? Really, it's butter and olive oil.

FAVORITE CUISINE: Very definitely French. Or Northern Chinese.

MOST USEFUL COOKING TIP: Take it seriously. The best French cuisine is called *cuisine soignée,* which means careful cooking. You don't have to be fancy, just be serious.

BEST SNACK: Don't snack. That's the way to get fat. If you want to snack, have a glass of water or tea.

MOST-USED COOKBOOK: *Larousse Gastronomique*

CAREER IF NOT A COOK: Veterinarian. I'd do cats—I'm a cat person, although dogs are nice, too.

ACTIVITY ON DAY OFF: Eating

Over her distinguished career, Julia Child has done more than any other culinary star to introduce Americans to better cooking. Her first television series, *The French Chef,* began airing in 1963 and educated Americans about classic French cooking in some two hundred shows. She went on to explore more contemporary cuisine in her next two series, *Julia Child & Company* and *Dinner at Julia's.* Child recently hosted two Emmy Award–winning series featuring well-known professional chefs, *In Julia's Kitchen with Master Chefs* and *Baking with Julia,* the first and only television cooking series to be awarded national Emmys. Child is the author of more than a dozen cookbooks, including her groundbreaking two-volume *Mastering the Art of French Cooking* and *The Way to Cook.* She is an active member of the International Association of Culinary Professionals, and a cofounder of the American Institute of Wine & Food.

Ben Barker

FAVORITE COOKING TOOL: Fish spatula

FAVORITE INGREDIENT: Fresh tomato

NEW SOUTHERN CUISINE IN A WORD (OR TWO): Not necessarily grits

BEST SNACK: Peanut butter and radishes

MENTOR: Grandmother—for her fried chicken

MOST-USED COOKBOOK: Paula Wolfert's *Cooking of Southwest France*

CAREER IF NOT A CHEF: Landscape architect

Ben and Karen Barker met on the first day of class as students at The Culinary Institute of America and have been cooking together ever since. In 1986, they converted an old grocery store into the Magnolia Grill. They have won many honors, including Ben's award for Best Chef: Southeast from the James Beard Foundation in 2000, and Karen's 1999 award for Best Pastry Chef from *Bon Appétit* and in 2001 the outstanding Pastry Chef award from the James Beard Foundation. Both husband and wife have cooked at Restaurant La Residence in Chapel Hill, and at The Fearrington House in Pittsboro, North Carolina, where Ben Barker succeeded Edna Lewis as head chef and established the "Cuisine of the New South" as the theme of the restaurant. They are coauthors of *Not Afraid of Flavor: Recipes from Magnolia Grill.*

Lidia Bastianich

FAVORITE COOKING TOOL: A spider to fish out cooked pasta

FAVORITE INGREDIENTS: Olive oil and garlic

FAVORITE CUTS OF MEAT: Tripe and shanks

AGE WHEN ARRIVED IN AMERICA: Twelve

BEST SNACK: A piece of Parmigiano-Reggiano drizzled with traditional balsamic vinegar

MOST MEMORABLE DINNER: When I returned to Pola in 1966 on my honeymoon, my maternal grandmother, Rosa, prepared *fuzi,* traditional Istrian pasta that looks like quills, with a courtyard hen *guazzetto.* It could have been that I had not been back for seven years. It could have been that I was in love and on my honeymoon. All I know is that I can still savor the complex, yet mellow flavor of the hen that had disintegrated and fallen off the bone into the sauce, spiked by the spicy cloves and the aroma of fresh bay leaves. The sauce coated each piece of fuzi like velvet and made my lips stick together with each bite. It was an intense, flavorful sensation.

MOST-USED COOKBOOK: Gossetti's *La Cucina Regionale*

CAREER IF NOT A CHEF: Pediatrician

ACTIVITY ON DAY OFF: Cooking for and with my grandchildren

Lidia Bastianich was born of ethnic Italian parentage in Pola, a fortified seaport on the southwestern tip of Istria, a peninsula about ninety miles northeast of Venice. This background has very much influenced her cooking: She is renowned as the "First Lady" of Italian cuisine. Bastianich had no formal culinary training; in fact, she studied biology. This science background has affected her culinary skills, however—she has said that understanding what

happens in the cooking process from a chemical standpoint is essential to successful dishes. Her restaurants have won many awards, including a three-star review in *The New York Times* for Felidia. Lidia Bastianich has two television shows, *Lidia's Italian Table* and *Lidia's Italian Table: Italian American Favorites*, and she produces a line of sauces. She is author of *Lidia's Italian Table* and *La Cucina di Lidia*.

Rick Bayless

FAVORITE COOKING TOOL: Mortar and pestle

BEST MEXICAN DISCOVERY: Chocolate

BEST SNACK: Garret's caramel popcorn

MOST MEMORABLE DINNER: The first time I tasted *mole poblano* in a converted gas station restaurant north of Mexico City when I was fifteen

AWARD MOST PROUD OF: Humanitarian of the Year

MENTOR: Julia Child

FUTURE ASPIRATIONS: A book and television series with my daughter, Lane

CAREER IF NOT A CHEF: Writer or visual artist

Rick Bayless helped to change the image of Mexican food in the United States by bringing authentic Mexican cuisine to Americans' palates. He was born into a family of restaurateurs specializing in the local barbecue of Oklahoma and, as a fourteen-year-old, planned a family vacation in Mexico, where his love for the culture and cuisine was born. He studied Spanish and Latin American culture as an undergraduate and was chosen to host the twenty-six-part PBS television series *Cooking Mexico* in 1978. He dedicated more than six years to culinary research in Mexico, culminating with the publication of his now-classic *Authentic Mexican: Regional Cooking from the Heart of Mexico* in 1987. That same year, Bayless and his wife and business partner, Deann, moved to Chicago and opened the Frontera Grill. He has won numerous awards as chef of this still-popular restaurant, as well as for the couple's second restaurant, Topolobampo, several from the James Beard Foundation. Bayless hosts his own PBS television series, *Mexico–One Plate at a Time.* He is the chairman of Chef's Collaborative, a national group of chefs in support of environmentally sound agricultural practices, and he is active in Share Our Strength, the nation's largest hunger advocacy organization. His books include *Mexico–One Plate at a Time,* a James Beard award winner in 2001, *Salsas That Cook: Using Classic Salsas to Enliven Our Favorite Dishes,* and *Rick Bayless's Mexican Kitchen: Capturing the Vibrant Flavors of a World-Class Cuisine.*

Daniel Boulud

FAVORITE COOKING TOOL: An induction cooker

FAVORITE INGREDIENT: Spring potatoes from back home in Lyons

BEST FRENCH DISCOVERY: The copper pot

BEST SNACK: A toss-up between popcorn and potato chips

TRANSFORMING MOMENT: At the age of fourteen in Lyons, meeting Paul Bocuse

AWARD MOST PROUD OF: Best Chef in America, James Beard Foundation, 1994

MENTORS: Georges Blanc, Roger Vergé, and Michel Guérard

CAREER IF NOT A CHEF: Wine maker in Provence

Daniel Boulud, a product of six generations of farmers and café keepers, was raised on his family's farm near Lyons. At age fourteen, he left home to apprentice at a bistro—and was nominated as candidate for best cooking apprentice in France. He went on to train under some of the country's most renowned chefs: Roger Vergé, Georges Blanc, and Michel Guérard. He made his way to America in the early eighties, where his first position was as chef to the European Commission in Washington, D.C. After opening the Polo Lounge in the Westbury Hotel and Le Régence in the Hôtel Plaza Athénée, Boulud became executive chef at Le Cirque from 1986 to 1992. His restaurant, Daniel, opened in 1993 and was quickly heralded as "one of the best ten restaurants in the world" by the *International Herald Tribune.* In 1998, he opened Café Boulud, named for the gathering place Boulud's great-grandparents owned and ran at the turn of the century. His other endeavors include Feast & Fêtes, the exclusive catering department of Daniel, and his "Private Stock" line of Caspian caviar and Scottish smoked salmon. One of the founding partners of Payard Pâtisserie & Bistro, which opened in August 1997, Boulud sold his interest in it to François Payard in September 2000. He is author of *Café Boulud Cookbook* and *Cooking with Daniel Boulud.*

Jeffrey Buben

FAVORITE COOKING TOOL: A ten-inch serated slicer

FAVORITE INGREDIENT: Onions

BEST SOUTHERN FOOD DISCOVERY: Grits and country ham

MOST USEFUL COOKING TIP: Use a recipe as a guide to cooking

SMARTEST MOVE: Becoming a chef

BEST SNACK: Fried chicken

MENTOR: Peter Van Erp

MOST-USED COOKBOOK: *James Beard's American Cookery*

ACTIVITIES ON DAY OFF: Family and fishing

A chef from Pennsylvania marries a businesswoman from North Carolina and Vidalia is born. Opened in 1993 by chef Jeffrey Buben and his wife, Sallie, the restaurant and its success encouraged the Bubens to open a bistro counterpart, Bistro Bis, five years later. Both win rave reviews, as does Buben. He describes his cooking as "modern American" influenced by classic training in French cuisine—it's been noted that his eclectic American style is also influenced by his wife's southern heritage. In 1999, the James Beard Foundation chose him as Best Chef: Mid-Atlantic. With more than twenty years experience in the industry, he has worked in New York City at The Sign of the Dove, Le Cygne, and Le Chantilly, and at several distinguished hotels, such as The Four Seasons, The Mayflower, and Hotel Pierre. Throughout the years, Buben has worked hard to contribute to organizations dedicated to hunger relief, AIDS, and homelessness.

Tom Colicchio

FAVORITE COOKING TOOL: An all-around metal spoon (for tasting, plating, saucing, etc.)

FAVORITE INGREDIENT: Salt

MOST USEFUL COOKING TIP: Keep your knives sharp

SMARTEST MOVE: Listening to my father when he told me that I should become a chef

BEST SNACK: Popcorn cooked in oil at home

MOST MEMORABLE DINNER: One fall dinner at a friend's farmhouse in Maryland, when a group of us plucked ingredients from the backyard garden and cooked an impromptu dinner together

MOST INSPIRATIONAL MOMENT: Watching the birth of my son

MOST-USED COOKBOOK: Jacques Pépin's *La Technique*

CAREER IF NOT A CHEF: Rock and roll star

As a teenager, Tom Colicchio taught himself to cook with the help of Jacques Pépin's legendary illustrated manuals on French cooking, *La Technique* and *La Méthode*. He made his kitchen debut at age seventeen at Evelyn's Seafood

Restaurant in his hometown of Elizabeth, New Jersey. Before opening his own restaurant, Colicchio gathered experience at notable New York eateries such as the Quilted Giraffe, where after just four months he was promoted to sous-chef, Gotham Bar and Grill, Rakel, and Mondrian. During his tenure as executive chef at Mondrian, he was selected as one of the Top Ten New Chefs in the United States. Gramercy Park opened in 1994; just two years later it was awarded three stars by *The New York Times*. Colicchio's interest in food extends to his community service: He donates his time to Share Our Strength and other organizations. His first book, *Think Like a Chef,* won a James Beard award in 2001.

Gary Danko

FAVORITE COOKING TOOL: I have a few. Hands down it would be Joyce Chen scissors; they are excellent for cutting fish bones, lobster shells, flowers, thin wire, etc. Once I turn a young chef on to them, they become essential. Number two is a clay tool used for cutting scallops of clay off a sculpture—it is excellent for coring pears. I showed it to Martha Stewart once, and by the time I had left her studio in Connecticut, she had already interviewed me about it, where I bought it and so on. It is now available on her Website. Funny enough, they never showed me using it on *Martha Stewart Living*.

FAVORITE INGREDIENT: Salt

MOST INSPIRATIONAL MOMENTS: Walking through the vineyards and orchards of Napa Valley, eating figs, plums, and walnuts

FIRST JOB: My first paid job was at The Village Inn in Massena, New York, at age twelve as a hatcheck boy. I later started washing dishes at age fourteen and I worked there for five years.

AWARD MOST PROUD OF: Best New Restaurant, James Beard Foundation, 2000

MENTOR: Madeleine Kamman

Gary Danko was reared in a small town in upstate New York; his interest in restaurants was launched when his father, an architect and builder, remodeled The Village Inn, a local eatery. Danko worked there through high school, then enrolled in The Culinary Institute of America in 1975. Always convinced of his calling, Danko gained deeper inspiration when he discovered Madeleine Kamman's *The Making of a Cook*. He continued to follow her career, even as his own was taking off: He spent three years cooking in San Francisco, then moved to Vermont, where he became the chef at Tucker Hill Inn. Inspired by the fresh local products there, such as butter, cheese, poultry, and produce,

Danko began to change his menu nightly, an uncommon practice at the time. In 1983, he finally introduced himself to Kamman and enrolled a year after that in her cooking school. A few years later, he took the helm of the restaurant of Beringer Vineyards' Chateau Souverain in Sonoma County, where he began to attract national attention. He moved to the Ritz-Carlton in San Francisco, where he won the James Beard Foundation's Best Chef: California award in 1995. He then helped launch Viognier in San Mateo, and, in 1999, opened Gary Danko.

Robert Del Grande

FAVORITE COOKING TOOL: A basting brush—I enjoy the art of basting anything.

THE ANNIE OF CAFÉ ANNIE: It's just a name, really. No one could decide, so we used it as a working name, thinking that we would find a "better" name later, and then the restaurant opened and the name stuck.

SOUTHWEST CUISINE IN A WORD: Rustic

BEST SNACK: Ripe mangoes

MOST INSPIRATIONAL MOMENT: The first time I met Julia Child—she was standing on a step above me, so she seemed seven feet tall. It was a great moment.

MOST INFLUENTIAL COOKBOOK: Very early on it would have been one of the Troisgros brothers' cookbooks or Michel Guérard's *La Cuisine gourmande*.

MOST-USED COOKBOOKS: Diana Kennedy's books on Mexican cuisine

Robert Del Grande's career began in California while he was earning a Ph.D. in biochemistry. Del Grande cooked dinner for his roommates for almost five years, reading every cookbook he could get his hands on. He then followed his girlfriend (now wife), Mimi, to Houston in 1981, where her sister and brother-in-law, Candice and Lonnie Schiller, had just opened Café Annie. Del Grande was completing his postdoctorate work in science and experimenting in the restaurant's kitchen. He soon became a partner and the executive chef. The cooking awards came next, and the self-taught chef abandoned the laboratory for the kitchen. The Del Grandes and the Schillers teamed up to open several other venues, including Taco Milagro, Rio Ranch, and the Café Express chain, which features healthy, quick meals.

Traci Des Jardins

FAVORITE COOKING TOOL: Chef's knife

FAVORITE INGREDIENT: Fat, i.e., butter, duck fat, olive oil

CHILDHOOD HOME: Firebaugh, California

MOST INSPIRATIONAL MOMENT: Watching Joachim Splichal work on my first day in a professional kitchen

AWARD MOST PROUD OF: Rising Star Chef, James Beard Foundation, 1995

ACTIVITY ON DAY OFF: Skiing

Food—in all its cultural diversity—was always at the center of activity in Traci Des Jardins' family. Her father was a rice farmer, her paternal grandfather was a skilled cook born in French Acadian Louisiana, and her maternal grandparents were from Mexico. The family prepared meals together with fresh produce from their garden and game that the men hunted. Des Jardins enrolled in the University of California at Santa Cruz with the intention of becoming a veterinarian, but soon abandoned college to work her way through the kitchens of Los Angeles and France. Her first job was with Joachim Splichal, who helped her win apprenticeships with such luminaries as Michel and Pierre Troisgros of Troisgros, Alain Senderens at Lucas-Carton, Alain Ducasse at Louis XV, and Alain Passard at Arpège. She came back to the United States and worked at Drew Nieporent's Montrachet, returned west to Splichal's Patina as the opening chef de cuisine (at age twenty-three), and helped open Aqua and Elka in San Francisco. Her work following this, as executive chef of Nieporent's Rubicon, garnered her national acclaim in 1993—success that has followed her to her own restaurant, Jardinière, which Des Jardins opened in 1997.

Rocco DiSpirito

FAVORITE COOKING TOOL: My palate

FAVORITE INGREDIENT: Salt and citrus

BEST SNACK: Cheese and pickle sandwiches

MOST MEMORABLE DINNER: Christmas Eve 1977, when my grandmother cooked a Feast of the Seven Fishes

MOST INSPIRATIONAL MOMENT: Seeing Gray Kunz cook at the fish station at Lespinasse

AWARD MOST PROUD OF: Winning the New York City spelling bee in 1980

RECIPE/DISH MOST PROUD OF: Taylor Bay Scallops with uni and mustard oil, because it so elegantly embodies my feelings about flavor and the power of great flavor combinations, i.e., sour, salty, sweet, bitter.

FUTURE ASPIRATIONS: Write the definitive guide to flavor

CAREER IF NOT CHEF: Satirist

ACTIVITIES ON DAY OFF: Reading, walking, and eating slowly

Before adopting Gray Kunz of New York's Lespinasse as his mentor, Rocco DiSpirito, moved from stove to stove, looking for a chef whose style would offer inspiration. He was not in a hurry even to open his own restaurant; after an initial, difficult effort, he waited another two years to learn more and try again. The result, Union Pacific, has received accolades, and DiSpirito has been hailed as one of the brightest starred chefs of his generation. He graduated from The Culinary Institute of America in 1986, and continued studying classical technique at Jardin des Cygnes in Paris with Dominique Cécillón. For nearly two years he immersed himself in French regional food and wine, wandering the local markets and touring vineyards. Back in New York, he worked under Jean-Michel Diot and Jacques Chibois, then earned a B.A. in business at Boston University. Later, in Mark Baker's kitchen at Aujourd'hui in Boston, DiSpirito first saw the combination of French technique and Asian ingredients—now a hallmark of his own style. Eager to explore the emerging cross-cultural cuisine, he returned to New York and studied with David Bouley, Charles Palmer, Gilbert Le Coze, and Gray Kunz. Kunz added DiSpirito to Lespinasse's opening team. In September 1995, DiSpirito as executive chef opened Dava Restaurant, and in 1997 opened his own restaurant, Union Pacific, where he continues to receive a host of honors and awards.

Tom Douglas

FAVORITE COOKING TOOL: Sausage stuffer

FAVORITE INGREDIENT: Duck

BEST SNACK: Barbecue potato chips

MOST MEMORABLE DINNERS: When my mom would make me barbecued beef for my birthday dinners when I was a kid

MOST INSPIRATIONAL MOMENT: Being a judge at the Jack Daniel's Barbecue Invitational and doing the "charcoal stroll" (talking to the teams before the event)

FAVORITE ETHNIC CUISINE: Vietnamese

FAVORITE COOKBOOK: Alice Waters's *Chez Panisse Menu Cookbook*

MOST-USED COOKBOOK: Barbara Tropp's *China Moon Cookbook*

A Delaware native, Tom Douglas started cooking at the Hotel Dupont in Wilmington, Delaware, before heading west to Seattle in 1978. He tried his hand at several jobs—house building, wine selling, railroad car repair—before making the obvious and final career choice of the restaurant business. Douglas never attended a culinary school; his cooking knowledge has come mostly from dining out across America and Europe, using his "taste memory" to re-create and develop recipes in his own style. Starting out at Seattle's Café Sport, Douglas helped define the northwestern style of cuisine, which borrows from many cultures, especially those of nearby Asia, Alaska, California, and Canada. He opened his own restaurant, the Dahlia Lounge, in 1989; five years later, he was awarded the James Beard Foundation's award for Best Chef: Northwest. Etta's Seafood, named after Douglas and wife-partner Jackie Cross's daughter, Loretta, opened to praise in 1995, followed a year later by Palace Kitchen, featuring rustic cuisine. Douglas has written a cookbook with recipes from all three restaurants, *Tom Douglas' Seattle Kitchen,* which won a James Beard award in 2001.

Wylie Dufresne

FAVORITE COOKING TOOL: Blender

FAVORITE INGREDIENT: Eggs

BEST SNACK: American cheese

MENTOR: Jean-Georges Vongerichten

STATIONS COVERED AT JO JO: All

MOST-USED COOKBOOK: Alice Waters's *Chez Panisse Cooking*

CAREER IF NOT A CHEF: First baseman for the New York Yankees

Wylie Dufresne grew up the son of a restaurant owner, but he didn't discover his passion for cooking professionally until mid-college. During a summer break from Colby College, he worked the pizza station at Al Forno in Providence and fell in love with "the buzz." After graduating in 1992, he enrolled at the French Culinary Institute in New York and worked nights at the Gotham Bar and Grill. He then applied for a job at Jean-Georges Vongerichten's Jo Jo, having been intrigued by the chef's book *Simple Cuisine.* Dufresne stayed at Jo Jo for three years, then completed a *stage* in L'Espérance in Burgundy, France. On his return, he worked the opening of Jean Georges, where he was eventually promoted to sous-chef, and then as chef de cuisine opened Vongerichten's

Prime Steakhouse in the Bellagio in Las Vegas. In 1999, Dufresne left Prime to work with his father and a number of other partners as the chef in his thirty-seat restaurant in New York's Lower East Side, 71 Clinton Fresh Food.

Todd English

FAVORITE COOKING TOOL: Japanese mandoline

FAVORITE INGREDIENT: Olive oil

MOST USEFUL COOKING TRICK: Toasting garlic

BEST SNACK: Blue corn sesame tortilla chips

MOST MEMORABLE DINNER: At home with Fredy Girardet

AWARD MOST PROUD OF: Coolest Dad by my kids

MENTOR: Jean-Jacques Rachou

FUTURE ASPIRATIONS: First restaurant on the moon

MOST-USED COOKBOOK: Escoffier's *Le Guide culinaire*

CAREER IF NOT A CHEF: Formula 1 race car driver

Todd English attended The Culinary Institute of America and honed his craft with Jean-Jacques Rachou at New York's La Côte Basque and then in Italy, where he began to draw from his Italian heritage through apprenticeships with Dal Pescatore in Canto Sull O'lio and Paraccuchi in Locando D'Angello. Returning to the United States at age twenty-five, he opened the award-winning northern Italian restaurant Michela's in Cambridge, Massachusetts, as executive chef. He opened his first Olives in nearby Charlestown in 1989. In spring 1991, English caught the culinary world's eye when the James Beard Foundation named him national Rising Star Chef of the Year, and then in 1994 named him Best Chef: Northeast. In recent years, English has opened other Olives locations, as well as many other restaurants nationwide, as his name has become recognized in the food world. Television credits include his public television series, *Cooking In with Todd English,* and appearances on *America's Rising Star Chefs.* He is very involved with local and national charities, including Big Brother and Share Our Strength. His cookbooks include *The Olives Dessert Table, The Figs Table,* and *The Olives Table.*

Bobby Flay

FAVORITE COOKING TOOL: Tongs

FAVORITE INGREDIENT: Mustard

FAVORITE SPICE: Black pepper

MOST USEFUL COOKING TIP: To keep fish or chicken from sticking to the pan, brush the meat with olive oil and season; heat a pan until almost smoking and place the fish or chicken skin side down in the pan. The next step is the most important: Don't touch it! If you immediately try to flip it, it is going to stick. You need to allow it to form a crust.

BEST MOVE IN THE KITCHEN: My pretty awesome ability to flip an omelet

BEST SNACK: Any flavor of Häagen-Dazs ice cream

MENTOR: Jonathan Waxman

MOST-USED COOKBOOK: The original *Joy of Cooking*

FUTURE ASPIRATIONS: To play pro golf

Bobby Flay asked his mother to buy him an Easy Bake oven when he was seven years old. She obliged, and a decade later Flay was working at the New York restaurant Joe Allen, where his father was a partner. There he so impressed the boss that Allen paid his tuition at the French Culinary Institute. After Flay graduated in 1984, restaurant owner Jonathan Waxman introduced him to the southwestern ingredients that influence his culinary style. His first job as an executive chef, at the Miracle Grill in New York's East Village, caught the eye of restaurateur Jerome Kretchmer, who then opened Mesa Grill with Flay as chef in 1991. It was so successful that Flay was made a partner, and he soon opened Bolo, a contemporary Spanish eatery. Flay's original style and innovative cuisine have earned him exemplary recognition, including Rising Star Chef of the Year from the James Beard Foundation in 1993. He has launched and starred in three national cooking shows, *Grillin' & Chillin'* and *Hot Off the Grill with Bobby Flay,* on the Television Food Network, and *The Main Ingredient with Bobby Flay* on Lifetime. He is author of *Bold American Food, From My Kitchen to Your Table,* and *Boy Meets Grill.*

Claudia Fleming

FAVORITE COOKING TOOL: Pastry scraper (*corne* in French)

FAVORITE INGREDIENT: Bourbon vanilla beans from Madagascar

MOST USEFUL COOKING TIP: Keep things clean and organized

MOST MEMORABLE DINNER: When I got engaged at Les Crayères in Champagne, France

MOST INSPIRATIONAL MOMENT: Tasting salt with chocolate with Philippe Conticini

MENTOR: Tom Colicchio

FUTURE ASPIRATIONS: A house on the Atlantic Ocean

MOST-USED COOKBOOK: Alice Waters's *Chez Panisse Dessert Cookbook*

ACTIVITY ON DAY OFF: Running

Claudia Fleming studied dance while growing up on Long Island and eventually moved to Manhattan to pursue it as a career. While working with a small modern dance company, however, she made her way to the restaurant world to support herself, starting in the dining rooms of Jams and Union Square Café. At the latter, Fleming found herself drawn to the kitchen—the pastry station in particular. In 1991, determined to hone her skills, she decided to go to Paris to study. After a stint at the prestigious Fauchon, she returned to New York and delved into pastry making at Montrachet, TriBeCa Grill, and Luxe. In 1994, she was hired as pastry chef at Gramercy Tavern. She has won many awards there, among them *Pastry Art & Design's* 10 Best Pastry Chefs of 2000. Fleming is author of *The Last Course: Desserts from the Gramercy Tavern.*

Suzanne Goin

FAVORITE INGREDIENTS: Roasted shallots and bread crumbs

MOST USEFUL COOKING TIP: Pay attention to detail!

BEST SNACK: Farro with cavolo nero and broccoli

MOST MEMORABLE DINNER: With Roger Vergé at Moulin de Mougin, summer 1978

MOST INSPIRATIONAL MOMENT: My first job at Ma Maison, summer 1984

MENTORS: The chefs of Chez Panisse

CAREER IF NOT A CHEF: Historian

The first thing Suzanne Goin ever cooked was crêpes for her younger sister and her friends. A Los Angeles native, Goin spent three weeks in the pastry kitchen at Ma Maison for her high school senior project. The next year, as a history major at Brown University, she tried to sell her desserts to Providence's Al Forno. Although the business plan failed, it won Goin a kitchen position there and she was hooked. After college, she and a former Al Forno chef opened a small restaurant. Soon she wanted a bigger challenge and applied for a position at Chez Panisse in Berkeley. After two years there, she left for Paris, working at the three-star, Arpège. Returning to the United States, Goin landed first at Boston's Olives and Alloro, then moved back to Los Angeles in 1995 as sous-chef at Campanile. When Mark Peel, Campanile's executive chef-owner, went on sabbatical, Goin replaced him in the kitchen. In 1999, she opened Lucques.

Christine Keff

HOMETOWN: Bakersfield, California

FAVORITE KITCHEN STATION: Sauté

MOST IMPORTANT RELATIONSHIP IN A KITCHEN: Between the chef and dishwasher/porter

BEST SNACK: Vietnamese noodle soup

FUTURE ASPIRATIONS: Retire and read for at least three years

MOST-USED COOKBOOK: Jeffrey Alford and Naomi Duguid's *Seductions of Rice*

Christine Keff knew she had found the right job during her two-year apprenticeship in New York's Four Seasons under chef Seppi Renggli. She trained at every kitchen station there, then moved on to work at Vienna 79 and O'Neal's before opening three separate restaurants for the Project Management Group. Leaving New York behind, Keff traveled extensively throughout the United States and Asia before relocating in Seattle, where she became executive chef at McCormick & Schmick's. In 1992, she became executive chef of the prestigious Hunt Club restaurant. Three years later she achieved her lifelong ambition by opening her own restaurant in Seattle, Flying Fish. She was awarded the James Beard Foundation's award for Best Chef: Pacific Northwest/Hawaii in 1999, and a year later opened her second restaurant, Fandango. Keff is dedicated to the Seattle community through her involvement with the March of Dimes, Northwest AIDS Foundation, Share Our Strength, and other organizations.

Thomas Keller

FAVORITE COOKING TOOL: My palette knife. It's a long, thin, extremely flexible knife—almost like a spatula. I use it for everything from icing cakes to turning and picking up food.

FAVORITE INGREDIENT: Food and anything to do with food!

MOST USEFUL COOKING TRICK: Have a great staff

MOST INSPIRATIONAL MOMENT: Shortly before I moved from New York to Los Angeles, some friends took me to Baskin-Robbins. I ordered an ice-cream cone. The guy put it in a little holder—you take it from a holder—and said, "Here's your cone." The minute he said it, I thought, "There it is," and invented our cornet: I took our standard tuiles, made cones with them, and filled them with tuna tartare. You can fill them with anything. Everyone who eats at our restaurant begins the meal with this cornet. People always smile when they get it.

BEST SNACK: Chocolate chip cookies

MENTOR: Roland Henin

MOST-USED COOKBOOK: Ferdinand Point's *Ma gastronomie*

CAREER IF NOT A CHEF: Shortstop for the New York Yankees—I want the opportunity to play in their stadium!

ACTIVITY ON DAY OFF: Sleep

Born in Southern California, Thomas Keller is a veteran of many of the great restaurant kitchens of the world. He first gained recognition at La Reserve and Restaurant Raphaël in New York, where he earned national exposure. To further his expertise, he moved abroad and served a *stage* throughout France in the kitchens of Guy Savoy, Michael Pasquet, Gerard Besson, Taillevent, Toit de Passy, Chiberta, and Le Pré Catalan. After Keller returned to New York he opened Rakel, where he received front-page coverage on *New York* magazine's "Ask Gael" issue. Four years later, Keller moved to California and joined the Ayala Hotel Group as executive chef at Checkers in Los Angeles. He purchased the French Laundry in 1994, with the goal of creating a three-star country French restaurant in the heart of Napa Valley. He has won numerous accolades, including Outstanding Chef: America, in 1997 from the James Beard Foundation. In addition, Keller is the founder and owner of EVO, Inc., a nationally distributed retail line of premium California olive oils and vinegar. He is author of *The French Laundry Cookbook*.

Bob Kinkead

BORN: Providence, Rhode Island

BEST SNACK: Hot dog, specifically a "gagger" made of a Seiler's hot dog with chili meat sauce, horseradish mustard, freshly chopped white onion, and celery salt, preferably on a potato roll

SMARTEST CAREER MOVE: To get back on the horse after my first restaurant, Twenty-One Federal, failed. I opened Kinkead's in the same town to take advantage of the goodwill and reputation that I'd earned.

MOST-USED COOKBOOK: *The Time-Life Good Cook* series, edited by Rich Olney

CAREER IF NOT A CHEF: Filmmaker

ACTIVITY ON DAY OFF: Check out other restaurants

The flavors of Bob Kinkead's youth, spent working summers in restaurants on Cape Cod, reappear in the cuisine he serves today. Kinkead was earning a degree in psychology at the University of Massachusetts at Amherst while cooking in some of New England's finer restaurants and hotels. He was head chef, and later a partner, at Twenty-One Federal in Nantucket; he also worked at Joseph's in Boston, the Sheraton Commander Hotel in Cambridge, and Chillingsworth in Brewster. It was his cooking at Twenty-One Federal in Washington, D.C., that brought Kinkead and his cooking to national prominence. In 1993, Kinkead's opened to great acclaim; Kinkead was awarded Best Chef: Mid-Atlantic by the James Beard Foundation in 1995.

Jean-Marie Lacroix

FAVORITE KITCHEN TOOL: Vertical blender

FAVORITE INGREDIENT: Saffron

MOST USEFUL COOKING TIP: Adding lemon juice to just about anything

SMARTEST MOVE: Coming to America

BEST SNACK: My wife's hot tomato and cheddar sandwich

MOST INSPIRATIONAL MOMENT: When a well-traveled guest commented that the Fountain is really a restaurant that happens to have 364 rooms on top

MENTORS: Michel Guérard and Fredy Girardet

FAVORITE PASTIME: Gardening when it's not raining

CAREER IF NOT A CHEF: Cabinetmaker

As executive chef at the Four Seasons Hotel in Philadelphia, Jean-Marie Lacroix is responsible for all kitchen operations of the acclaimed Fountain Restaurant and Swann Lounge & Café, as well as the hotel's banquet and room service operations. Lacroix, a native of Epinal, in France's Franche-Comté region, received his formal training at Thonon les Bains on Lake Geneva. Before coming to the Four Seasons in Philadelphia at its opening in 1983, Lacroix was executive chef at Le Quatre Saisons (Four Seasons) Montreal. He is recognized for his encouragement and development of young talent—many of the kitchens in Philadelphia's starred restaurants boast of having a Lacroix graduate. Lacroix and the Fountain Restaurant are notable for their support of various philanthropic organizations, such as Share Our Strength and PhillyMeals on Wheels. In 1998, Lacroix became the first Philadelphian to receive the Robert Mondavi Award for Culinary Excellence.

Nobuyuki Matsuhisa

FAVORITE FISH: Shellfish

FAVORITE INGREDIENT: Soy sauce

BEST SNACK: Senbei Japanese crackers

MOST MEMORABLE DINNER: At Daflore in Venice

DRAMATIC MOMENT: One of the customers proposing in our restaurant—he hid the ring in an oyster shell

FUTURE ASPIRATIONS: Restaurants worldwide

CAREER IF NOT A CHEF: Professional golfer

Born and raised in Japan, Nobuyuki Matsuhisa was fluent in sushi by the age of twenty, after having apprenticed in some of Tokyo's finest sushi bars. He soon ventured overseas to Lima, Peru, where he opened his own sushi bar. There he studied the culture and regional ingredients; the combination contributed to his inventive style. Three years later, he moved to Buenos Aires, Argentina, then returned to Japan. Anchorage, Alaska, was Matsuhisa's last stop before moving to his current base, Los Angeles. His first restaurant, Matsuhisa, was opened in Beverly Hills in 1987; Nobu, in New York, opened in 1994 in partnership with Robert De Niro—a year later it was honored as Best New Restaurant by the James Beard Foundation. Many more restaurants followed, representing Matsuhisa all over the world. In 2000, he opened Nobu in Milan, Italy, with Giorgio Armani. Matsuhisa travels often, overseeing his fleet.

Nancy Oakes

FAVORITE INGREDIENT: Corn

MOST USEFUL COOKING TRICK: Confit garlic in the microwave

BEST TEACHERS: The time I spent in the kitchens of France and Italy

FAVORITE KITCHEN STATION: Saucier

MOST IMPORTANT RELATIONSHIP IN THE KITCHEN: With my co-chef, Pamela Mazzola

BEST SNACK: Osetra caviar on toasted English muffins with lots of butter

MOST INSPIRATIONAL MOMENTS: Every trip to the farmers' market

AWARD MOST PROUD OF: Second place in the sand castle competition on Carmel Beach, age nine

MENTOR: My father

MOST-USED COOKBOOK: Louis Pullig De Gouy's *Gold Cook Book*

Nancy Oakes and her chef de cuisine, Pamela Mazzola, want every diner at Boulevard to feel personally cared for. Self-taught, Oakes enhanced her philosophy with knowledge she gained from great teachers under whom she served informally. From Girard Boyer and Taillevant to Guy Savoy and Joel Robuchon, these chefs taught her to cherish all aspects of food preparation and serving. She had already established herself in the San Francisco food world before the 1993 opening of Boulevard, with stints at Alexis on Nob Hill; the popular waterfront restaurant she opened with a friend, Barnacle; and her neighborhood bistro, L'Avenue. Boulevard and its chef have won much acclaim, including being voted the number one restaurant in the San Francisco Bay Area in 1998 and 1999 by the *Zagat Survey*. In 2001, Oakes received the Best Chef: California award from the James Beard Foundation.

Patrick O'Connell

FAVORITE DECORATION: Our dog, Rose, who is the inspiration for our chef's outfits and an entire line of Dalmatian-spotted products

BEST SNACK: Lumps of aged Parmesan cheese

MOST MEMORABLE DINNER: Corn on the cob and sliced tomatoes just out of my garden, with Hellmann's Mayonnaise.

AWARD MOST PROUD OF: Outstanding Chef of the Year, James Beard Foundation 2001

197

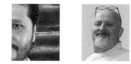

MENTORS: Julia Child, Mimi Sheraton, and Janis Joplin

MOST-USED COOKBOOK: Julia Child's *Mastering the Art of French Cooking*

CAREER IF NOT A CHEF: Psychiatrist or butler

Patrick O'Connell, a former acting student, is as inspired about the food he serves as the table he sets. Self-taught chef O'Connell, a native of Washington, D.C., and his partner, Reinhardt Lynch, began their restaurant careers as caterers working out of their farmhouse, using only a wood-burning stove and an electric frying pan. They were so successful they decided to open a restaurant. In 1978, they rented half of a defunct garage for two hundred dollars a month in the village of Washington, Virginia—population 158. Within weeks of opening, critics proclaimed The Inn to be the best restaurant in the Washington, D.C., area. It has won multiple culinary and hospitality awards, from becoming America's first five-star country house hotel to O'Connell's being named the James Beard Foundation's Best Chef: Mid-Atlantic in 1993 and Outstanding Chef in 2001. A sense of drama and whimsy is evident throughout the Inn and in its restaurant; its kitchen was recently refurbished to seem as if it belonged in a grand old private residence, with the sense of a film set from another era. O'Connell wants guests to feel as if they've dropped in on a "fabulous house party." He is the author of *The Inn at Little Washington Cookbook: A Consuming Passion.*

Tadashi Ono

TO IMPROVE ANYTHING: A touch of soy sauce

FAVORITE INGREDIENT: Bluefin tuna

MOST MEMORABLE DINNER: When I was little, my father took me to a fisherman friend's house, and we had fish right off the boat—sashimi, grilled, and poached.

MOST INSPIRATIONAL MOMENTS: Coming up with new dishes; when I see my customers happy

GOALS: To be a good father

MOST USEFUL COOKING TIP: Less is more

MOST-USED COOKBOOK: Kitaohji Rosanjin's *Cooking Kingdom*

ACTIVITY ON DAY OFF: Making pottery

Tadashi Ono was born in Tokyo, Japan, where he enjoyed sculpting and wood carving as a child. At age seventeen, he began working part-time in a Japanese restaurant in the evenings after school. His career took him first to California

and then to New York. Drawing on his memories of his mother's Western-style cooking and that of his uncle, who worked as a French chef, Ono began to move toward using more French cooking techniques and ingredients. He won a position in 1985 at La Petite Chaya, a top Los Angeles restaurant serving a fusion of Japanese and French cuisines. When the restaurant closed, he found himself working in the kitchen of L'Orangerie, under the direction of two executive chefs—a Frenchman who had worked with Jean Troisgros in France, and a Swiss who had worked with Fredy Girardet in Switzerland. For a year the two chefs competed to best each other, and to his profit, Tadashi was caught in the middle. In 1988, he decided to move to New York and began to work as sous-chef at La Caravelle, where he was the executive chef from 1990 to 1995. Little by little he introduced some influences of his native Japan into his primarily French dishes until, in 1995, he left La Caravelle with the desire to exhibit his culinary expertise—Japanese, French, California fusion, New York—in his own restaurant. In 1999, he opened Sono.

Michel Richard

MOST USEFUL COOKING TRICK: Using plastic wrap. I use it for sausage casing, for marinating, for storage, and for baking. For example, to prepare a salmon in puff pastry, I wrap the salmon in plastic and then in a thin layer of puff pastry and bake. The plastic helps keep the moisture in the fish and the pastry dry. When I'm ready to serve, I remove the plastic wrap.

SMARTEST MOVE: Going from Champagne, France, to Lenôtre in Paris, to New York, to Los Angeles, to Washington, D.C.

BEST SNACK: Fresh asparagus in vinaigrette

MOST INSPIRATIONAL MOMENT: As an eight-year old I spent a week in a restaurant baking cookies. It was then that I decided to be a chef.

MENTOR: Gaston Lenôtre

CAREER IF NOT A CHEF: Glassblower. It is still a dream. I could also have been a wine maker or farmer.

Michel Richard's trip to Washington, D.C., was a long and winding one, starting in France, where he apprenticed at Gaston Lenôtre's esteemed pastry shop. When Lenôtre decided to open shop in the United States, Richard was sent to run it. The pâtisserie closed, but Richard remained, traveling first to New Mexico, where he bought and ran a café, and then to Los Angeles to open Michel Richard Pâtisserie in 1977. The success of his pastry shop afforded Richard the opportunity to travel back and forth between the United States

and France, eating, learning, and cooking. In 1987, he opened Citrus in Los Angeles. It put Michel Richard on the culinary map and paved the way for his next restaurant, Citronelle, in Santa Barbara. In 1994, he opened another Citronelle in Washington, D.C., where the streets, the seasons, and the markets remind Richard of France. In early 1998, the newest Citronelle underwent a massive renovation and Richard moved from Los Angeles to Washington, D.C., to cook full-time. He has been featured on numerous television shows and is involved with philanthropic ventures. Richard is author of *Michel Richard's Home Cooking with a French Accent.*

Eric Ripert

FAVORITE INGREDIENT: Truffles

MOST USEFUL COOKING TRICK: Using a lemon to clean your hands and the cutting board after chopping garlic or onion

MOST MEMORABLE PASTRY AT CAFÉ DE PARIS: The entire pastry cart

SMARTEST MOVE: To come to Le Bernardin

MOST MEMORABLE DINNER: At Robuchon in Paris

ACTIVITY ON DAY OFF: Eating meat

Born in Antibes, France, in 1965, Eric Ripert developed the Mediterranean palate that informs his cooking by tasting, watching, and learning at his grandmother's elbow. When the family moved to Andorra, he expanded his repertoire to include Spanish flavors and ingredients, from fish to saffron. On holidays and birthdays, Ripert insisted his family travel to the very best restaurants so he could sample their menus. When the Riperts visited the legendary Café de Paris in Biarritz, he polished off an entire tasting menu, a half dozen à la carte items, and a sampling of each of the café's thirty-odd desserts. With encouragement from his parents, Ripert attended culinary school, École du Moulin à Vent in Perpignan, and in 1982 he moved to Paris to work at La Tour d'Argent, a temple of luxurious French cuisine that dates back more than four hundred years. In December 1983, Ripert moved to the Michelin three-star Jamin, where he soon was promoted to assistant chef de partie. He left to fulfill his military service in 1985, then returned at the request of Jamin chef-owner, Joel Robuchon, as chef poissonier. In 1989, Ripert moved to the United States to work as sous-chef at Jean-Louis (under chef Jean-Louis Palladin) in the Watergate Hotel in Washington, D.C. In 1991, he moved to New York, where he worked briefly as sous-chef under David Bouley until he was hired as the chef of Le Bernardin a few months later. He has credited Joel Robuchon with teaching him technique and discipline, Gilbert Le

Coze (Le Bernardin's original chef, under whom Ripert had worked) with showing him how to run a kitchen and restaurant, and Jean-Louis Palladin with opening his mind. In 1995, Ripert earned a four-star rating from *The New York Times*; he and the restaurant were applauded in publications nationwide. In 1996, chef Ripert became a part owner of Le Bernardin. His first cookbook, *Le Bernardin Cookbook: Four-Star Simplicity,* was published two years later.

Marcus Samuelsson

MOST USEFUL COOKING TRICK: Find flavors everywhere—even in a juice bar. Technique is secondary; you must first learn to recognize a flavor, then you can bring it into your own cooking.

SMARTEST MOVE (IN RETROSPECT): I was given the opportunity to go to France to study early in my career, but my father wouldn't let me go. He wanted me to do my other *stage* first, so that I was at my best when I got to France. It was smart.

BEST SNACK: Dried Japanese rice crackers

MOST MEMORABLE DINNER: First time eating Thai food—I was cooking in Switzerland and my colleagues and I would cook from our native countries for one other. Getting the ingredients was not easy for the Thai chef, but he did it and it was amazing.

FUTURE ASPIRATIONS: I look forward to my food journey, to continue building teams, and to growing as a professional. Everything else is detail.

ACTIVITY ON DAY OFF: I love to run in the morning. Or play tennis.

Marcus Samuelsson has been changing Americans' perception of Scandinavian food since 1995, when he took over the kitchen at Aquavit. The Ethiopian-born chef, who, along with his sister, was adopted by a couple in Sweden after being orphaned at age three, calls himself "the food ambassador for Scandinavia." He decided on a career in the kitchen when he was sixteen, encouraged by years learning the arts of preparing seafood and game, baking, canning, and pickling under his grandmother's watchful eye. He attended the local culinary institute, Estamosesson, then, mapping out his plan with his father, went to Switzerland to learn organization, later to Austria to learn pastries, and then to France for the language and classical technique. In 1993, he interned at Aquavit under executive chef Chister Larsson, then consolidated his cooking skills on a Swedish luxury cruise ship. Next came an apprenticeship at Georges Blanc, the three-star restaurant near Lyons, before returning to Aquavit in 1994 to work under executive chef Jan Sendel. Just eight weeks after the pair began working together, Sendel died unexpectedly and Samuelsson became

executive chef the next year. Samuelsson and his cooking received much praise, such as a three-star review in *The New York Times* and an award for Rising Star Chef from the James Beard Foundation in 1999. He opened a branch of Aquavit in Minneapolis, Minnesota, in 1998, a location chosen for its high concentration of Americans of Swedish descent. Aquavit also recently launched a new line of traditional Swedish prepared foods.

Lydia Shire

FAVORITE COOKING TOOL: Any supersharp, thin-bladed knife and any one of my All-Clad stainless pans

MOST USEFUL COOKING TIP: Seasoning—be bold, make your food memorable. Don't be afraid of salt; coarse sea salt is best.

FAVORITE ITALIAN FLAVOR: Bitter almonds. We make a wonderful bitter almond milk tart to serve with roast pork, with a "crackling" skin (so crisp) left on the pork rack itself.

SMARTEST MOVE: Opening my own restaurant—total freedom plus I can close on Christmas!

BEST SNACK: Bacon sandwich

MOST INSPIRATIONAL MOMENT: Watching live shrimp cooked in front of me in a glass teapot in China

MOST-USED COOKBOOK: Marion Cunningham's *The Fannie Farmer Cookbook*

ACTIVITY ON DAY OFF: Cooking for my friends while we watch football

Chefs Lydia Shire and Susan Regis have been cooking together since the early 1980s, when Shire was executive chef at Seasons Restaurant in the Bostonian Hotel. Shire received her initial training at the Cordon Bleu in London, graduating in 1970, then returned to Boston to work at Maison Robert. She continued her early career at the Harvest restaurant in Cambridge, then as restaurant chef of Café Plaza in the Copley Plaza Hotel. In 1981, Shire moved to the Parker House to become chef of the hotel's formal dining room and soon opened Seasons Restaurant in the Bostonian Hotel with Jasper White. Shire soon succeeded White as executive chef, with Regis working her way up through the kichen. Regis has said that those days were quite exciting, with chefs collaborating to define what American cuisine really was. When Shire was asked to open the new Four Seasons Hotel in Beverly Hills as executive chef (the first woman to hold the position in a luxury hotel), Regis went as sous-chef. Ultimately Shire wanted to own a restaurant, so in 1989 she returned to Boston to open Biba—named after a favorite shop in London.

In 1994, she opened Pignoli, winning a number of prestigious awards along the way. Regis oversees the kitchens of both restaurants as executive chef. Shire was awarded the James Beard Foundation's award for Best Chef: Northeast in 1992; Regis took the honor in 1998.

Katy Sparks

FAVORITE INGREDIENT: Lemongrass

MOST USEFUL COOKING TRICK: Tasting everything in stages

SMARTEST MOVE: Sticking it out during the lean years

BEST SNACK: Cheese

MOST-USED COOKBOOK: Patricia Wells's *Bistro Cooking*

ACTIVITY ON DAY OFF: Sleeping

As a child, Katy Sparks ran among the pastures of Vermont. Her father kept cattle and chickens, and the family always made good dining a priority. From an early age, she knew that she wanted to cook. Sparks graduated from Johnson and Wales in 1986, and embarked on her career at Campagne, a Provençale restaurant in Seattle. After perfecting her art of seafood preparation there, she moved to New York to work at the Quilted Giraffe with its owner-chef, Barry Wine. She won an interview with Bobby Flay a year later and credits her attentive manner for landing the job as sous-chef at Flay's Mesa Grill: "I was the only one taking notes." When Flay opened Bolo, he appointed Sparks chef de cuisine. The job whet Sparks's appetite to become a chef in her own right. While searching for the right position, she consulted and worked with chef Elka Gilmore at Kokachin. Sparks found her chef's post at Solstice, which only lasted four months, but on the restaurant's closing, Sparks discovered Quilty's. As head chef there, she has won much acclaim. In 1998, she was named one of the Ten Best New Chefs by *Food & Wine*.

Susan Spicer

FAVORITE COOKING TOOL: Paring knife

FAVORITE INGREDIENT: Lemon

MOST USEFUL COOKING TRICK: Using lots of shallots

SMARTEST MOVE: Opening Bayona

MOST MEMORABLE MEAL: At an outside café in Turkey

MENTOR: Daniel Bonnot

MOST-USED COOKBOOK: Paula Wolfert's *World of Food*

Susan Spicer began her cooking career in New Orleans as an apprentice to chef Daniel Bonnot at the Louis XVI restaurant in 1979. After a four-month *stage* with chef Roland Durand (Meilleur Oeuvrier de France) at the Sofitel in Paris in 1982, she returned to New Orleans to open the sixty-seat bistro, Savoir Faire, in the St. Charles Hotel as chef de cuisine. In 1985, she traveled extensively in California and Europe for six months, returning to work in the kitchen at the New Orleans Meridien Hotel's Henri (consultant chef, Marc Haeberlin of the Auberge de l'Ill). In 1986, she left to open the tiny Bistro at Maison de Ville in the Hotel Maison de Ville. After nearly four years as chef, she formed a partnership with Regina Keever and, in spring of 1990, opened Bayona in a beautiful two-hundred-year-old Creole cottage in the French Quarter. With solid support from local diners and critics, Bayona soon earned national attention. In May 1993, Spicer was the recipient of the James Beard Foundation's award for Best Chef: Southeast Region, and in 1995 was chosen for the Mondavi Culinary Excellence Award.

Joachim Splichal

FAVORITE COOKING TOOL: A slotted wooden spoon that I use for pasta

FAVORITE INGREDIENT: Tomatoes

MOST USEFUL COOKING TRICK: My ability to chop onions very fine

BEST SNACK: Fuji apples

MOST MEMORABLE DINNERS: Every meal with my wife and sons

MENTOR: Jacques Maximin

MOST-USED COOKBOOK: My Patina cookbook and my own inspiration

FUTURE ASPIRATIONS: I would like to be a wine maker

ACTIVITY ON DAY OFF: Playing with my children

California's bountiful resources and a receptive business community in Los Angeles has provided Joachim Splichal with the perfect environment in which to cook creatively. He was born and raised in Spaichingen, a small village in Germany. He left Germany at the age of eighteen to work in the hotel industry, traveling around the world—Canada, Morocco, Israel, Sweden, Norway, and Switzerland. He worked in France as chef saucier at La Bonne Auberge, a Michelin three-star restaurant in Antibes, and at the legendary L'Oasis in La Napoule. At age twenty-three, he was hired as sous-chef by Jacques Maximin,

who became his professional mentor, and worked at his side for four years at the Chantecler restaurant in the Hôtel Negresco in Nice. During this period, Splichal accumulated numerous culinary awards, including first prize for Youngest and Most Creative Chef from the Cercle Épicurien Society. With nothing but trunks filled with personal belongings, Splichal came to the United States in 1981 to serve as executive chef for the newly established Regency Club in Los Angeles. His reputation spread, and he moved to the Seventh Street Bistro in downtown Los Angeles, an establishment he helped develop from the ground up. He left to open Max Au Triangle in 1984, where his memorable meals were the talk of Los Angeles's food aficionados. in 1989, with his wife, Christine, he opened the famed Patina in Los Angeles. They have since gone on to expand their restaurant holdings, with bistro-style Pinot restaurants in several locations. Splichal is author of *Joachim Splichal's Patina Cookbook: Spuds, Truffles & Wild Gnocchi* and *Joachim Splichal: Cooking Without Recipes*.

Allen Susser

FAVORITE INGREDIENT: MANGO madness here. Moving to South Florida twenty-five years ago, I ran into a mango tree in my neighborhood and it was love at first bite. I cook with them both green and ripe. With one hundred twenty different varieties available here, it is an amazing lot of fun each summer in mango season.

FAVORITE COOKING TOOLS: Citrus reamer and mango fork

COOKING TIP: I love cooking with citrus. The essential oils that you get from the zest of the skin are wonderfully aromatic and flavorful in many dishes. Using either a zester or rasper works well.

BEST SNACK: Mango Batido (a mango smoothie)

MOST MEMORABLE DINNER: Cooking a fund-raising eightieth birthday dinner party for Julia Child in Boston

MENTORS: Paul Bocuse, Julia Child

MOST-USED COOKBOOK: Elisabeth Lambert Ortiz's *The Book of Latin American Cooking*

ACTIVITY ON DAY OFF: Fishing with my girls

Allen Susser has been credited with transforming South Florida cuisine from nondescript to nouvelle. Using the exotic spices and produce found in the Caribbean and Asia, including the subcontinent of India, Susser combined these flavors with the Old World techniques of the Mediterranean to create

the "New World Cuisine" served at his signature restaurant. With degrees from New York City Technical College and the Cordon Bleu, he began his on-the-job training in the kitchen of the Bristol hotel in Paris. From there, he went on to other kitchens in both Florida and New York—most notably Le Cirque in New York City, and Turnberry Isle Resort & Club in Florida—before establishing Chef Allen's Restaurant in 1986. He has written three books: *Allen Susser's New World Cuisine and Cookery, The Great Citrus Book,* and *The Great Mango Book.*

Rick Tramonto

FAVORITE COOKING TOOL: My Braun hand blender

FAVORITE INGREDIENT: Garlic. In everything, as God meant it to be!

BEST SNACK: Italian beef

MENTOR: Alfred Portale

MOST-USED COOKBOOKS: Any of Julia Child's. I always find myself going back to them.

FAVORITE COOKBOOK: *The French Laundry Cookbook* by Thomas Keller

CAREER IF NOT A CHEF: Something to do with spreading the gospel

ACTIVITY ON DAY OFF: Anything with my son

From humble culinary roots, Rick Tramonto has become the award-winning chef-owner, with pastry chef, Gale Gand, of Tru in Chicago and, previously, of Brasserie T in Northfield, Illinois. Tramonto began working his way through the ranks of the kitchen when he was only sixteen, helping to support his family by flipping burgers at Wendy's, then moving on to the Strathallen Hotel, where he both met his wife and learned the French technique for which he is renowned today. Gand has always been an artist and, upon working in a restaurant, discovered that her skills translated well to cuisine. She started her own catering company before joining the Strathallen Hotel in Rochester, New York. In 1984, the couple decided to move to New York City, where Tramonto worked at Tavern on the Green and Gotham Bar and Grill, the latter with Gand. The couple then participated in the opening of Chapel's under chef Greg Broman. Feeling homesick for Chicago, they moved back in 1987, where Tramonto cooked at Scoozi! and Charlie Trotter's; Gand also worked at Carlos's restaurant, the Pump Room, and opened a number of new restaurants including Cafe 21, Bice, and Bella Luna. England was next: They transformed the kitchen and cuisine at Stapleford Park, a hotel outside London. Between establishing Brasserie T in 1995 and Tru in 1999—both showered with stars by critics for their inventive spin on classical French cuisine—the duo has

collaborated on two cookbooks: *American Brasserie: 180 Simple, Robust Recipes Inspired by the Rustic Foods of France, Italy, and America* and *Butter, Sugar, Flour, Eggs: Whimsical Irresistible Desserts.*

Charlie Trotter

FAVORITE COOKING TOOL: Chef's knife

FAVORITE INGREDIENT: Good-quality salt

BEST SNACK: Fruit with organic yogurt

MENTOR: Father

MOST-USED COOKBOOK: Ferdinand Point's *Ma gastronomie*

CAREER IF NOT A CHEF: Film

ACTIVITY ON DAY OFF: Anything with my son

Charlie Trotter entered the culinary world in 1982, after graduating from the University of Wisconsin with a degree in political science. Never formally trained in the culinary arts, he instead embarked on an intense four-year period of work, study, and travel, including stints with Norman Van Aken, Bradley Ogden, and Gordon Sinclair. He lived in Chicago, San Francisco, Florida, and Europe, reading cookbooks, working, and eating out incessantly. In 1987, he opened his eponymous restaurant and began serving his hallmark complex dishes with unexpected combinations of flavors. He's won many awards for his work, including, in 1999, Outstanding Chef: America from the James Beard Foundation. Trotter is involved with a variety of charitable organizations, including The American Cancer Society and Make-A-Wish Foundation. His cooking show, *The Kitchen Sessions with Charlie Trotter,* is aired nationally on public television; his sixth cookbook, *The Kitchen Sessions with Charlie Trotter,* was released simultaneously. He's the author of six other cookbooks: *Charlie Trotter's Cookbook, Charlie Trotter's Vegetables, Charlie Trotter's Seafood, Charlie Trotter's Desserts, Charlie Trotter's Meat and Game,* as well as *Gourmet Cooking for Dummies.*

Ming Tsai

FAVORITE COOKING TOOL: Benriner slicer

FAVORITE INGREDIENT: Ginger

SURPRISE MOMENT ON YOUR TELEVISION SHOW: Falling off an ostrich
(on *Ming's Quest*)

FAVORITE EAST-WEST FLAVOR COMBINATION: Champagne and sushi

BEST SNACK: Any kind of garnish—fried onions, shallots

MOST MEMORABLE DINNER: By Ken Oringer at Clio: five hours (from 11:30 P.M.
to 4:30 A.M.), twenty courses

MOST INSPIRATIONAL MEAL: Making Jasmine tea soufflés for Ken Hom and
Julia Child, both of whom said to stick with the East-West technique

FUTURE ASPIRATION: Work less, eat more

Ming Tsai started cooking at his family's Chinese restaurant in Dayton, Ohio,
as a teenager. A mechanical engineering degree from Yale proved to be merely
a brief detour in a career that would lead him to Paris to study at the Cordon
Bleu and work at Fauchon and Natasha, where he encountered East-West
cuisine for the first time. Back in the United States, Ming returned to school
and received a master's degree in hotel administration and hospitality
marketing from Cornell before working several years in the hotel industry as
food and beverage director at the Hotel-Intercontinental Chicago. In 1992,
the kitchen lured Ming back and he arrived at Silks, an East-West restaurant
in the Mandarin Oriental Hotel in San Francisco. After that, he served as
executive chef for Ginger Club, a new Southeast Asian restaurant in Palo Alto.
Ming then moved on to Santa Fe as executive chef of Santacafe. In 1997,
he and his wife opened Blue Ginger in Wellesley, Massachusetts, to many
awards. Ming's hit television series, *East Meets West with Ming Tsai,* debuted
in September 1998 on The Food Network. In May 1999, he was awarded a
Daytime Emmy for Outstanding Service Show Host. Ming recently published
his first cookbook, *Blue Ginger: East Meets West Cooking with Ming Tsai.*

Norman Van Aken

FAVORITE COOKING TOOL: Curiosity

FAVORITE INGREDIENT: Creativity

MOST USEFUL COOKING TRICK: Turning hard work into fun

MOST INSPIRATIONAL TRAVEL: Wherever I can go to markets and see the
local cooking

SMARTEST MOVE: Never working just for money

BEST SNACK: Yogurt with dried fruits and roasted unsalted nuts

AWARD MOST PROUD OF: Three—Food Arts Silver Spoon, Robert Mondavi,
James Beard

MENTOR: My mother

MOST-USED COOKBOOK: *Gourmet* magazine's *Gourmet Cookbook,* volume one

Norman Van Aken's first connection to the restaurant world was his mother.
She worked as a waitress and hostess in numerous Illinois restaurants, bringing
Van Aken in to help if the dishwasher or busboy was out. When he was
nineteen, Van Aken and a group of friends drove from Illionis to Key West in a
day and a half. The trip made him more aware of other culinary influences in
the South, and he began to drive around Florida to learn more about Spanish,
Caribbean, Central and South American cuisine. Van Aken learned about wine
from his mother, too—she opened a liquor store in a tiny town in Illinois, where
Van Aken worked in the early 1980s. He spent time talking to wine purveyors
and tasting their wares while saving up money to open his own restaurant. Van
Aken worked in the kitchen of Louie's Backyard in Key West, from 1985 to
1990, and it was there that he found his style: a combination of regional
American and Caribbean with an overlay of Asian touches. Next he cooked in
the South Beach section of Miami, at A Mano. He opened Norman's in 1991
and has received numerous accolades, such as the 1997 James Beard
Foundation's award for Best Chef: Southeast. He is author of *Norman's
New World Cuisine, The Great Exotic Fruit Book,* and *Norman Van Aken's
Feast of Sunlight.*

Marc Vetri

FAVORITE COOKING TOOL: My hands

FAVORITE INGREDIENT: Artichokes

MOST MEMORABLE DINNER: At Louis XV in Monaco; I was there by myself
and they didn't have any room for me, so they sat me in the kitchen. I watched
them and ate for about four hours, probably ten courses, then the chef sat
with me. When I asked for the bill, they asked, "Did you enjoy yourself? Did
you have a memorable evening?" When I said yes, they told me that I was a
guest of Alain Ducasse.

BEST SNACK: Ice cream

MOST INSPIRATIONAL MOMENTS: When someone walks into the restaurant and asks me to make a menu for them—I have those moments every day.

CAREER IF NOT A CHEF: Jazz blues musician

Marc Vetri, born in Philadelphia, was perhaps destined to be a chef: His grandfather had run a popular neighborhood restaurant, and dinners at his grandparents' home were veritable feasts of lasagna, sausage, broccoli rabe, smelts, mussels, and more. His first job was washing dishes at Down Beach Deli in Margate, New Jersey. In college he studied business, and after graduation he moved to California to play jazz guitar. Eventually, he returned to cooking, getting a job (through dogged persistence and a few weeks of working without pay) in the kitchen of Wolfgang Puck's Granita. With the encouragement of the chef, Vetri went to Italy, where he remained for a year working in six different restaurants. His training there was so rigorous that it included butchering animals, and making prosciutto and lard. He was taught to make wine and press olive oil. Back in the United States, he helped to design and open an Italian seafood restaurant, Pier il Ristorante, in Juneau, Alaska. In New York, his next venture was as a consultant with Coco Pazzo, and then as executive chef at Bella Blu and Baraonda restaurants. In 1998, Vetri returned to Philadelphia and opened Vetri, a traditional Italian restaurant that soon attracted a loyal following.

Jean-Georges Vongerichten

FAVORITE COOKING TOOL: A plancha (a griddle that reaches high temperatures)

SMARTEST MOVE: Coming to New York

BEST SNACK: Chocolate

MOST MEMORABLE DINNER: Live sushi menu in Tokyo

AWARD MOST PROUD OF: Twice receiving four stars from *The New York Times* (Lafayette and Jean Georges)

FUTURE ASPIRATIONS: Creating new concepts or new flavors

CAREER IF NOT A CHEF: Clothing designer

ACTIVITY ON DAY OFF: Walking around New York

Born and raised on the outskirts of Strasbourg in Alsace, Vongerichten's earliest family memories are about food. The Vongerichten home centered on the kitchen, where each day his mother and grandmother would prepare lunch for almost fifty employees in their family-owned business. "I would wake every morning to the most wonderful smells," reminisces Vongerichten, "and I quickly became known as 'the palate' to my family, tasting each sauce and dish, recommending salt or some more herbs." For his sixteenth birthday, he was brought to the Auberge de l'Ill for dinner and that evening he chose his career path. Training at the Auberge de l'Ill as apprentice to chef Paul Haeberlin and then later working with French chefs such as Paul Bocuse and Louis Outhier at L'Oasis gave him the experience to win a position at the Oriental Hotel in Bangkok. From 1980 to 1985, he opened an impressive ten restaurants around the world, many in Asia; it was during this time that he would learn the aromatic flavors of the East that would figure into his distinctive Asian-French style. Vongerichten arrived in the United States in 1985, opening the Marquis de Lafayette restaurant in Boston. He was then asked to open Lafayette in New York in the Drake Hotel. Over the next twelve years, six new culinary endeavors of his opened, all well received, especially his namesake and flagship restaurant, Jean Georges, in the Trump International Hotel and Tower, as well as the much celebrated Vong, known for its exotic Thai-influenced French cuisine. Vongerichten is the author of three cookbooks, *Simple to Spectacular: How to Take One Basic Recipe to Four Levels of Sophistication*, *Jean-Georges: Cooking at Home with a Four-Star Chef*, and *Simple Cuisine: The Easy, New Approach to Four-Star Cooking*.

Bob Waggoner

FAVORITE INGREDIENT: Wine

FAVORITE COOKING TOOL: Vitamix blender

MOST USEFUL COOKING TIP: Always give roasted meats and fish time to rest before serving

SMARTEST MOVE: Going to France when I was twenty years old and staying for eleven years

FAVORITE SNACK: A true Mexican taco

MENTOR: Jean-Pierre Silva at Le Vieux Moulin in Bouilland, France

MOST-USED COOKBOOK: *Le Répertoire de la cuisine*

CAREER IF NOT A CHEF: Photographer

Bob Waggoner likes to cook with local southern products in new ways—he dubs his style "Contemporary Lowcountry Cuisine." His commitment to supporting local farmers and growers and encouraging them to cultivate new and unusual products has won him praise from both the agricultural community and his guests. In January 1998, only four months after his arrival, Charleston

Grill became the only restaurant in South Carolina to be awarded Four Mobil Stars. Waggoner, a California native, received his formal training with Michael Roberts at Trumps in Los Angeles from 1981 to 1983, and later in France at a constellation of Michelin-rated restaurants with chefs Jacques Lameloise, Charles Barrier, Pierre Gagnaire, Gerard Boyer, and Mark Meneau. At twenty-three, he spent one year in Caracas, Venezuela, where he worked alongside renowned chef Jean-Paul Coupal in his private club, Members. He then returned to France to become chef of Hôtel de la Poste in Avallon. In 1988 he became the first American to own his own restaurant in France, the much acclaimed Le Monte Cristo. In 1991, chef Waggoner was offered the opportunity to join chef Jean-Pierre Silva at Le Vieux Moulin in Bouilland, France. He returned to the United States in 1993 to cook at the award-winning Turnberry Isle Resort & Club in Florida, before joining the Wild Boar in Nashville, where he earned the restaurant a coveted AAA Five-Diamond Award. In 1998, he joined the Charleston Grill as executive chef.

The Restaurants

Ben and Karen Barker

MAGNOLIA GRILL
1002 Ninth Street
Durham, NC 27705
Tel. 919 206 3600

www.magnoliagrillcookbook.com

Lidia Bastianich

BECCO
355 West 46th Street
New York, NY 10036
Tel: 212 397 7597

FELIDIA
243 East 58th Street
New York, NY 10022
Tel: 212 758 1479

ESCA
402 West 43rd Street
New York, NY 10036
Tel: 212 564 7272

LIDIA'S
101 West 22nd Street
Kansas City, MO 64108
Tel: 816 221 3722

LIDIA'S PITTSBURGH
1400 Smallman Street
Pittsburgh, PA 15222
Tel: 412 552 0150

www.lidiasitaly.com

Rick Bayless

FRONTERA GRILL
445 North Clark Street
Chicago, IL 60610
Tel: 312 661 1434

TOPOLOBAMPO
445 N. Clark Street
Chicago, IL 60610
Tel: 312 661 1434

Daniel Boulud

DANIEL
60 East 65th Street
New York, NY 10021
Tel: 212 288 0033

CAFÉ BOULUD
20 East 76th Street
New York, NY 10021
Tel: 212 772 2600

DB – BISTRO MODERNE
55 West 44th Street
New York, NY 10036
Tel: 212 391 2400

www.danielnyc.com

Jeffrey Buben

VIDALIA
1990 M Street, NW
Washington, D.C. 20036
Tel: 202 659 1990

BISTRO BIS
15 E Street, NW
Washington, D.C. 20001
Tel: 202 661 2700

Tom Colicchio

GRAMERCY TAVERN
42 East 20th Street
New York, NY 10003
Tel: 212 477 0777

CRAFT
43 East 19th Street
New York, NY 10003
Tel: 212 780 0880

www.gramercytavern.com

Gary Danko

GARY DANKO
800 North Point
San Francisco, CA 94109
Tel: 415 749 2060

www.garydanko.com

Robert Del Grande

CAFÉ ANNIE
Galleria
1728 Post Oak Boulevard
Houston, TX 77019
Tel: 713 840 1111

TACO MILAGRO
2555 Kirby Drive at
    Westheimer
Houston, TX 77019
Tel: 713 522 1999

RIO RANCH
9999 Westheimer
Houston, Texas 77042
Tel: 713 952 5000

CAFE EXPRESS
3200 Kirby Drive
Houston, TX 77098
Tel: 713 522 3994

210 Meyerland Plaza
Houston, TX 77096
Tel: 713 349 9222

1101 Uptown Park Blvd.
Houston, TX 77056
Tel: 713 963 9222

5601 Main Street
Audrey Jones Beck Bldg.
Lower Level
Houston, TX 77005
Tel: 713 639 7370

1422 West Gray
Houston, TX 77019
Tel: 713 522 3100

780 West Sam Houston Pkwy.
N. Houston, TX 77024
Tel: 713 586 0800

10150 SW Freeway
Houston, TX 77074
Tel: 713 596 3940

6570 Woodway Drive
Houston, TX 77057
Tel: 713 935 9222

4101 Beltline Road
Addison, TX 75244
Tel: 972 991 9444

3230 McKinney Avenue
Dallas, TX 75204
Tel: 214 999 9444

5600 West Lover's Lane
Dallas, TX 75209
Tel: 214 362 2211

2525 East Camelback Road
Phoenix, AZ 85016
Tel: 602 522 9199

www.cafe-express.com

Traci Des Jardins

JARDINIÈRE
300 Grove Street
San Francisco, CA 94102
Tel: 415 861 5555

Rocco DiSpirito

UNION PACIFIC
111 East 22nd Street
New York, NY 10010
Tel: 212 995 8500

www.unionpacificrestaurant.com

Tom Douglas

DAHLIA LOUNGE
2001 Fourth Avenue
Seattle, WA 98101
Tel: 206 682 4142

ETTA'S SEAFOOD
2020 Western Avenue
Seattle, WA 98121
Tel: 206 443 6000

PALACE KITCHEN
2030 Fifth Avenue
Seattle, WA 98121
Tel: 206 448 2001

www.tomdouglas.com

Wylie Dufresne

71 CLINTON FRESH FOOD
71 Clinton Street
New York, NY 10002
Tel: 212 614 6960

Todd English

OLIVES
10 City Square
Charlestown, MA 02129
Tel: 617 242 1999

3600 Las Vegas Blvd. South
Las Vegas, NV 89108
Tel: 702 693 8181

World Center Building
1600 K Street, NW
Washington, D.C. 20006
Tel: 202 452 1866

315 East Dean Street
Aspen, CO 81611
Tel: 970 920 7356

201 Park Avenue South
New York, NY 10003
Tel: 212 353 8345

KINGFISH HALL
South Market Building
Faneuil Hall
Boston, MA 02109
Tel: 617 523 8862

FIGS
42 Charles Street
Boston, MA 02108
Tel: 617 742 3447

67 Main Street
Charlestown, MA 02129
Tel: 617 242 2229

1208 Boylston Street
Chestnut Hill, MA 02167
Tel: 617 738 9992

92 Central Street
Wellesley, MA 02181
Tel: 781 237 5788

MIRAMAR
2 Post Road West
Westport, CT 06880
Tel: 203 222 2267

**GREG NORMAN'S
AUSTRALIAN GRILLE**
4930 Highway 17, South
North Myrtle Beach, SC
29582
Tel: 843 361 0000

Bobby Flay

BOLO
23 East 22nd Street
New York, NY 10010
Tel: 212 228 2200

MESA GRILL
102 Fifth Avenue
New York, NY 10011
Tel: 212 807 7400

Claudia Fleming

GRAMERCY TAVERN
42 East 20th Street
New York, NY 10003
Tel: 212 477 0777

Suzanne Goin

LUCQUES
8474 Melrose Avenue
at La Cienega, West
West Hollywood, CA 90069
Tel: 323 655 6277

Christine Keff

FANDANGO
2313 First Avenue
Seattle, WA 98121
Tel: 206 441 1188

FLYING FISH
2234 First Avenue
Seattle, WA 98121
Tel: 206 728 8595

Thomas Keller

FRENCH LAUNDRY
6640 Washington Street
Yountville, CA 94599
Tel: 704 944 2380

www.sterba.com/yountville/
frenchlaundry

Bob Kinkead

KINKEAD'S
2000 Pennsylvania Avenue,
NW
Washington, D.C. 20006
Tel: 202 296 7700

COLVIN RUN TAVERN
8045 Leesburg Pike
Vienna, VA 22082
Tel: 703 356 9500

www.kinkead.com

Jean-Marie Lacroix

FOUNTAIN RESTAURANT
Four Seasons Hotel
Philadelphia
One Logan Square
Philadelphia, PA 19103
Tel: 215 963 1500

www.fourseasons.com

Nobuyuki Matsuhisa

NOBU
105 Hudson Street
New York, NY 10013
Tel: 212 219 0500

3835 Cross Creek Road
Malibu, CA 90265
Tel: 310 317 9140

At Hard Rock Hotel
4455 Paradise Road
Las Vegas, NV 89109
Tel: 702 693 5090

15 Rue Marbeuf
Paris 75008
France
Tel: 33 1 5689 5353

6-10-17, Minamiaoyama
Minato-ku
Tokyo, Japan
Tel: 011 81 03 5467 0022

The Metropolitan Hotel
19 Old Park Lane
London W1Y4LD
United Kingdom
Tel: 011 44 171 447 4747

NOBU NEXT DOOR
106 Hudson Street
New York, NY 10013
Tel: 212 334 4445

MATSUHISA
129 North La Cienega Blvd.
Beverly Hills, CA 90211
Tel: 310 659 9639

303 East Main Street
Aspen, CO 81611
Tel: 970 544 6628

UBON
8530 Beverly Boulevard
Los Angeles, CA 90048
Tel: 310 854 1115

Nancy Oakes

BOULEVARD
1 Mission Street
(at corner of Steuart)
San Francisco, CA 94105
Tel: 415 543 6084

Patrick O'Connell

**THE INN AT LITTLE
WASHINGTON**
Middle and Main Streets
Washington, VA 22747
Tel: 540 675 3800

Tadashi Ono

SONO
106 East 57th Street
New York, NY 10022
Tel: 212 752 4411

www.sonorestaurant.com

Michel Richard

CITRONELLE
at The Latham Hotel
3000 M Street, NW
Washington, D.C. 20007
Tel: 202 625 2150

CITRONELLE
at The Santa Barbara Inn
901 East Cabrillo Boulevard
Santa Barbara, CA 93103
Tel: 805 963 0111

Eric Ripert

LE BERNARDIN
155 West 51st Street
New York, New York 10019
Tel: 212 489 1515

www.le-bernardin.com

Marcus Samuelsson

AQUAVIT
13 West 54th Street
New York, NY 10019
Tel: 212 307 7311

AQUAVIT, MINNEAPOLIS
IDS Center
75 South 7th Street
Minneapolis, MN 55402
Tel: 612 343 3333

Lydia Shire

BIBA
272 Boylston Street
Boston, MA 02116
Tel: 617 426 7878

PIGNOLI
79 Park Plaza
Boston, MA 02116
Tel: 617 338 7500

Katy Sparks

QUILTY'S
177 Prince Street
New York, NY 10012
Tel: 212 254 1260

Susan Spicer

BAYONA
430 Rue Dauphine
New Orleans, LA 70112
Tel: 504 525 4455

www.bayona.com

Joachim Splichal

PATINA RESTAURANT
5955 Melrose Avenue
Hollywood, CA 90038
Tel: 323 467 1108

PINOT BISTRO
12969 Ventura Boulevard
Studio City, CA 91604
Tel: 818 990 0500

PINOT PROVENCE
686 Anton Boulevard
Costa Mesa, CA 92626
Tel: 714 444 5900

CAFÉ PINOT
700 West Fifth Street
Los Angeles, CA 90071
Tel: 213 239 6500

PINOT BRASSERIE
3355 South Las Vegas
    Boulevard
Las Vegas, NV 89109
Tel: 702 414 8888

PINOT BLANC
641 Main Street
St. Helena, CA 94574
Tel: 707 963 6191

NICK & STEF'S
330 South Hope Street
Los Angeles, CA 90071
Tel: 213 680 0330

601 F Street NW
    at the MCI Center
Washington, DC 20004
Tel: 202 661 5040

9 Pennsylvania Plaza
    at Madison Square Garden
New York, NY 10001
Tel: 212 563 4444

Allen Susser

CHEF ALLEN'S
19088 N. East 29th Avenue
North Miami Beach, FL 33180
Tel: 305 935 2900

www.chefallen.com

Rick Tramonto

TRU
676 North Saint Clair Street
Chicago, IL 60611
Tel: 312 202 0001

Charlie Trotter

CHARLIE TROTTER'S
816 West Armitage Avenue
Chicago, IL 60614
Tel: 773 248 6228

www.charlietrotters.com

Ming Tsai

BLUE GINGER
583 Washington Street
Wellesley, MA 02482
Tel: 781 283 5790

www.ming.com

Norman Van Aken

NORMAN'S
21 Almeria Avenue
Coral Gables, FL 33134
Tel: 305 446 6767

www.normans.com

Marc Vetri

VETRI
1312 Spruce Street
Philadelphia, PA 19107
Tel: 215 732 3478

Jean-Georges
Vongerichten

LIPSTICK CAFÉ
885 Third Avenue
    (at 54th Street)
New York, NY 10022
212 486 8664

THE MERCER KITCHEN
99 Prince Street
New York, NY 10012
Tel: 212 966 5454

JEAN GEORGES
Trump International Hotel
    and Tower
1 Central Park West
New York, NY 10023
Tel: 212 299 3900

VONG
6 West Hubbard Street
Chicago, IL 60610
Tel: 312 644 8664

VONG
200 East 54th Street
New York, NY 10022
Tel: 212 486 9592

VONG
The Mandarin Oriental Hotel
5 Connaught Road
Central Hong Kong
Tel: 011 852 2825 4028

VONG
The Berkeley Hotel
Wilton Place
Knightsbridge SWIX 7RL
United Kingdom
Tel: 011 44 171 235 1010

PRIME STEAKHOUSE
Bellagio Hotel
3600 Las Vegas Blvd. South
Las Vegas, NV 89109
Tel: 702 693 7111

Bob Waggoner

CHARLESTON GRILL
224 King Street
Charleston, SC 29401
Tel: 843 577 4522

www.charlestongrill.com

Acknowledgments

I would like to thank the following:

Cees Nouwens, with whom I made all the portraits;

My team in Holland: Bea Tamminga, Barbara Baving, Mike Boissevain, Coco Bijman, Ruud Mol, Henk Raam, Linda Wagner, Danielle Nes, and Christian Maat;

Jan Karel Schreuder and Elisa Reichek for their support;

My publisher, Artisan, and the people there: Ann Bramson, Ann Treistman, Deborah Weiss-Geline, Nancy Murray, Dania Davey, LeAnna Weller Smith, Burgin Streetman, Thea Hetzner, and Rachel Godfrey;

Kimberly Yorio, for selecting and scheduling all the chefs;

Stephanie Lyness, for her introduction to the book and her work on the recipes;

Sherrill Rose, for writing the text;

The designers of P*h*.D: Clive Piercy, Marie Reese, and Traci Swartz;

Jonnie Boer of Restaurant the Librije in Holland and Henny Botman of Restaurant D'Artiste for patiently posing while holding a large fish, even though they didn't make the cover;

Duikelman BV in Amsterdam for lending me all the kitchen equipment I needed for shoots;

Ruparo Graphical Services for the scanning;

David Pryor at Toppan Printing;

Marisa Perry of Dairyland for supplying us with great cheeses;

All the chefs for their contributions and letting us stay for dinner;

My wife, Eveline, and my children Boris, Julian, and Nina, for all their great support;

Last but not least: my mother and father. And my aunt Jopie for giving me my first camera.

Jan Bartelsman

210

Index

213